S0-CPS-070

MASTERS OF THE SYMPHONY

BY

PERCY GOETSCHIUS, Mus. Doc.

AUTHOR OF

Lessons in Music Form;
The Larger Forms of Musical Composition;
Homophonic Forms of Musical Composition;
Material used in Musical Composition; etc.

Fifth Year

OF

A STUDY COURSE

IN

MUSIC UNDERSTANDING

ADOPTED BY

The National Federation
of Music Clubs

$2.00

BOSTON: OLIVER DITSON COMPANY

NEW YORK: CHAS. H. DITSON & CO.   CHICAGO: LYON & HEALY, INC.
LONDON: WINTHROP ROGERS, LTD.

MADE IN U. S. A.

Copyright MCMXXIX, by Oliver Ditson Company
International Copyright Secured

To my esteemed friend
WILLIAM ARMS FISHER
this book is cordially inscribed.

PREFACE

To begin our book with the declaration, inspired by absolute conviction, that music is more ennobling and refining than any other art—than almost anything else in life; more far-reaching in its influences for good; and that its exercise brings more joy and solace to the average soul than any other occupation—is but to repeat what has already been said times without number. Its repetition sounds trite, stereotyped, and some individuals do not react sympathetically to it. But Shakespeare knew it and said it; and the greatest, profoundest observers and philosophers of all ages have averred it. So let it be impressed here again upon the willing student, for it is the Truth.

But there are various ways of listening to music. Some take it in with their ears only, some with their mind, some with the soul, and some, apparently, only with their feet. And so the question arises: Which class of listeners derives the greatest benefit from it? Since music, in what we regard as its best sense, has become a highly developed, many-sided and intricate art, with meanings that reach far beneath the surface of things, and touch the finest sensibilities of our being, it appears obvious that the degree of enjoyment must be commensurate with the degree of understanding; must depend upon the degree to which we penetrate its secret chambers and comprehend its methods and purposes. Grandfather derives immense comfort, in a way, from "Auld lang syne"—*with the words*; and the bulk of humanity enjoys its musical experiences in something of the same fashion. But how utterly primitive is this kind of enjoyment, compared with

PREFACE

the unspeakable experience of one who hears *and understands* (if only in part) the message of a Symphony of Beethoven! Such understanding may be partly intuitive, though only in rare cases and in small proportion. It is rather the reward of study; of earnest, well-directed and patient *study;* and that is the opportunity which this book aims to provide for the student and lover of what is best and noblest in the art of music.

This attitude is so essential and so difficult to apprehend in its fullest sense, that it will bear defining in another form: The key to the fullest enjoyment of a work of art is Appreciation, and this can result only from *Knowledge*. One must possess, in music, a sufficient knowledge of the fundamental harmonic relations to supply, so to speak, the artist's canvas; and must acquire an insight into the details of form and structure in order to obtain a full, clear perception of the artist's creative purpose, and of his mental and emotional operations in achieving that purpose. In exact proportion to the extent of this insight is the measure of his enjoyment. It is not the sound of the music alone which can deeply move us—any more than the sound of the words in a poem; but the *meaning,* the true and deep significance of those factors which the sound helps to convey to our intelligence. That is what our judgment rests upon, and the recognition of this deeper significance should therefore be the goal of the earnest-minded student.

It is undeniably true that no amount of mental effort can fathom all the emotional depths, or wholly disclose the *spiritual* contents, of the work of genius. But all such effort tends in the right direction, and carries us ever nearer to the solution of some of its mysteries.

The author is also fully aware of the justice of the objection often raised against analytic or dissecting operations in the music

PREFACE

art—when carried to excess; and he has faithfully endeavored to point out only those historic, structural and technical elements that may aid in placing the mind and attitude of the student in closer touch with the intentions and methods of the creator.

* * *

The student will find his efforts materially supported and furthered in the present course of musical education, first, by obtaining good pianoforte arrangements of the Symphonies whose demonstration has been attempted, either for two, or for four hands; and to these must be adjoined the miniature orchestral scores, which are amply provided in various published editions, and are both easily procurable and inexpensive. These may be used by the student for parallel reference while pursuing the text-explanations, either alone or in classes, in the studio—or in the concert hall during an actual orchestral performance. And finally, in the absence of piano versions, if such be wanting, the student can resort to the ample lists of rolls and records for the player-piano and the phonograph; and, perhaps best of all, may avail himself of the radio to hear and enjoy such symphonic recitals as are freely and regularly broadcast from large cities.

The inquisitive music lover who would make an abstract study of the Symphonies from the piano-version, independently of the above-named adjuncts, should first memorize the principal Theme, and trace its manipulation in the Exposition up to the subordinate Theme; the same with the latter up to the Codetta, and so on to the "double bar." This done, he should play the Exposition through without interruptions. The study of the Development is particularly fascinating; the contents of each Section should be examined with reference to their connection with (derivation from) the material of the Exposition; also to verify the under-

PREFACE

lying thematic or emotional causes which lead from each Section into the next; also, in the final Section, to recognize the manner in which the Retransition achieves the "return to the beginning." The Recapitulation should be compared minutely with the Exposition, noting to what extent and in which places the composer has restated the previous material exactly, and where modifications are made—also searching out the reasons for such changes. In the Coda, as in the Development, the relation to foregoing thematic factors should be investigated.

This course will acquaint the student with the physical or technical details of the Symphony, and will furnish him with valuable clues to the emotional or spiritual message it carries. But when he attends a public performance of the masterwork, he will do well to relegate this knowledge to the subconscious realm, and yield himself to unobstructed communion with its Spirit. Thus will his joy be complete.

Percy Goetschius

CONTENTS

CHAPTER		PAGE
	Introduction	1
I.	The Development of Orchestral Instruments, and Evolution of the Symphony	10
II.	Haydn and Mozart	40
III.	Beethoven	89
IV.	Schubert and Mendelssohn	158
V.	Schumann and Brahms	204
VI.	Liszt, Tchaikovsky, Dvořák, Sibelius	258
VII.	Berlioz, Franck, Saint-Saëns, d'Indy	293
VIII.	Bruckner, Elgar, Mahler, Strauss, and other Symphonists of the 19th Century and the Modern Era	323
	Epilogue: American Symphonists	360

INTRODUCTION

There is much difference of opinion as to which form of composition represents the highest type of musical art. Such diversity of view, in this as in all similar fields of ethical, scientific and artistic life, is due to two weighty causes: partly to the difficulty of recognizing and fixing an accurate and reliable standard; and also, probably chiefly, to the influence of individual taste and personal preference. A great many persons, of intelligence and generally sound judgment, will insist that a certain form is the highest, simply because they like that form best, forgetting or ignoring the impersonal criterion, with which alone a correct estimate can be made.

Probably a large majority of music lovers and students, if asked the question, would unhesitatingly point to the Opera and Oratorio as the most eminent grades of musical creation. They certainly are the largest; but magnitude is not by any means synonomous with true greatness; the short *Ave verum corpus* of Mozart contains more traits of transcendent artistic refinement and worth than many an Opera—even the most popular—over a hundred times as long. The Opera does, undeniably, present a broad panorama of extremely attractive factors: the drama, the action, the music, the singing, the orchestra, and the scenic background; and what the Oratorio lacks in the allurements of the stage and visible dramatic action, is fully compensated by the sacredness and dignity of the subject, and the seriousness of the musical setting. But it is this very multiplicity of captivating and impressive qualities in the Opera, and to a lesser degree in the Oratorio, that, no matter how skillfully interwoven and balanced, impairs the *unity* and concentration absolutely essential to a work of purely artistic aim. ⁄The Opera can not reasonably be regarded as the highest type of musical creation, for the simple reason that it is not music alone. The music which it contains, though an integral part of the whole, is associated with many other sensuous appeals, and therefore it is only partly, not wholly, a musical form. Whatever extraneous elements are thus added to music, be they never so artistically excellent in themselves, must inevitably hamper the free, unconstrained unfolding of the true, pure musical spirit, and adulterate or obscure the main issue. This is even true (theoretically at least) of every Song, which can never be "absolute" music, because of its comradeship with Words that lay equal claim to poetic independence, and exercise an unavoidable constraining influence upon their musical companion—excepting perhaps in those cases where the words are treated with such indifference by the composer that their embarrassing effect is negligible, as in so many of the Songs of Schubert, in which the poetic appendage seems merely to direct, in a general way, the current of the composer's conception, and to assist in creating the "mood" or atmosphere of the music. Hence it is apparent that the very highest type of musical art must consist exclusively of pure, unalloyed, music.

This reasoning leads to the consideration of pianoforte compositions, wherein it is possible to meet the requirements of absolute music, and create works of lofty artistic quality, as attested in the Sonatas of Beethoven and other masters. But pianoforte music is hedged about by many and insurmountable limitations (chiefly digital, but also as concerns variety of tone-color) which check its highest flights, and prevent it from reaching up to the last pinnacle of artistic effectiveness.

The organ overcomes some of these limitations, by virtue of its greater abundance of tone-color (all artificial, it is true), and its wider range of dynamic possibilities, from the faintest pianissimo up to the overpowering, gloriously sonorous volume of the full organ,—but only to weaken, on the other hand, under other restrictions that render it as powerless to climb the heights as is the pianoforte.

Far more numerous are the resources of Chamber music, and here it is the string-quartet which shines forth with such radiance that very many serious critics and discriminating music lovers point unreservedly to this as the most aristocratic, refined and eminent type of musical creation. And surely this claim is well based. The indescribable beauty, emotional appeal and mobility of the tone of these stringed instruments, uniform in tone-quality and yet distinctive in each of the registers of the 'cello, viola and violin, at once intensely human and divine; the transparency of the whole quartet texture, which prohibits every attempt to cover up structural defect or weakness by a cloak of fustian, or gaudy technical superficialities; the almost imperative employment of the polyphonic style of writing in order to maintain the individual melodic independence of each instrument, thus presupposing the highest degree of technical mastery,—these conditions unite to elevate the string-quartet far above the average level of musical conception and presentation. And still, there are here again limitations. The lack of emphatic accentuation, and of diversity of tone-color in this company of four instruments of identical pedigree, is relieved only in the scantiest degree by *sordini* (mutes), *pizzicato* (plucking the strings), and one or two other superficial technical devices; hence the spectre of monotony dogs even this paragon of artistic excellence.

Other kinds of Chamber-music in which the *ensemble* includes instruments of radically different tone-color, as when the pianoforte joins forces with the strings, or when some wind instrument (clarinet, horn, flute, etc.) is admitted into the company,—these more diversified *ensembles* fare somewhat better than the string-quartet, and, when conceived and consummated with serious purpose, they do approach a higher level of expressiveness and effectiveness, so far as Variety, the vital condition of true tone-art, is

INTRODUCTION

concerned. Still, it is only an approach, which again falls short of the purest and highest ideal.

Further search for this ideal along the paths last traced leads inescapably to the orchestra, and orchestral music. Therein every *desideratum* seems supplied, every condition amply fulfilled.

For the orchestra, besides possessing all the merits of the other, less exalted styles of music setting, goes farther and surmounts their limitations. It presents a canvas of fully sufficient breadth and width, and an opulent palette of tone-colors and nuances that outshine Joseph's famous Biblical coat. The ordinary orchestra of today comprises about ten different instruments or families of instruments, of strings, wood or brass, each of which has its distinctive *timbre* or tone-quality, namely: the quartet of *Strings*, increased to a quintet by the addition of the larger Double-bass, and powerfully augmented by *ripieni*—multiplication of each part up to ten, twenty or more, which constitute the solid foundation of the entire iridescent edifice, and whose divinely-human voices give such rare value to the string-quartet; further, the dulcet, purling, incredibly flexible *Flute*, intensified to a pert, shrill tonal delivery in its diminutive offspring, the *Piccolo*; the plaintive, appealing (now and again saucy) *Oboe*, with its larger, more resonant companion, the *English Horn*; the suave, gurgling *Clarinet*, whose lower "chalumeau" is so luscious, augmented in richness in the larger *Bass-clarinet*; the hollow-voiced, mildly grotesque *Bassoon*, with its redeeming, rich lower register, greatly magnified in resonant power in the *Contra-bassoon;* the stirring, white-hued, martial *Trumpet;* the golden-throated, mellow *Horn;* the majestic *Trombones,* whose gamut of tone-shades extends from an unspeakably tender pianissimo up to a blaze of glorious resonance and power; and the *Drum,* the chief exponent of the rhythm, embracing a range of volume from the low ominous murmur of its softest roll, to a veritable crashing din of enveloping sound-waves.

To this array of color-material, which represents the normal bounds of the ordinary classic orchestra, are often added, for special effects, the *Harp, Organ, Bass-drum, Snare-drum, Cymbals, Triangle, Bells,* and other instruments of unique quality though of doubtful legitimacy, which swell the turmoil, but detract from, rather than add to, the genuine, authentic effectiveness of the consistent, discreetly equipped symphonic orchestra.

It may be argued that these orchestral attributes, since they merely supply color but in no way contribute to the essential musical contents, are as extraneous as the words and dramatic action of the opera. That may be true in some sense; but they are nevertheless vital, for, without affecting the *tonal* contents, they impart emotional character to the melodic contours, and, what is still more essential, they serve to chromatize and emphasize all the lines of the design, thus accentuating and vitalizing the various interlacing threads of the musical pattern, and transforming the picture from a "flat" copy into a living, speaking thing, replete with force and beauty.

For these very reasons any transcription of a Symphony or other orchestral composition for the piano, especially a version for two hands, must necessarily be inadequate for the recognition and full enjoyment of all the details of the original. But, on the other hand, the piano arrangement has very positive value inasmuch as it presents all the *tonal* elements, and the physical structure, in a precise and distinct form, thus bringing the student into immediate touch with the actual reflective process of the composer, and—in the case of those who have already heard a performance of the work in its orchestral presentation—it *recalls* the complete impression and invites the hearer to restore, to some extent, the vision of the colorful original.

* * *

The student may need to be warned against placing a hasty, superficial interpretation upon all of the above. Our Introduction aims to furnish a logical reply to the question: Which is the highest *type* of musical composition? It does not imply comparison as to the just claims to eminence, or popularity, of musical creations of any kind. A Symphony is not *per se* a great work, merely because it is a Symphony. There are many Symphonies of mediocre quality, and there are numberless Operas, Oratorios, String-quartets, piano Sonatas, Songs, etc., of extremely lofty artistic quality—as, for example, Bach's *St. Matthew Passion* and *B-minor Mass*, Beethoven's *Fidelio* and *D-major Mass,* the Operas of Mozart and those of Wagner, the *German Requiem* of Brahms, and many other choral, vocal or purely instrumental compositions that are not Symphonies. But the fact remains that symphonic conception and form constitute the highest *type* of musical art. In other words: all things being equal, a masterly Symphony will be a "greater" musical work than any example of, say, the vocal class, for the simple reason that it is *pure, absolute, unembarrassed Music.*

QUESTIONS FOR REVIEW

1. What two causes are cited for difference of opinion regarding the classification of artistic musical types?
2. What militates against the pre-eminence of the Opera and Oratorio?
3. . . . . of the Song?
4. What limitations operate similarly to consign piano and organ music to a comparatively lower level?
5. Define the status of the String-quartet.
6. . . . . of other Chamber-music.
7. In which type of composition are these objections and limitations lifted?
8. Define in detail the apparatus of the ordinary modern orchestra.
9. Why is it untenable to regard tone-colors as extraneous?
10. What are the shortcomings, and what the advantages, of a piano version of the orchestral score?
11. Against what misconception is the student warned?

REFERENCES

Goepp	Symphonies and their Meaning.
Upton	Standard Symphonies.
Surette	Development of Symphonic Music.
Porte	Famous Symphonies and how to understand them.
Mason	From Song to Symphony.
Lee	Story of the Symphony.
Hamilton	Epochs in Musical Progress.
Hamilton	Outlines of Music History.
Pratt	History of Music.
Landormy	A History of Music.
——	The Oxford History of Music.
Grove	Dictionary of Music and Musicians.
Coerne	Evolution of Modern Orchestration.
—	The Art of Music (The Orchestra).
Newmarch	Concert-Goers' Library of Descriptive Notes.
Wilson	Music and the Gramophone.

Chapter I

THE DEVELOPMENT OF ORCHESTRAL INSTRUMENTS, AND EVOLUTION OF THE SYMPHONY

IT is perfectly obvious that the first, most primitive utterances of the human family were vocal, and that very many centuries must have passed before anything in the nature of instrumental experiments could have been made. An infant uses his lungs long before he makes conscious use of his hands; and in music, the human race must have remained in the infantile stage for a tremendously long time.

The author can not bring himself to recognize, or place any confidence in, the "music" of ancient peoples—two to five thousand years back — notwithstanding the copious, ofttimes glowing and enthusiastic visions that able historians have placed before us, bearing upon ancient music. Besides, this is not the place, and it cannot be our purpose, to delve into the psychological depths of the musical mystery, fascinating and illuminating though it might prove to be, to some students. Our aim is, mainly at least, a practical one, and deals exclusively with those comparatively recent ages whose influence upon the musical creations of our own era can be traced and defined with some measure of accuracy and authority.

The evolution of the Symphony is so inseparably identified with, and dependent upon, the history and development of musical instruments that it is imperative to begin with the latter.

Just when the first musical instrument was fashioned and used, no one can tell; but there is proof positive of the existence of such contrivances, some very crude, and others remarkably refined (at least in appearance), dating back to the dawn of history. The ancient Egyptians did surely possess and manipulate an array of *Harps* (*tebuna*), besides many other more or less inviting tone-producing instruments; the Hebrews had their sacred *Shofar* and numerous other mediums of mechanical tone-production, enumerated in the Bible; the Chinese their venerable and venerated *Cheng* and *King;* the Hindus their *Vina;* the Greeks their various *Lyres* and *Kitharas*, also *Flutes*, single and double; the Romans their *Flutes* and *Trumpets*. But the greater part of these mechanical agents are so remote, and have exerted so little influence upon the instruments that form the modern orchestra, that they may be dismissed with complaisant mention. The only ones of these ancient instruments that appear to have persisted and to have become approximate models for later days are the *Flutes*, the rounded metal *Buccina*, and the straight *Tuba* (or *Lituus*, when slightly curved at the end) of the Romans, whose general resemblance to the present flute, horn and trumpet is noteworthy.

Of far greater significance are three more recent contrivances of the Arabs and Persians, the *Rebab* and *Kemangeh* — stringed instruments that passed over quite directly into our present viola or violin and 'cello; further, the *Lute* (*"el aud"*—aloe wood) which became the type for the prodigious number of Italian lutes; and the *Zurna,* an instrument of nasal quality which probably led to the European *Pommer* family (sixteenth century), the highest member of which is practically identical with the modern oboe. These were familiarized through the crusades, that brought many European nations into contact with the Orientals. The lute, though wholly banned from the modern orchestra, nevertheless promoted greatly the cultivation of the instrumental style, since its qualities were peculiarly adapted to accompaniments in detached chords, thus favoring the harmonic style and furthering precise rhythmic accents, and, in general, inviting independent treatment.

It should be borne in mind that serious music, up to and far into the sixteenth century, was almost exclusively vocal. The Masses of the Church, and the Madrigals of the secular world, were the predominating channels of musical expression, and they neither sanctioned nor tolerated co-operation with instruments. Madrigals and other secular forms were sometimes transcribed for and played upon the lute (no doubt clumsily enough); and rustic dances, serenades, minstrel activities, and other musical inducements certainly furnished occasion for brief, more or less skillful instrumental practices from earliest historic times. But these inartistic musical occupations with the still rather imperfect instruments of early days, unpolished and unemotional (in the deeper sense), have no appreciable bearing upon the birth and development of the later artistic forms of instrumental music, excepting in that they did their share in preparing the soil for future accomplishments, and aided materially in bringing music closer to the common people, in a congenial form—more than the elaborate and exclusive music of the Church, or the artistic performances of trained singers could do.

The inception of a distinctive and independent instrumental style came very late. History associates the names of Giovanni Gabrieli (1557-1612) and Claudio Monteverde (or Monteverdi, 1567-1643) with the first conscious attempts to separate the vocal and instrumental styles, and to impart greater independence to the instrumental accompaniments and the purely instrumental preludes and interludes which were added to the vocal scores. Of these two distinguished composers it was Monteverde who became active in the promotion of the Opera (called into life about 1600), and herein he found the greatest and most natural inducement to develop and advance the co-operation of instruments, not only, as stated, in the accompaniment, but in numerous interspersed instrumental passages. He is called the father of the art of Instrumentation.

The instrumental apparatus of that day was exceedingly copious, including, besides several varieties of the organ, and of the harpsichord and clavichord, a large number of different sized lutes, a complete family of fiddles (fidula, viola, vielle, giga, violino, etc.), an equally complete set of wood-wind instruments (flutes, pommers or schalmeien, zinken), and numerous metal ones (horns, trumpets, trombones, tubas), also drums, and a quantity of other mechanical agents which it is not necessary to mention here.*

The first three of these groups—organ, harpsichord and lute—were not destined to become incorporated in the subsequently established orchestral family; but they were used, for a time only, and in an inferior capacity, in eking out the meagre resources of the primitive "orchestra" in the operatic music of the earlier periods; or they were employed for other purposes better suited to their character, in other kinds of secular music.

Of the instruments that were to survive ruthless elimination, the family of violins were far the most important. These were brought to a degree of perfection never yet excelled, by the famous Italian violin makers Amati (end of the sixteenth and far into the seventeenth century), Stradivarius (beginning of the eighteenth century), Guarnerius (seventeenth and eighteenth centuries), and others;

---

*Since it is the purpose of this chapter to present only the *essential* matters and facts involved, no further details are here given. The student is advised to consult such books as *Grove's Dictionary of Music*, *The New Encyclopedia of Music and Musicians* by Waldo Selden Pratt, or Theodore Baker's *Biographical Dictionary*, for fuller information concerning these diverse instruments, composers, and other items presented in these pages.

and as quintet, embracing the full musical compass, nearly equal to that of the modern pianoforte, the violin-family became the unchallenged basis of the symphonic orchestra.

Next in value came the wood-wind instruments; (1) those with reeds: the pommers, schalmeien and zinken, produced in five or six different sizes, and developing into the oboes (about 1700), bassoons (sixteenth century), and clarinets (about 1700); and (2) those without reeds: the flutes, of which there was also a complete quartet, of different sizes (fifteenth to seventeenth centuries), finally reduced to one standard form and admitted into the select company of the symphonic orchestra. The flutes maintained a worthy standing in the musical practices of the seventeenth and eighteenth centuries, not alone as accompanying, but also as solo instruments. While the violins enjoyed the preference among the Italians, the flute was the almost unrivalled favorite of the French, who found its sweet, languorous tone congenial (especially in aristocratic circles), and it was, and is, of all symphonic solo instruments the easiest to play.* Reams upon reams of music were written for the ordinary flute, not only in France—even as late as 1792, when no less a master than Beethoven composed a "little duo for two flutes without bass,"—and beyond that date.

The reed-instruments held their own, and, passing through many successive stages of mechanical improve-

---

*A comprehensive and illuminating account of this by Louis Fleury appears in the *Musical Quarterly* of Oct. 1923, under the title *The Flute and Flutists in the French Art of the Seventeenth and Eighteenth Centuries*.

ment, became a significant contingent of the symphonic orchestra, in four sizes: the oboe (or hoboe, from the French *haut bois*)*, the English horn (curiously misnamed, for it is in reality neither a horn nor is it English), the bassoon, and the contra-bassoon.

The clarinet belongs to the same tribe of wood-instruments, but is more intimately related to the early French *chalumeau*, from which it was differentiated, and greatly refined, about the year 1700. Though of exquisite tone-quality, infinite capacity for nuances, and eminently adapted to and qualified for orchestral purposes, it did not find its way into the orchestra as an essential factor until the days of Haydn and Mozart. It is used in three slightly different sizes, to render its extremely difficult manipulation more convenient for different keys.

The brass instruments underwent but little modification, and were incorporated into the orchestra in nearly their original ancient form. The most momentous improvements were the invention of the sliding mechanism for the trombones (beginning of the sixteenth century), and the adoption of independent valves for the trumpet and horn (1770 to about 1850), whereby these instruments were transformed from the "bugle" type, limited to the aliquot or harmonic overtones, into full chromatic instruments of vastly enhanced capacity and facility. The four horns ("rounded" tube) generally employed in the modern or-

---

*Oboes were made in several sizes and used by Bach and others in the accompaniments to their vocal compositions, not, however, to any extent as solo instruments.

chestra are all exactly alike in size; but the other, "straight" tube group, forms a complete family of four or five members in different sizes: the trumpet, the alto-trombone, tenor-trombone, bass-trombone, and tuba—though the latter is, strictly speaking, not a legitimate member of the trombone family (with which it is always associated), but is more closely allied to the horn type. The tuba superseded the ophicleide, which in its turn was derived from the (wooden) Serpent.

About the kettledrums no more need be said than that they very early found their way into every orchestral body without challenge, because of their immense rhythmic importance; and the same applies, though not for this especial reason alone, to the other percussive contrivances.*

This list represents, then, the legitimate constituents of the modern symphonic orchestra; limited somewhat in number up to, and during, the epoch of Haydn and Mozart, but unfolding into full bloom through Berlioz and his successors—not infrequently expanding beyond these normal confines.†

* * *

Allusion was made above, in connection with the operas of Monteverde, to the custom of employing musical instru-

---

*See further *From Song to Symphony* by D. G. Mason, Chapter VII. See also *Musical Instruments* by Edgar Stillman Kelley, wherein will be found an account of all these musical contrivances, as comprehensive as it is masterly, and with very copious cuts illustrating the appearance and relative sizes of the various instruments.

†An interesting and significant side light is thrown upon the choice and application of instruments as *accompaniments* to church music (that is, not independently) in an article by Orlando A. Mansfield in the *Musical Quarterly* of April, 1916.

ments *independently of the vocal parts*, in Preludes, and in Intermezzi or Interludes. These purely instrumental numbers were naturally brief; but little more, at first, than unpretentious passages, barren of thematic relation to the rest. Therefore they must have appeared inconsequential at the time; but it was out of them that a wholly new and glorious phase of musical expression was to emerge, culminating in the monumental Symphonies of our day. *They were at first called "symphonies" (Sinfonie).*

This would seem to locate the starting point of our Symphony. But such a conclusion would be partly erroneous; for the word "symphony" was not an innovation; it had been used now and then in a musical connection ever since it was first pronounced in ancient Greek theories, where it signified "sounding together"; just as the analogous word "sonata" ("sounding piece") was occasionally employed, primarily for vocal compositions, long before it became the distinctive title for a type of instrumental music. But why the term "symphony" chanced to be applied to these instrumental passages it is not easy to determine. Later on, the word was applied only to the *first* or opening passage, while the other (interspersed) phrases were called "ritornelles."*

At the same time, or shortly afterward, this introductory "Symphony" began to differentiate itself to a marked degree, assuming a decidedly more significant character

---

*The use of the term *Sinfonia* for the first movement of the Suite, in keeping with the old custom of marking thus the opening number of the preludes to the early opera, is confirmed in the second of Bach's six *Partite* (another name for Suites, particularly in Italy) for the clavichord.

than the ritornelles possessed. The object of the symphony was to prepare the hearer for what was to follow, and it therefore adopted a larger form and more serious pose; whereas the ritornelles served solely to alternate briefly with the vocal parts, in a lighter fashion, and consisted of chords, runs, and short ornamental figures of specifically instrumental effect.

In time the term "Overture" superseded the word "symphony" for this opening instrumental number, an innovation which is ascribed to Alessandro Scarlatti (1659-1725), who was the first to attach greater importance to the Overture, and who not only gave it a far more serious and refined bearing, but also established its structural pattern. This pattern, known as the Italian Overture, consisted legitimately of three sections: the first one in rapid tempo, the second in slow tempo, and the third again rapid—*allegro, adagio, allegro.*

As the Overture grew in importance and in popularity, these three tempi—in other words, Movements—were detached from each other, and each one developed into a separate and independent piece. And here it is that we recognize the point of departure, *the actual beginning, of the modern Symphony.*

The following example is given, not as an illustration of the complete Overture (for it consists of one section only), but as a specimen of instrumental music as it appeared in connection with the early opera. It is the prelude (or "symphony") to Monteverde's *L'Orfeo,* given in Mantua in

1607, and is scored for no fewer than thirty-three instruments—viola, tromboni, cornetti, flautino, clarino, regal, chitaroni, and one or two others:

MONTEVERDI, *L'orfeo*

Note the persistent adherence to the tonic harmony throughout,* with but occasional transient allusions to the dominant; the persistent bass tones; the uniformity of the

*An idea adopted by Wagner—in a vastly higher artistic sense—in the Prelude to his *Rheingold*.

tenor, and also of the alto, relieved by the quaint and highly effective rhythmic patterns. The only *musical* thread is at the top, as quasi melody; and it is, despite a certain monotony, decidedly interesting and expressive. As a whole, this "symphony" creates a singularly spirited impression even upon modern ears, and is by no means totally devoid of musical beauty.

It was not until nearly a century later that the Overture was extended in Italy, as indicated above, to three separate sections or Movements: *allegro, adagio, allegro*. And when Jean Baptiste Lully (1633-1687), the pioneer of the opera in France, began his remarkable career with *Les fêtes de l'Amour et de Bacchus*, in 1672, he soon fell in with the Italian plan of the Overture in three sections, but *reversed the order of the tempi,* so that the French Overture consisted thereafter always of a rapid movement between two slow ones. It was not this arrangement, it will be remembered, that was adopted in the nascent Symphony, but the earlier order which had become distinctive of the *Italian* Overture.

An example of the French type is here given, chiefly to confirm the progress that this early era of the instrumental art was making in independence, ingenuity of treatment, and more genuinely musical expression. It is the Overture to Lully's opera *Phaëton*, produced in Paris in 1683. The make-up of his orchestra is not indicated, but it probably included kettledrums, since Lully is known to have led in the introduction of these into the orchestral body.

Hand in hand with the mechanical perfecting of the instruments, the advances made in their technical manipulation, and the ever increasing realization and conscious recognition of what absolute music offered to the yearning spirit of human expression, went the steady evolution of a style of music that was destined to reach undreamt-of heights, and to bear fruits of transcendent beauty and power, such as we more fortunate beings now taste and enjoy—that, in a word, led to the magnificent symphonic achievements of our day (to mention only that type of artistic musical accomplishment which directly concerns the present reader). It is manifestly important that the student of the Symphony should trace the course of this development, at least in its broader outlines.

There were at this early epoch three distinct styles of instrumental music in vogue, each complete in itself and outwardly independent of the others, and yet all overlapping each other at certain points, and exerting a stimulating influence upon one another, namely: the Suite, the Sonata and the Symphony.

I. The Suite (seventeenth century) was primarily, and always chiefly, a mere collection of Dances, though other pieces of a more poetic and not infrequently of pictorial (descriptive) character were often interspersed, especially in France, to the number of from four to six as a rule, all in the same key, and usually in the same form—either a double-period or a primitive Two-Part form. This latter form was gradually elevated to the more refined and artistic design that became characteristic of the Sonata-movement, cultivated by François Couperin, Domenico Scarlatti and many other devotees of instrumental music (in France, Italy, England and Germany), and which, after a few additional perfecting strokes, was to evolve into the fixed structural type of the Symphony-movement.

An early example of this popular Two-Part form, selected from the copious *Pièces de clavecin* by François Couperin (*le Grand*, 1668-1733) illustrates very clearly the embryo of that structural scheme from which the modern Sonata-allegro form was to emerge. It is entitled *Le réveille-matin*, and is of that descriptive order to which allusion was made above.

EVOLUTION OF THE SYMPHONY

The First Part is a double-period of eleven measures, modulating in the fourth measure and closing with a cadence in the *dominant* key. It contains *one Theme only*, although a different motive sets in, in measure seven, which foreshadows the significant separation or "split," that, in the case of more expanded, broader examples, provides for a second (subordinate) Theme—to be demonstrated later on. The Second Part is considerably longer, and utilizes material from Part I, quite in accordance with the manner of the "Development" in the symphonic *Allegro*. It adds phrase to phrase in this fashion up to the twenty-seventh measure, at which point the third phrase (*not* the first) of the First Part reappears—from measures five and six—but this time transposed to the principal key (F major); and in measure thirty-two the former new motive is resumed, also in the principal key this time, and restated exactly as before, to the end. *Thus the Second Part is both Development and "Recapitulation," in an embryonic stage.* Each Part is repeated.

The student may supplement this line of analysis by scanning other easily procurable examples, from the harpsichord compositions of Domenico Scarlatti, Couperin, Rameau, J. S. Bach and others.

II. The Sonata is much older than the Suite, the title, at least, having been in use (affixed to both vocal and instrumental pieces) during the preceding century or longer.

It consisted for quite a time of one single Movement, the structural plan of which advanced gradually from the simplest phrase-group up to the expanded Two-Part form illustrated in Ex. 3. This latter design appears to have owed its inception to Couperin *le Grand,* though rudimentary traces of it are found in still earlier works. It was regarded, in a sense, as the established structural scheme for the One-movement Sonatas; but it gradually widened out into a *Three-Part* form, with fairly definite presentation of two motives in the First Part—the germs of the later principal and subordinate Themes of the classic sonata-allegro form.

This "widening out" of the Two-Part form is somewhat similar to the enlargement demonstrated in Ex. 3, but it differs in one exceedingly important respect, namely: The tentative separation or "split" of the material of the first Part into two recognizable motives, and the recurrence of these two thematic members in the second Part, accomplished nothing more than this increase in the number of thematic impressions, and did not actually extend the scheme to *three* Parts; the form remains *Two-Part* only, for the manifest reason that there is no detached third Part in evidence. So that in leading over into the genuine sonata-allegro design, this transformation into a Three-Part form had first to be accomplished, and it is of this latter act that we are now speaking, an operation which took place along with the growth of the One-movement Sonata, at least principally.

The simple Three-Part form, as the student of musical architecture doubtless well knows, differs from the Two-Part form in that it contains a *return to the very beginning,* and a sufficiently clear presentation of the first motives of the first Part; all that follows this recurrence, from that point to the end, constitutes the Third Part.

There is something so supremely natural in this order of the structural factors: a Statement, a Digression for variety, and a return to the Statement for confirmation and a satisfactory closing of the circle—A-B-A,—that one wonders why any other arrangement should have been accepted from the very outset. It did occur, to be sure, though not as commonly as would appear natural. Its first pronounced application took place in the *da capo* Aria of early Italian operas, and thence passed over into instrumental music through the partly conscious and partly fortuitous transformation and expansion of the then almost universal Two-Part form, demonstrated in Ex. 3. Illustrations of the simple Three-Part form are so numerous—nine-tenths of our ordinary pianoforte literature being molded in this design—that no special example need be given here. The student will discover convenient masterly models of it in the Songs Without Words of Mendelssohn, for instance, No. 25.*

A diagram will aid the student in unraveling the somewhat involved demonstration:

$\vee$ indicates a semi-cadence;

$\|$ indicates a perfect cadence.

1. The Phrase-group:

    $\|$————$\vee$————$\vee$————$\vee$————$\vee$———— etc. $\|$

2. The Double-period:

    $\|$————————$\vee$————————$\vee$————————$\|$

3. The simple Two-Part form (very similar to the Double-period):

    $\|$ I. ————$\vee$———— $\|$ II. ————$\vee$———— $\|$

---

*As an aid in this quest, the student is referred to the *Analytic Edition* of the Songs Without Words (Oliver Ditson Company).

4. The expanded Two-Part form, common in the single Sonata movement (Ex. 3):

|| I. ~~~ || II. ~~~ ||
    New   New
   motive   motive, transposed.

5. The simple Three-Part form:

|| I. ~~ || II. ~~~ III. ~~~ ||
                        Like I.

6. The expanded Three-Part form, as Sonata- (or Symphony-) allegro (the combination of 4 and 5):

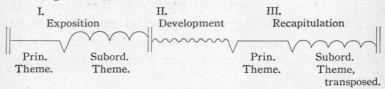

In view of the fact that the Symphony is a "Sonata for Orchestra," it is obvious that the evolution of the Sonata has very direct bearing upon that of the Symphony. The steady development and perfecting of the instrumental Sonata, beginning with Andrea Gabrieli (1586) and carried along by Couperin, Johann Kuhnau, Domenico Scarlatti, the great Bach and his son Philipp Emanuel Bach, and many others, achieved its highest fulfilment in the classic era of Haydn, Mozart and Beethoven.

Although the Sonata in one Movement was for awhile typical, it was not uncommon to enlarge it to two, three and even four Movements, under the influence, no doubt, of the contemporaneous Suite. As early as 1683, the eminent Italian violin-master Corelli wrote Sonatas in four short Movements: *adagio, allegro, adagio, allegro;* and the plan of three Movements finally became general, in both the Sonata and its more pretentious companion, the Symphony, the first Movement (at least) of which adopted the characteristic Two-Part form, as a very general rule.

III. The Symphony proper comprised from the beginning three separate Movements, and was originally, as has been shown, but little more than an expansion of the connected and homogeneous *Sections* of the Italian Overture— a slow Movement between two rapid ones.* The first step in the artistic unfolding and growth of the Symphony concerned chiefly the first one of its three Movements. This was so lengthened that one Theme did not suffice; or, perhaps more probably, the desire for a greater amount of thematic material, and also for an increase in variety, made an expansion of the form necessary. Be that as it may, it soon became customary to add a second (in a sense an auxiliary or "Subordinate") Theme, in a different key, a tentative specimen of which is clearly seen in Ex. 3 (Couperin). And the next significant step was the unfolding of the structural scheme out of the prevalent Two-Part into the far more artistically adequate and perfect

---

*This calls to mind, albeit there is not the remotest historic connection involved, the famous First, Second and Third Music of the English stage, in the eighteenth century. These were three wholly different instrumental "selections," with reasonable pauses between, designed to occupy the attention of a motley audience predisposed to disorderliness, while awaiting in a darkened theatre the beginning of the Play. The Third Music was called the "curtain piece" and corresponded to the Overture proper. As stated, there is no relation whatever here to the continental Overture; still, it is an engaging analogy, and, if nothing more, it confirms the universal instinctive predilection for a three-fold arrangement.

Three-Part form, by returning to the *beginning* after the second part had done its work, and restating the entire First Part, as Third,—whereby the second one of the two Themes was transposed to the principal key, thus providing for at least that kind and degree of diversity.

When thus magnified, the "Parts" assumed the proportions and qualities of "Divisions," the first of which is known as the Exposition (that is, the statement of the two Themes, with possible additions in the nature of Codettas, or concluding motives), the second as Development, and the third as Recapitulation (with the indicated transposition). See the diagram, No. 6. This design of the first (allegro) movement was maintained more or less persistently, and was handed over to Haydn, who recognized its superiority and firmly established it as standard for the classic structural design. It is now known as the Sonata-allegro—or, since the terms are synonymous, as the Symphony-allegro form. This, be it noted, does not refer to the complete Symphony, but to one, usually the first, *Allegro-movement*. It may be, and of course is, applied likewise to the other Movements, when their contents call for such a plan.

* * *

The earliest symphonist of whom music history makes respectful mention was *Giovanni Battista Sammartini* (1705-1775), whose first Symphony was performed in 1734 in Milan. He was credited with at least twenty-four such works.

He was followed by the celebrated *Stamitz* family, which contributed three or four members to the list of eighteenth-century celebrities, active in Germany and in France as eminent violinists and composers. The founder and probably the most illustrious of the family was *Johann Karl Stamitz* (1717 or 1719—1761), who may deserve credit as the most vigorous and successful promoter of the symphony, prior to the era of Haydn. Accounts of his output differ; it is certain that he produced twelve Symphonies, and some historians place the number as high as fifty. His eldest son, *Karl Stamitz* (1746-1801) was apparently even more prolific and generally popular than his father, the number of his Symphonies being estimated at seventy. An outline of one of the Symphonies of the elder Stamitz gives a sufficiently clear view of the status of the form at this momentous juncture. It is in D major, and is scored for the body of strings, plus nothing more than two oboes and two horns. The first movement is an *Allegro maestoso* in 4/4 measure, without Introduction. In the Exposition there is, besides the principal theme, a subordinate theme in A major, the conventional dominant relationship. The design is much like the prevailing Two-Part form, but a trifle more sharply delineated, since at least a fragment of the principal theme recurs, as Recapitulation, before the restatement of the subordinate Theme—this time in D major. The second movement, *Andante*, in 2/4 measure, is a miniature sonata-allegro design, well outlined. The third movement (Finale) is an *Allegro assai*, 6/8 measure, in the expanded Two-Part form. The music is respectable, and not wholly wanting in genuine musical qualities.

The next important names are those of *Christian Cannabich* (1731-1798, almost exactly contemporaneous with Haydn); and *François Joseph Gossec* (1733-1829), who has been called the creator of the French Symphony. The following example sketches a Symphony of Gossec in C major. It is scored for the usual quintet of strings, two oboes, two trumpets, two bassoons, two horns, three trombones and kettledrums (tuned, as is almost invariably the case in the classic orchestra, in the tonic and dominant of the key):

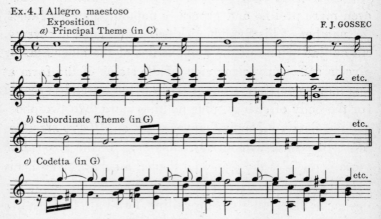

The first Division of this first Movement corresponds closely to the regular "Exposition" of the classic symphonic-allegro form, with its two themes and codetta. There is no Introduction. The codetta is repeated and extended. A "Development," forty-seven measures in length follows, consisting of obvious and commonplace references to the thematic material of the Exposition. The "Recapitulation," or recurrence of the Exposition, is abbreviated, but presents both themes—the subordinate one transposed as usual to the principal key; the codetta is omitted, and the final "Coda," derived directly from the principal theme, is very short.

The second Movement, in slow tempo, in the minor mode of the same key, is but little more than a Three-Part Song-form, beginning thus (flutes are here substituted for the trumpets):

The third Movement (Finale) is a sprightly *Presto*, after the traditional manner, based upon these themes:

The form is very similar to the expanded Two-Part design of the sonata (Ex. 3); that is to say, there is no complete "Recapitulation"; after the "Development" the principal Theme does not reappear—in its place stands the subordinate Theme, in the principal key.

One cannot gainsay this Symphony a certain vigor and some measure of genuine musical feeling. The second Movement is melodious and makes a mildly emotional appeal. But it is, on the whole, pedantic, stereotyped, and impresses a modern ear as decidedly sterile and unsophisticated. There are but few changes of key, and these only into the closely related ones; and there is the scantiest possible evidence of harmonic or rhythmic ingenuity—not a trace of inspiration or of any deeper purpose than that of entertaining a class of listeners unwonted to take a serious view of the tone-art.

A somewhat later composer, *Andrè E. M. Grétry* (1741-1813), author of the justly famous opera *Richard Cœur de Lion*, has six Symphonies to his credit, which manifest finer conception and workmanship than those of his predecessors.*

Strange to say, the symphony received no direct impulse from the two titanic geniuses, *Johann Sebastian Bach* and *Georg Friedrich Handel* (both born in 1685), though an immense influence was exerted by them upon this, as upon all other vehicles of musical utterance, indirectly, through the allied form of the *Concerto grosso* (a type akin to the Suite, and dating back to Corelli, 1712), of which Handel produced his magnificent twelve (in 1739), and Bach his still more masterly and momentous six *Brandenburg* Concertos (in 1721).

---

*An exceedingly interesting account of symphonic activities in Paris at this period will be found in the *Musical Quarterly* of Oct. 1924, pages 525-531. The entire article, by J.-G. Prod'homme, is instructive and worthy of careful perusal.

EVOLUTION OF THE SYMPHONY

QUESTIONS FOR REVIEW

1. Which medium of musical expression is the older?
2. Which early instruments served as models for some of the material of the modern orchestra?
3. What names are associated with the first conscious attempts to create an independent instrumental style?
4. Define the instrumental inventory of their day.
5. Which group proved to be the most important, and which came next?
6. Outline the history of the wood-wind group, and of the metal group.
7. In what connection with the opera were these instruments first used independently?
8. What were these passages called; to which one was the term later limited; and what name was finally assigned to the opening number?
9. Define the pattern of the Italian Overture.
10. In what respect did the French Overture differ from the Italian, and which of these became the pattern for the Symphony?
11. Which three types of instrumental music were in vogue in the 17th and 18th centuries?
12. Define, in general terms, each of these.
13. Outline the expanded Two-Part form, as commonly employed in the Sonata and in the first Movement of the early Symphony.
14. In what manner did this form expand into the Three-Part design?
15. Define the processes through which the Three-Part design developed into the established Sonata-allegro form.
16. Name some composers who successively contributed to the progress of the Symphony.

*　　*　　*

CHRONOLOGICAL LIST OF NOTED SYMPHONISTS

(MOSTLY PRIOR TO THE MATURE CREATIVE PERIOD OF HAYDN)
WHOSE NAMES OCCUR ON CONCERT PROGRAMS IN BOSTON,
NEW YORK AND PHILADELPHIA, PRIOR TO 1800

BACH, PHILIPP EMANUEL (1714-1788), credited with 18 Symphonies.

WAGENSEIL, G. C. (1715-1777), 30 Symphonies.

STAMITZ, JOHANN KARL (1717 or 1719-1761), 12 Symphonies.

ABEL, KARL F. (1725-1787), many Symphonies.

GOSSEC, F. J. (1733-1829), 26 Symphonies.

BACH, JOH. CHRISTIAN (1735-1782), many Symphonies.

DITTERSDORF, KARL D. VON (1739-1799), over 50 Symphonies.

WANHAL, J. B. (1739-1813), 100 Symphonies.

PICHEL, W. (1741-1805), 88 Symphonies.

PAISIELLO, GIOV. (1741-1816), 12 Symphonies.

STAMITZ, KARL (1746-1801), 70 Symphonies.

WRANITSKY, PAUL (1756-1808), 27 Symphonies.

PLEYEL, IGNAZ J. (1757-1831), 29 Symphonies.

GYROWETZ, ADALBERT (1763-1850), 60 Symphonies.

* * *

REFERENCES

JOHNSTONE	Instruments of the Modern Symphony Orchestra.
KELLEY	Musical Instruments.
ELSON	Orchestral Instruments and their use.
NATHAN	The Orchestra, and how to listen to it.
LEE	Story of the Symphony.
HENDERSON	The Orchestra and Orchestral Instruments.

MASON	Orchestral Instruments and what they do.
COERNE	Evolution of Modern Orchestration.
SCHLESINGER	Instruments of the Modern Orchestra.
GROVE	Dictionary of Music and Musicians.

ILLUSTRATIVE RECORDS

V—Victor

Records of Orchestral Instruments.

Chapter II

HAYDN AND MOZART

CAREFUL comparison of dates (a matter not to be ignored in the study of any evolutionary process) discloses the fact that some of the symphonic composers cited near the end of Chapter I were born *after* Haydn (1732-1809); therefore it may seem inconsistent to rank them, as it is customary to do, as forerunners of Haydn. The latter produced his first Symphony, in D major, in 1759, and it can not be said to foreshadow the epochal achievements of his later career. In the first place, however, it must be borne in mind that Haydn did his distinctive work in symphonic composition at a comparatively advanced age, after the other, older and younger men, had lost their hold upon the music-hungry public; and, furthermore, Haydn's immense superiority, in every respect, reduced the youngest of them to the rank of precursors, artistically, if not chronologically. Hence it is that the history of the Symphony as musical art creation of the most eminent type, and the outstanding monument of musical conception, is assumed to begin with Haydn.

But there is one name which received only passing mention in our list of Haydn's predecessors. For, because of its peculiarly direct bearing upon Haydn's productions, and because of its historic significance in itself, it is entitled to detached consideration—and that is the name of *Philipp Emanuel Bach*, son of the "great" Bach. He belongs properly, though inferior in rank, to the era of Haydn and his successors, and is rightfully designated their most important forerunner.

PHILIPP EMANUEL BACH

Philipp Emanuel Bach, the third son (second surviving one) of Johann Sebastian Bach, was born (1714) in Weimar, and died (1788) in Hamburg. Having made the latter town his principal residence, he is known as the Hamburg Bach—a mark of identification which serves to distinguish conveniently one particular member of so very numerous and individually famous a family. The family council decreed that Philipp should study law, but his inherited passion for music prevailed, and under his father's training he soon became proficient and ultimately almost as famous in his particular way as his immeasurably greater progenitor. He was a brilliant harpsichord player, and it was the elegance and refinement of his taste, rather than depth and power of real genius, that made him more accessible to the public and won for him far greater popularity and admiration—for a time— than were commonly bestowed upon his father. His famous book, *Experiments in the true Art of Clavier Playing* (1759), betrays the trend of his musical preferences. But he was a prolific composer, and his music (chiefly instrumental), though more graceful and ingratiating than profound in character, was sufficiently original and significant to serve as an inspiration and model for succeeding generations. His music exerted an immense influence on Haydn, whose early Symphonies are conceived in the selfsame spirit and manner.

Philipp Emanuel Bach wrote eighteen Symphonies, the third of which, composed in 1776, is here outlined as a specimen of his orchestral style. It is scored for the quintet of strings, two flutes, two oboes, one bassoon, one horn, and cembalo (harpsichord). The first Movement, to which there is no Introduction, presents the following thematic material:

The form is rather obscure. There is no double-bar to mark the end of the Exposition, though the presentation of the usual two well-defined Themes seems to round out the first Division recognizably; a sort of Development, not quite genuine in its relation to the foregoing, leads over into the subordinate Theme, without a return to the beginning—thus corroborating the expanded Two-Part form (diagram, No. 4). Several allusions to the principal motive, in various keys, are interspersed throughout, imparting to the whole a loose "sectional" impression. The

Movement closes on the dominant of D minor, and passes without a break over into the second Movement:

This is a lyric Movement of very real melodic beauty. The melody is carried almost constantly by the viola. The concise design approximates the Two-Part Song-form. There is but one Theme.

Note the similarity of this phrase to the first Theme of the first Movement—especially the second measure. This Movement, like the first one, closes with the dominant chord of the following *Presto*, and is joined to it without a pause.

The third, and final, Movement is a conventional lively *Presto*, inclining more toward the graceful than to the rollicking style:

The subordinate Theme is extended by a Codetta, and the close of the Exposition is emphatic. But, as in the first Movement, there is no complete Recapitulation; the Development merges into the recurrence of the subordinate Theme (transposed, as usual), and the design therefore does not exceed the expanded Two-Part form.

The similarity of thematic invention between the themes of this Symphony and many of those of Mozart, in both his youthful and more mature periods, is as unmistakable as it is striking and noteworthy. It is, however, more of an external coincidence than a conscious imitation; for though Mozart was as familiar with the music of the younger Bach as was Haydn, and also admired him greatly, he (Mozart) was a radically original genius, and such outward analogies as one frequently finds between his music and that of his contemporaries are due solely to the influence of the prevailing style.

Joseph Haydn

With Haydn we ascend, almost abruptly, a vastly higher plane of musical thought and feeling, rising steadily through Mozart, and attaining its summit in Beethoven.

Haydn's music bears witness to a new, advanced point of view; in it is revealed a newborn and deeper consciousness of the possibilities of musical expression, a finer sense of tonal beauty, a keener penetration into the apparent mysteries of the universal language of Tone. There still remain, naturally, some traces of the influence of tradition and habit; but from the very outset Haydn manifests a more lively imagination, greater freedom and originality, and a far superior grasp upon, and mastery of the technical and structural elements of composition. The rigidly pedantic, stereotyped, sterile qualities prevalent in much foregoing music are completely banished from the works of Haydn. His melodies are more spontaneous and more eloquent; his harmonies and modulations incomparably richer, freer, more exuberant and searching; his rhythms more manifold and vital; his counterpoint, though not abundant and never conspicuous, is as perfect and finely effective, in its modest measure, as is that of Mozart.

The salient, preëminent attribute of his muse is *cheerfulness;* his is the happy, gleeful, ardent voice of the carefree child, that could not be silenced by the very real discomforts, and even misery, which surrounded his earlier years. Therefore, Haydn's music is never genuinely pathetic, sentimental or passionate—the bulk of it is in major;—his face is always turned toward the light, and its radiant reflex illumines his every utterance. Hence, also, his pronounced sense of humor, proofs of which crop up at frequent intervals in all of his works.

Joseph Haydn was born March 31, 1732, in the Austrian village of Rohrau, near the Hungarian frontier, of humble parents. He received some early musical guidance from a relative, Matthias Frankh, who was chiefly instrumental in deciding that Joseph should make music his life work. Haydn's boyhood was spent as a choir boy in the church of St. Stephen in Vienna, in which stimulating surroundings he studied diligently, and composed a Mass at the age of thirteen, to which he referred in later life with satisfaction and pride. When his voice changed he left the choir and was thrown upon his own resources, which were slender enough to have broken the courage of a less optimistic youth. But he persevered in his studies, and one day he stumbled upon a volume of Sonatas by Philipp Emanuel Bach. Late in life, with the memory of this momentous hour vividly in mind, Haydn said: "I could not leave the clavier until I had played all the Sonatas through; and those who know me best must recognize that I owe a great deal to this master, that I understood him, and made a thorough study of him; he himself once sent me a compliment thereupon." Many years later (1782) a distinguished musical critic, J. F. Reichardt, wrote: "If we possessed no more than one Haydn, and Philipp Emanuel Bach, we Germans could boldly lay claim to an original style, and declare that our instrumental music is the most interesting of all."

In 1758 Haydn was appointed music-director by Count Morzin, and in 1759 Prince Esterhazy, who had heard Haydn's First Symphony (in D, 1759) induced Morzin to "let him have his composer." This put an end to the hardships of Haydn's youth, and his life thereafter, in the honorable capacity of "First Kapellmeister" to several successive members of the noble Esterhazy family, was free from privations, devoted assiduously to the outpouring of his musical genius in an incredible quantity of works of every form and style.

In 1781 Haydn first met Mozart, and the kinship of their genius, their sincere appreciation and admiration of each other, coupled with warm personal sympathy, gave birth to a friendship that was inspiring and beneficial to both. His encounter with Beethoven, in 1792, was less fruitful.

Early in 1791 Haydn accepted an invitation from the noted violinist Salomon, and spent eighteen months in London. The visit to England was repeated in 1794.

The remainder of his life was devoted chiefly to the composition of *The Creation* and *The Seasons*.

Haydn died May 31, 1809, in Vienna.

The number of his Symphonies is variously estimated as from 119 to 150. Out of this formidable list there are eighteen which constitute the best and most mature of his orchestral creations—six Paris Symphonies and the twelve English ones which he composed during his two sojourns in London; and it is upon these that his fame as creator of the first *Master-Symphonies* rests.

Those which sprang from his early period were written with more speed than reflection, no doubt, usually a half-dozen at a time; but they all contain some original and lovely touches, which reveal the rare genius of the youth; and are an earnest of the choicer fruits of his maturer years. The quaint titles of many of his early Symphonies (the first forty, from 1759 to 1770) imply a disposition on Haydn's part to adopt some poetic or dramatic basis for the work. Thus we encounter: *Le Midi, Le Matin, Le Soir* (closing with a thunderstorm), *Philosopher, Absent-minded, Farewell* (or "Candle" Symphony), *Schoolmaster, Fire, La Chasse, L'Ours, Children's* Symphony, and many others. This descriptive tendency, however, is not to be taken seriously; it does not detract in the slightest degree from the seriousness with which Haydn prosecuted his art —notwithstanding the utterly unconquerable buoyancy and cheerfulness of his temperament. It may be accounted for largely as a transient concession to the widespread custom of the day (compare the titles of many of the harpsichord compositions of Couperin, Rameau, Kuhnau, etc.).

And, in any event, it afforded Haydn an effective means of fathoming the powers of tone from this *natural* angle.

It must be admitted that the music of Philipp Emanuel Bach already presages many of the excellent traits that are so abundant and distinctive in that of Haydn, and this would account for Haydn's veneration of him.

What immense influence the imposing works of the "great" Bach might have exerted upon Haydn's whole manner, had he known them, it is hard to determine. But these works, excepting the *Well-Tempered Clavichord*, were for many reasons only locally familiar to North German music lovers, and even there they were soon neglected, and might have been forgotten, but for the resurrection of the *St. Matthew Passion*, by Mendelssohn in 1829, which led to the restoration of much of the greatest music that has ever been penned.

Haydn's Early Symphonies

One of Haydn's very earliest Symphonies (probably his second) exhibits the following contents and character. It is scored for the quartet of strings (a double-bass is not indicated), two horns, and two oboes. The first Movement opens without Introduction:

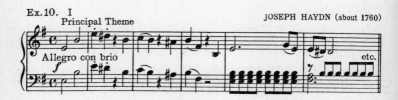

Ex. 10. I
Principal Theme
JOSEPH HAYDN (about 1760)
Allegro con brio

The choice of key is remarkable; E minor was for a long time the tonality most rarely adopted for the Symphony (No. IV of Brahms is the first "Master-Symphony" in that key). Three brief Codettas follow the themes and complete the Exposition. The Development is regular. The Recapitulation is greatly abbreviated—only a brief fragment of the subordinate Theme recurs (in the principal key), and one of the Codettas is omitted.

The second Movement is a Menuetto, with Trio:

Ex. 11. II Minuetto

The principal Division is conducted throughout in octave-canonic imitation. The Trio, in E major, is homophonic.

The third Movement is the traditional "slow" one, a beautiful lyric *Adagio*:

Ex. 12. III Principal Theme

Its structural design is the expanded Two-Part form (diagram, 4). The themes are clearly drawn, and the Exposition is normal; but there is no complete Recapitulation; the Development leads pointedly into the subordinate Theme (transposed).

The Finale is a *Presto*, but less breezy in character than the conventional last Movement:

The subordinate Theme is spun out to a considerable length, and one Codetta is appended. The form is the same as that of the preceding *Adagio*—expanded Two-Part; that is, there is no return to the principal Theme after the Development; but the entire lengthy subordinate Theme is presented (in the principal key), and the Codetta is enlarged to a Coda.

The student will perceive that all four Movements of this Symphony are in the same key—minor and major. This was the prevailing manner, and discloses another point of contact between the early Symphony and the Suite.

* * *

Haydn's Innovations

Haydn must be credited with two extremely important and far-reaching innovations, in his efforts to standardize the type of the Symphony, and give it a more adequate and perfect character and form. These are: (1) the insertion of one of the Dance-forms (most commonly a Minuet) borrowed from the Suite; and (2), the adoption and confirmation of the sonata-allegro plan, as the most consistent design for a composition of the lofty scholastic and artistic rank of the Symphony. His genius quickly discerned the psychologic interrelation of the Movements (increased by himself from three to four).

The Psychological Scheme of the Symphony

A Symphony opens, in its first (*allegro*) Movement, with that dignity and seriousness of bearing which immediately proclaim the lofty purpose of the whole. And for the proper fulfilment of this purpose, nothing short of the most perfect structural design, that of the Expanded Three-Part, or sonata-allegro form, with its firmness of line, its provision for contrast and confirmation, and its wholly satisfactory total effect, could be tolerated. To emphasize this weighty quality still further, it became customary with Haydn, especially in his later Symphonies, to prefix an Introduction, in slow tempo (generally *largo*), serious in tone, but arresting, and sometimes mildly dramatic. All the succeeding masters of the Symphony adopted the idea of the Introduction, and either applied it or omitted it, as swayed by the specific conceptive quality and aim of the work in its totality.

In the second Movement the atmosphere changes from this sterner aspect to a more intimate, lyric, emotional, altogether sympathetic mood, in slow or stately tempo. Now, the subsequent abrupt transition from this gentler mood to the hilarity and bustle of the Finale might well prove to be too startling; and for this reason Haydn drew upon the Suite for one of its most congenial dances (as stated, this was usually the Minuet); its complacent, graceful, partly subdued and partly rhythmically animated character fitted into this transitional purpose admirably, without interfering with the lively spirit, the rollicking gaiety of the last Movement.

The Finale itself naturally adopts the only medium of contrast that is left to choose from—the spirited, light-hearted, brilliant mood, which matches each of the foregoing phases sufficiently well, and leaves the hearer at the end with a sensation of exhilaration and complete satisfaction that crowns the enjoyment of the whole work.

These are the established qualities which earned for Haydn the title of Founder of the modern Symphony.

The proof of his wisdom lies in the fact that this four-square disposition of the symphonic Movements, with its well-defined and sensibly bridged contrasting moods, was accepted by Haydn's successors and has held its own without essential modification to the present day. Any deviation from it seems to lower the standard, and has necessitated the use of other titles, such as Tone-Poem, Orchestral Suite, and the like.

In the above example, Haydn, it is true, places the Minuet after the *Allegro* as *second* Movement; but the Dance soon gravitated to its established place as *third* Movement. Further, it was Beethoven who, by quickening the tempo of the Minuet and calling it a *Scherzo* in many of his works, established a slightly different and in some instances even more effective alternation and merging of moods.

The sonata-allegro design was occasionally adopted for the slow Movement, especially in larger and more pretentious works; and it was not unusual to apply it also to the Finale—although for a Movement of so light a nature, the more perspicuous and recognizable design of the *Rondo* appears to be the more consistent and effective. We shall return to this later on.

The "Candle" Symphony

There is something so quaintly humorous, so thoroughly in unison with Haydn's genial, sunny disposition, in his

Farewell Symphony (known also as the *Candle* Symphony), that a brief description of it is here given. The story runs thus:

In the summer of 1772, Haydn and his men, exhausted from their confining labors, looked forward to their early release from duty. But Esterhazy suddenly decided that they should remain two months longer. With ready wit, Haydn hit upon a musical method of voicing a protest, which could not irritate the Prince, and, should it fail of its aim, would at least give them all a hearty laugh. Very soon the task was completed (for Haydn wrote with incredible rapidity, and had only to adjust his scheme to the last movement of an already finished Symphony), and rehearsed; and the hour of performance drew near—

The entire Symphony, in the unusual key of F# minor, is music of finest fibre, and holds its own with the best that Haydn's genius and eminent workmanship ever consummated in the symphonic domain. It embraces the usual four Movements, of which only the Finale is here illustrated, since that is the only one involved in Haydn's humorous plan. This Finale, scored for full quintet of strings, two oboes and two horns, is in the regular sonata-allegro form, tersely presented. Its thematic material is as follows:

This Movement, although completely finished so far as the form is concerned, ends with a semicadence on the dominant of F♯, and thence passes over into an extra, fifth, Movement, which is to witness the perpetration of the musical jest. It is a graceful slow Movement (*adagio*) in A major, of gentle, ingratiating character, thus:

Ex. 15.

It is cast in the Three-Part Song-form, extended by a fourth Part (or Coda) which consists of the material of Part I, but transposed to F♯ major (the principal key of the Symphony).

At the cadence of the First Part, the 2nd horn and the 1st oboe players (following the direction *si parte* in the score) blow out their candles, quietly close their books, and with their instruments walk off the stage, as if too weary to continue. The other players keep on, but twenty-three measures later, near the end of Part III, the 2nd oboe and the 1st horn leave in the same manner; a few measures farther along, the double-basses, then the 'celli, then all but one of the first and second violins, then the violas—puff out their candles and walk away, leaving only the two solo-violins, playing alone. The closing phrase, given to these, runs thus:

Prince Esterhazy saw the point, interpreted the innocent pantomime in the kindliest spirit and said: "Haydn, I understand you; the gentlemen may leave tomorrow."

Haydn's Mature Symphonies

As stated above, the best of Haydn's symphonic production is recorded in his last twelve Symphonies, composed in London from 1791 to 1794. Some of these carry distinctive titles, as the *Drum-roll* (No. I), the *London* (No. II), the *Drum-beat* (or *Surprise*, No. VI), and the *Military* (No. XI). There is also an *Oxford* Symphony, written in 1788 for Paris, but first performed in London, July, 1791; it was so named in recognition of the distinguished honor accorded to Haydn by Oxford University, in conferring upon him the honorary degree of Doctor of Music on that occasion.

The title *Drum-roll* is due to the singular opening of the Symphony with a solo roll of the drum, one measure:

The history of the *Drum-beat* (not to be confounded with the "Drum-roll") again discloses Haydn's unconquerable humor, and his love of a good musical joke. The second (slow) Movement of the Symphony is an extremely simple melody, of folk-song character, the first Period of which runs thus:

Ex. 17. II JOSEPH HAYDN (1792)

At the end of the Period, on the heels of the softest pianissimo repetition, there is a sudden terrific crash of the drum (and entire orchestra). One explanation of the origin of this jest is to be sought in a remark of Haydn's at the time: "It was my intention to give the audience something new that would surprise them." But the real underlying impulse was Haydn's determination to check the inclination of his hearers to fall asleep (after their customary heavy dinner), during the performance of his music. It was a genuine surprise, and led to the nickname *Surprise,* by which the Symphony was thereafter known.*

---

*For more details, structural and otherwise, of this Symphony, see the *Analytic Symphony Series,* No. 1.

58 *MASTERS OF THE SYMPHONY*

The *Military* Symphony was so called chiefly because Haydn, in the second Movement (based upon a most charming French Romance), augmented his orchestra in a very unusual manner by the addition of a bass-drum, cymbals and triangle—strong percussion instruments which give the 4/4 measure the character of a military parade. But there are still other traits which contribute to the "military" impression.

(See the *Analytic Symphony Series*, No. 19.)

Haydn's last, and in many respects best and most mature Symphony (No. XII of the London group) exhibits the following thematic factors. The first Movement begins with an impressive Introduction—an addition to the form for which Haydn manifests a more positive inclination in his later than in his earlier Symphonies:

The form is a regular sonata-allegro of unusual length and breadth of conception. The Development is masterly, and indicates plainly the important advance in Haydn's musical thought. The early type of the Development-sections, practised by Haydn's predecessors and for quite a period by Haydn himself—the dry, perfunctory, haphazard (or worse still, purely mechanical) recurrences of the motives of the Exposition, with no fixed purpose, and no higher aim than to occupy the hearer's attention until it was about time to go back to the beginning—this lifeless type was gradually supplanted, in Haydn's works, by the *genuine* Development, in which the material of the Exposition was made to serve a definite progressive plan, with ingenuity, originality and spirit. Such is this one of Haydn; and it exhibits some of the fine artistic qualities that entered so vitally into the supreme methods of Beethoven. Herein Haydn was unquestionably influenced by the last three great Symphonies of Mozart, written in 1788 (six years before these of Haydn). It is a curious historic phenomenon: Mozart, at first the pupil and emulator of Haydn, becomes finally his preceptor and model.

The second Movement, which reveals marked affinity with Mozart's most characteristic slow Movements, is a regular Three-Part Song-form (Part I repeated), opening thus:

Ex. 19. II

Its message is serious, but delivered affably and without sentimentality, in a delightfully smooth, flowing rhythm.

The third Movement is the Menuetto with Trio—already a firmly established conventionality:

Ex. 20. III. Menuetto

Of especial charm is the Trio, with its interesting melody, and the singularly attractive cadences, in which (see measures 8-9, 15-16) the flute lays a lovely tonal arc over the cadence-lines of the other instruments—six times in all, and always the same tones, *f-d*. Note the altered rhythmic location of these tones, as indicated by the cadence-marks V—at first *over*, and then *at* the cadence.

The Finale is, as usual, a rollicking *Presto* Movement, sparkling, and permeated with humor. It is cast in the Third Rondo-form (explained below), and presents the following thematic factors:

Ex. 21. IV
Principal Theme

It would require a whole chapter to point out all the marvels of ingenuity, imagination and technical dexterity with which Haydn manipulates this material. The reader is urged to make a thorough study of this felicitous Finale; he will discover the source upon which Beethoven freely drew, even in his later works, for many a clever conceit that we are accustomed to appraise as original with Beethoven (for example, the episode in the Coda). Note the manifold treatment of the first three-tone figure. Note, also, that the two subordinate Themes employ the motives of the principal Theme, in a different manner and environment.*

Thus did Haydn round out his symphonic activity, and crown his final concept with a genius and mastership that vindicate his rank as Founder and Father of the Classic Symphony.

The Rondo-forms

The Rondo design is simply an *alternating* presentation of principal and subordinate Themes. Its age may be inferred from this very simplicity of purpose; it is found among the earliest specimens of instrumental music, oftenest as Dance, consisting of a short principal Period *alternating* with equally brief, different, subordinate Periods, often to the number of five, six or more, after the pattern of the French poetic "Rondeau"—whence the name.

In its more modern (classic) shape the Rondo appears in three dimensions:

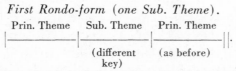

*This similarity of the two chief Themes, instead of the contrast that would be expected, was very common—almost the rule—in Haydn's day, and rested upon the universal, and in that era particularly prevalent, demand for thematic *Unity*. It is encountered a little less frequently in Mozart, but was recognized as valid by Beethoven, Mendelssohn, Brahms and others, gaining, rather than losing, its structural authority among present-day composers. Conspicuous examples are: Beethoven, last Movement of the piano Sonata, Op. 26; first Movement of his Fifth Symphony; Brahms, First Symphony, slow Movement; Glazounov, first Movement of the piano Sonata, E minor, Op. 75; d'Indy, first Movement of the String Quartet, E major, Op. 45.

Second Rondo-form (two Sub. Themes).

Pr. Th.	I. Sub. Th.	Pr. Th.	II. Sub. Th.	Pr. Th.
|————|	|————|	|————|	|————|	|————|
	(different key)		(different key)	

Third Rondo-form (Second Rondo, extended).

Pr. Th.	I. Sub. Th.	Pr. Th.	II. Sub. Th.	Pr. Th.	I. Sub. Th.	Pr. Th.
|————|	|————|	|————|	|————|	|————|	|————|	|————|
	(different key)		(different key)		(transposed to prin. key)	(or Coda)

* * *

Wolfgang Amadeus Mozart

With Haydn, music was an absorbing, serious Plaything—in the highest and best sense, be it understood. He derived as much enjoyment and amusement from his occupation with tones as any child could get out of his most inviting toys. And yet it was always a momentous game that he played; in all of the immense volume of his works there is not a trivial note, not the faintest suspicion of superficiality, or indifference to the rules of the game.

With Mozart, music was that too, at times, for the disposition of these two great masters was fundamentally alike. But Mozart's spirit reached out farther; he saw things that Haydn did not. He felt that music was more than a passive Plaything; saw that it was a Language with a life of its own and pregnant with the power of speech; a medium of communication, the bearer of spiritual messages from soul to soul. This quality in music Mozart *felt*, and he gave evidence of his prescience, not infrequently, in episodes that seem to convey a deeper spiritual Meaning, far more significant and touching than the supreme beauty of the music itself; a Meaning still vague and elusive in Mozart's communications—for it was reserved for Beethoven to penetrate still deeper into the mysteries of the Language of music, and to deliver spiritual messages that are as vital and unmistakable as they are indefinable.

Wolfgang Amadeus Mozart was born January 27, 1756, in Salzburg, Austria. His father, Leopold Mozart, a violinist and composer of considerable reputation, was well fitted to guide the musical development of his amazingly precocious son, and he devoted his life to this great and responsible task. So rapidly did the genius of Wolfgang unfold that when he was only six years old (by which time he had already composed a set of violin sonatas) his father felt justified in undertaking an extensive concert tour with the lad, through Munich to Vienna, Paris and London, lasting over three years.

While in London, Wolfgang composed his first Symphony (1764) which, with others that promptly followed, were publicly performed and "greatly admired."

Although his musical occupations had been conducted chiefly in the instrumental domain, Mozart's mind early turned to dramatic music, for which he always evinced a decided preference, and in 1768 he wrote, in Vienna, at the Emperor's request, his first opera, *La finta semplice*.

In 1769 his father took him to Italy, and this journey was one of unintermittent triumphs, besides contributing in the most propitious and powerful manner to the general education and the unfolding of the character of the youth. Unspoiled by the adulation and enthusiastic recognition of the public, and of the musically learned class as well, Mozart retained the unassuming, gentle, lovable and noble qualities which characterized his whole life. In Milan his opera *Mitridate* was given (in 1770) with tremendous success, and this was followed by a series of masterly dramatic works that carried his fame to its summit in the unparalleled operas *Figaro* (1786), *Don Giovanni* (1787) and *The Magic Flute* (1791).

At the same time, he did not neglect the instrumental style, but produced a profusion of concerted works for orchestra, with piano, and with other instruments; also compositions for piano alone; many string quartets, quintets, and other types of Chambermusic; further, quantities of orchestral works, including about fifty Symphonies.

Mozart's existence was far from being one of unclouded happiness. In one way or another circumstances seemed to conspire against his comfort and financial well-being; he was often reduced to absolute poverty, and suffered positive distress. Still, his thoroughly happy, optimistic disposition; the appreciation which was seldom denied his glorious artistic achievements; and the unquenchable joy he found in his beloved art—these things seem to have outweighed the misery which from time to time he could not escape, and to have kept the sacred fire alive in his breast. At last, however, suffering, illness, overwork, and the nervous strain incidental to his creative labors exacted their toll, and with his premature death—December 5, 1791—one of the most lovable, most phenominally gifted, purest and most masterful musical spirits passed away.

Mozart's First Symphony

No little historic interest attaches to Mozart's very first Symphony, written in London in 1764 (at the age of eight!) a fragment of which is here given. It is scored for the quartet of strings, two horns and two oboes. The first

Movement is a simple but regular sonata-allegro, with the following principal Theme:

This is followed by a second Movement, *Andante,* and a Finale, *Presto.* (There is no Minuet.)

One extraordinary thing about it is that it is the work of a child of eight years; and another thing that compels our amazement, is the ambition, self-assurance, temerity of the youngster in assailing such a problem. Regarded as artistic music, it has, assuredly, no special value. But you cannot expect much of a boy of eight, especially in an encounter with so formidable an object as the Symphony. On the other hand, it must not be forgotten that Mozart was preternaturally precocious, equipped with an intelligence and experience far beyond his years. He already possessed more *instinctive* knowledge of the language of tone than many a professional musician can boast of having acquired at the end of a long and studious career. He was saturated with a consciousness of the basic principles of tone-relation and tone-organization; he was quick to apprehend the operation of these principles in the music he so dearly loved and eagerly devoured; the "rules" of the art were second nature to him. But besides this the youthful Mozart possessed—as the future confirmed—a musical imagination of extraordinary scope, originality and vitality, and was strongly impelled by the desire to pour out his musical feelings, reproduce his musical visions, and record them in tangible form.

Passing over a few other Symphonies composed by Mozart in his next succeeding youthful years, it is instructive to pause at one of the later ones (his twelfth), written in July, 1771—at the age of fifteen,—and to verify the marked progress in assurance and technical grasp.

The first Movement, scored for full quintet of strings, two oboes and two horns, presents these thematic lines:

The design is sonata-allegro, regular and very concise. The Development is short; the Recapitulation complete. Note the similarity of the two Themes, a structural feature demonstrated under Ex. 21.

In the second Movement, an *Andante*, two flutes are substituted for the two oboes. The Themes run thus:

Ex. 24. II
Principal Theme

The design is sonata-allegro, but so concise that it barely reaches beyond the Three-Part Song-form. Both this and the first Movement are fine illustrations of the expanding process from the Three-Part Song-form into the sonata-allegro form. See the diagram in Chapter I, Nos. 5 and 6.

A keen ear will sense in the Themes of this *Andante* the distinctive quality of Mozart's melodic conception, nascent and unpronounced, but not to be mistaken. Haydn would not have written them thus; perhaps no one but just Mozart, even in this, his formative, period. Note the imitation in the inner voice.

For the third Movement, Mozart, following Haydn's lead, inserts a Minuet with Trio:

Ex. 25. III Menuetto (regular 3-Part form)

The Finale is animated, but heroic rather than gay. The design is that of the Dance, Song with Trio, each in the regular Three-Part form (the same as in the third Movement). The principal Theme begins thus:

The Trio-Division is in G minor, and is followed, as always, by a recurrence of the entire first Division.

Mozart's Last Symphonies

The finest, ripest fruits of Mozart's orchestral creation are recorded in five of his last Symphonies, two in D major (Nos. 35 and 38), and the three great masterworks in E♭ major, G minor and C major (Nos. 47, 48 and 49).*

The one in D, numbered 35, is known as the *Haffner* Symphony, having been designed for a festivity in the house of Siegmund Haffner, the "Mayor" of Salzburg, July, 1782. It has no Introduction but—as is somewhat

---

*All five are included in the *Analytic Symphony Series*, and may there be examined in minute detail.

more common with Mozart—begins abruptly with an exceedingly spirited Theme, worthy of quotation:

The subordinate Theme assumes a shape so similar, outwardly, to the principal one, that the hearer might question its own identity. But it must be recalled that, as pointed out in the footnote following Ex. 21, such thematic *unity* was considered not alone permissible but desirable. Here, the necessary contrast is secured by the difference in statement (it appears at first "upside down"), and by the new motives which grow naturally out of this one. Further, it seems to have been Mozart's express purpose to lay almost exclusive emphasis upon this festive Theme throughout. The form of the first Movement is sonata-allegro. It is scored for the "full" orchestra of that day: the quintet of strings, full octet of wood-wind (two each of flute, oboe, clarinet and bassoon), two horns, two trumpets, and the kettledrums.

The usual slow Movement; Minuet; and Finale, complete the Symphony.*

The student's attention is directed to the dramatic gesture in the third measure of this principal Theme, and he should compare these two rather pompous staccato beats with those in the second measure of Ex. 7 (Ph. Em. Bach); also with the second measure of Ex. 10 (Haydn); of Ex. 13; and Ex. 22 (Mozart, third measure). It is a "dramatic gesture" that was exceedingly popular and, as these examples show, astonishingly common in the earlier Symphonies. It occurs in many other Themes of Haydn and Mozart, but with diminishing frequency—like a mannerism whose hollowness was being detected. A lingering echo of it occurs in the Finale of Beethoven's Second Symphony (in the 2nd and 6th measures); but it is not unlikely that Beethoven, who abhorred "gestures" of any kind, was here, in this humorful Movement, good-naturedly mimicking the empty bombast of bygone days. Still, he uses the figure seriously in the 2nd measure of his piano Sonata, Op. 2, No. 3; also in the 1st and 2nd measures of Op. 22, and even in the 2nd measure of his prodigious Sonata, Op. 106. It was completely repudiated by Schubert, Mendelssohn, Schumann and Brahms, in their Symphonies—although Brahms makes fine, *genuine* dramatic use of it in his first piano Concerto, Op. 15, second measure.

The other D major Symphony of Mozart, numbered 38, and known as the *Symphony without Minuet* (finished December 6, 1786), stands upon an equally eminent plane with the great "last three." Many critics esteem it one of the most admirable products of symphonic literature up to the close of the eighteenth century. The score, otherwise "full," includes *no clarinets*. It begins with an imposing

*See the *Analytic Symphony Series*, No. 23.

Introduction, followed by these thematic components of the Exposition:

Ex. 28. I Introduction W. A. MOZART (1786)

Note the number and variety of thematic figures (motives) in the principal Theme; each one of these plays an important part in the formation of the Exposition. The beautiful subordinate Theme, a Period of eight measures, is immediately repeated in the minor mode, with singularly telling effect. Three or four Codettas are added. The

Development is an ingenious manipulation of these thematic factors, culminating in a Returning-passage of great beauty, in the minor mode, over a dominant organ-point. The Recapitulation is a nearly exact recurrence of the Exposition, with the usual transpositions.

This Movement is followed by an *Andante*, and a *Presto* Finale, both, like the first Movement, in the sonata-allegro form.

(See the *Analytic Symphony Series*, No. 24.)

* * *

The last three "great" Symphonies of Mozart were all written during one year (1788), an almost startling confirmation of the spontaneity and rapidity of Mozart's creative method. And they do not betray the slightest evidence of superficiality or haste; nothing that the master ever brought forth manifests greater depth, finer artistic discrimination, or more flawless technical workmanship than these three wonderful Symphonies. They occupy together such a uniformly high plane of excellence that it is futile to single out any one of the three as the "best" or most enduring, although they represent, viewed broadly, three clearly differentiated moods—the one in E♭ suave, that in G minor sombre, and that in C major heroic.

The Symphony in E♭, No. 47, scored for the ordinary full orchestra: quintet of strings, full wood-wind octet, two horns, two trumpets and two drums, has an Introduction, and the following thematic factors, in its first Movement (sonata-allegro form):

Ex. 29. I Introduction   W. A. MOZART (1788)

One or two short Codettas are added. The Development is terse, the Recapitulation almost exact—with the customary transpositions.

The other three Movements: a supremely beautiful *Andante* (in the sonatine-form, that is, the sonata-allegro form *without a Development*); a stirring Menuetto; and a Finale of the conventional bright, animated type (sonata-allegro design)—are based upon these respective principal Themes:

(See the *Analytic Symphony Series*, No. 18.)

The Symphony in G minor (No. 48) is serious, almost sombre in character, and signalizes Mozart's nearest approach to genuine, conscious dramatic expression in his instrumental works. The choice of score is unusual and striking: there are no clarinets (only flutes, oboes and bassoons); two horns but no trumpets; and *no drums*, throughout, notwithstanding the strong emotional emphasis which characterizes the Symphony. There is no Introduction. The Themes of the first Movement are as follows:

The Development deals constantly with the principal Theme, in various keys and various combinations.

The second Movement is an *Andante* of surpassing loveliness. The design is sonata-allegro, with these Themes:

Ex. 32. II

The Minuet, which follows as the usual third Movement, is of that animated, quickened type, introduced by Haydn, that induced Beethoven to substitute for it the name *Scherzo* (in his Second, Third, and other Symphonies, and in many of his piano Sonatas and Chamber-music works). The rhythmic swing of the principal Division is vigorous and exhilarating; the Trio assigns an important rôle to the wood-wind body. The Themes run thus:

Ex. 33. III. Menuetto, Principal Division

Note the spacing in 3-measure Phrases, and the effective syncopation at the beginning. The Trio is in the major mode.

The Finale is more serious, more "symphonic," than the traditional closing Movement. Its thematic material is as follows:

The Development begins with an extremely curious, rhythmically and melodically disjointed extension of the principal motive, weirdly humorous. The rest is made up completely of the principal Phrase, in masterly contrapuntal and modulatory elaboration. The Recapitulation is a nearly exact reproduction of the Exposition, with the prescribed transpositions.

(See the *Analytic Symphony Series*, No. 2.)

This brings us to the last, and crowning creation of Mozart's in the symphonic domain, the Symphony in C (No. 49), to which some unknown enthusiast attached the name by which it has since been called—the *Jupiter* Symphony. It is Mozart's greatest, most scholarly Symphony, though probably not the most popular with the majority of music lovers; for here, as in the case of all works of genius, that which is most scholarly does not make as strong an appeal to the average heart, as a work which lies nearer to the level of human sympathy and comprehension.*

It is scored for the usual classic orchestra, but without clarinets. It opens without Introduction. The first Movement, in sonata-allegro form, comprises this thematic material:

*See the fine essay by Harold D. Phillips: *The Anomalous Place of Mozart in Music*, in the *Musical Quarterly* of July, 1922.

The Development utilizes chiefly the first Codetta, especially its easily recognizable second Phrase.

The second Movement, *Andante cantabile*, is perhaps the finest of all of Mozart's slow Movements. It is wrought out of the following thematic factors, cast in the sonata-allegro form:

The Menuetto is of the traditional graceful type, thus:

Ex. 37. III Menuetto, Principal Division

The Trio is unique: it *begins* with a perfect cadence, against which the violins seem gently to remonstrate.

In the Finale, Mozart assumes a serious, almost austere attitude (somewhat after the manner not uncommon with Haydn), and creates a contrapuntal masterpiece worthy of the great Bach, sacrificing to this end, it must be admitted, the winning qualities of sheer musical beauty to some extent. Its Exposition is woven out of these five Themes, each one a proper thematic contingent as in any regular Exposition:

HAYDN AND MOZART

Ex. 38. IV Finale

(Theme 5 partly resembles Theme 4.) After the statement of the subordinate Theme, the Exposition is spun out with contrapuntal manipulation of Themes 2, 3 and 4, interspersed with a few extra motives. The Development, also, naturally deals with these Themes (including No. 1), rather briefly, but in a great variety of shapes (inversion, stretto, diminution, shifted measure, even "retrograde"). The Recapitulation copies the Exposition closely (with the transpositions), but is slightly abbreviated. Then follows the Coda, and this Coda becomes a stage for the most remarkable polyphonic feat in symphonic literature—a feat that is very rarely encountered in *any* type of published music. After twenty-seven measures of polyphonic network involving Themes 1, 4 and 3, *all of the five Themes are announced simultaneously,* and thus carried through a complete fugal "exposition" in five successive presentations, and, of course, in Quintuple-counterpoint, so applied that each voice presents the entire set of Themes in succession.

The first announcement is thus scored (in the string-quintet, duplicated in the wind-body):

The combination starts in G major, and alternates with C, so that the final (fifth) announcement shall be in C, the principal key. A very few additional homophonic measures bring the Symphony quickly to an end.

(See the *Analytic Symphony Series*, No. 11.)

* * *

Viewed in its total scope, the music of Mozart manifests two fundamental qualities whose presence may be taken for granted in the work of any true Master, but which stand out here in almost unparalleled prominence.

First, a frank and unquestioning affirmation of the basic, *natural*, conditions of tonal relations and discipline. Any inclination to abandon or modify these simple paths, any grotesque subversion of Nature's law, was absolutely foreign to Mozart's musical creed; such orginality, such emotional or dramatic impulses as his music reflects, are all held firmly within these natural bounds. His melody wells up pure and sweet out of the most wholesome and productive musical soil, and this elemental outflow is graced with melodic and rhythmic adornments that we associate with Mozart and no one else.*

Second, truly exquisite workmanship in every technical respect—melody, harmony, modulation, counterpoint, and structural adjustment.

---

*A concrete illustration of what is here meant is supplied by the following example—selected at random from his Symphony in E♭: the principal Theme, given in Ex. 29. This Period originates in these normal harmonic progressions: *Tonic* (3 measures), *Dominant* (4 measures plus two beats), *Tonic* (one beat); then one measure of *Subdominant*—and so forth.

This method of melodic generation is, of course, characteristic of every classic composer; but with no one else (save perhaps Schubert) does it operate with such apparent, simple, primitive force as with Mozart.

It is these qualities that make Mozart so universally revered and beloved, and assure him the unique distinction of being "the finest and truest model, the safest and surest guide, for every student of musical expression."

QUESTIONS FOR REVIEW

1. Which distinguished composer is regarded as the most important forerunner of Haydn?
2. Which structural design predominates in the symphonic Movements of Ph. Em. Bach?
3. What superior qualities become apparent, at once, in the music of Haydn?
4. What is the pre-eminent attribute of Haydn's character?
5. Outline Haydn's biography. Emphasize years of birth and death.
6. What is said of his earlier Symphonies?
7. Which structural form predominates in the 3rd and 4th Movements of Haydn's Second Symphony?
8. With what two momentous innovations is Haydn credited?
9. Outline the psychological scheme of the Four-Movement Symphony.
10. What episode led to the composition of the *Farewell* (or *Candle*) Symphony; and what peculiarity does its performance exhibit?
11. When and where did Haydn compose his best twelve Symphonies?
12. What gave rise to the title of the *Surprise* Symphony; and by what other title is it known?
13. Define some of the eminent qualities of Haydn's last Symphony.

14. Why do the two chief Themes in the sonata-allegro form often resemble each other?
15. Outline the three classic Rondo-forms.
16. What comparisons are drawn between the genius of Haydn and that of Mozart?
17. Outline Mozart's biography, emphasizing years of birth and death.
18. What is remarkable about Mozart's very first Symphony?
19. What peculiar rhythmic trait appears at the beginning of Mozart's *Haffner* Symphony (3rd measure); and what is its history?
20. Which Symphonies did Mozart write in 1788?
21. What contrasting moods do his last three Symphonies reflect?
22. What by-name is sometimes given to Mozart's last Symphony?
23. What is the character of its Finale; and upon what elaborate contrapuntal scheme is it based?
24. What two fundamental qualities does the genius of Mozart manifest?

References

BRENET	Haydn.
HADDEN	Life of Haydn.
SEEBURG	Joseph Haydn. The Story of his Life.
RUNCIMAN	Haydn.
TOWNSEND	Joseph Haydn.
HADOW	Haydn, a Croatian composer.
JAHN	Life of Mozart.
BREAKSPEARE	Life of Mozart.
GEHRING	Mozart.

Holmes	Life of Mozart.
Kerst	Mozart.
Nohl	Life of Mozart.
Wilder	Mozart.
Hussey	Mozart.
Hull	Music: Classic and Romantic.
Mason	Beethoven and his forerunners.
Hamilton	Epochs in Musical Progress (Chapter IV).
Surette	Symphony Music.
Grove	Dictionary of Music (article on C. P. E. Bach).
—	Oxford History of Music (Vol. 5).

ILLUSTRATIVE RECORDS AND ROLLS

Records: B—Brunswick; C—Columbia; E—Edison;
H—His Master's Voice; O—Odeon; Pa—Parlophone;
Po—Polydor; V—Victor; Vo—Vocalion.
Rolls: A—Ampico; D—Duo-Art; M—Melodee; Pl—Pleyela;
Q—QRS; U—Universal; W—Welte-Mignon.

Music Mentioned in Chapter II:

Haydn Symphonies

No. 6, in G major (*Surprise*)   C, Pa, Po, V; M, Pl, Q, U.

No. 11, in G major (*Military*)   H, V; M, D.

No. 12, in B♭ (*Oxford*)   Vo; Pl.

Mozart Symphonies

No. 35, in D major (*Haffner*)   C.

No. 38, in D (*without Minuet*)   Pl, Q.

No. 47, in E♭ major   C, Pa, Po, V; M, Pl, U.

No. 48, in G minor   V; M, Pl, Q, D.

No. 49, in C major (*Jupiter*)   C, V; M, Pl, U.

Chapter III

BEETHOVEN

THE three great masters of the classic Symphony, Haydn, Mozart and Beethoven, through whom this type—the highest in music—was brought into being and carried to an apparently unpassable limit of perfection, were singularly alike, fundamentally, in their outlook upon absolute music, and their conception of what it should be; its mission; its inherent potentialities; its structural requirements; and its qualities as a medium of spiritual intercourse. The three were of one and the same spiritual family. And it is only under such auspices that an art can fulfil its evolutionary course free of conflicting agencies, and successfully attain, through unimpeded, straightforward progressive stages in the one proper direction, to its full development. Thus, each one of these masters fostered the same artistic ideals and carried them forward to the highest plane of realization.

The characteristic difference in their individual attitude and methods of musical utterance may be aptly likened, with a moderate portion of poetic license, to three successive periods in the life of the same being.

Haydn's music emanates from the spirit of the Child. An exceedingly engaging and beautiful child, but with a gaze that reveals little or no depth of expression; always smiling, gay, absolutely carefree, full of fun and even mischief, reflecting but little knowledge of the experience of life, its sorrows and passions; no realization of the "good and evil" in the world.

That of Mozart voices the spirit of Youth, and reveals a wider outlook upon life. There is still a goodly remnant of juvenile gaiety, and the predominating note is Joy, the joy of living, and of loving in an innocent, dispassionate way; here and there a tinge of adolescent melancholy, now and then a burst of grief or dramatic emotion, which, however, does not seem quite convincing; the humor is more rare and more subdued. But it is the same Child, with a considerably advanced consciousness, and a more serious spirit.

In Beethoven's music we are confronted with the spirit of the full-grown Man. The outlook upon life is vastly broader, the influences of progressive living and learning far more obvious. Gaiety is by no means wholly banished, for it is still the same noble-hearted, wholesome individual; but this quality has become more dignified and refined; the joys are more serene and profound; the sorrows more genuine and touching; the outbursts of emotional passion reveal a wider experience of human conflict, and are more convincing. But the glorious rays of wisdom, the radiance of a noble, matured benevolence, shine forth with a brightness that affords prophetic glimpses of heavenly visions. Withal, there is the dexterous hand of the master of expression, that fashions the thought and its presentation with all but superhuman skill and forcefulness:*

Ludwig van Beethoven was born December 16, 1770, at Bonn on the Rhine. The *van* (not *von*) in his name confirms his Belgian descent, on the paternal side; and although his whole life was spent under German influences, and his music is essentially German in character, the Netherlands lay some just claim to Beethoven, as another illustrious link in the great chain of music masters beginning with Okeghem, and including Josquin des Prés, Dufay and many others.

Beethoven's father and grandfather were professional musicians in the Electoral Chapel at Bonn; and the former, a man of disagreeable temper, thought he saw, in the extraordinary talent of the lad, a source of profit for himself; and so he speeded up Ludwig's musical training in a manner that gave the boy much distress. Ludwig soon became a proficient pianist, whereby the *Well-Tempered Clavichord* of the great Bach seems to have been his chief inspiration and delight; and also acquired great facility upon the violin and the organ.

These branches, and composition as well, were vigorously promoted by the Court Organist Neefe and the distinguished violinist Franz Ries, both of whom took a lively interest in Beethoven's talent. As early as 1782 he had written and published a set of Variations and three Sonatas.

In 1787, Beethoven's ambition to profit by the guidance of Mozart was fulfilled, though little came of it through personal contact — all the more, however, through the compositions of

---

*The reader is urged to make a thoughtful study of an essay on *Beethoven's Instrumental Music* by the famous German writer E. T. A. Hoffmann (author of the *Kreisleriana*), with commentary by the translator, Arthur Ware Locke, in the *Musical Quarterly* of Jan. 1917.

Mozart, for which Beethoven cherished an admiration verging on idolatry, and which he studied with consuming ardor.

In 1792 he moved to Vienna; came into contact with Haydn, from whom he received a few unfruitful lessons, and with the famous theorist Albrechtsberger, under whose tutelage his technical mastery advanced rapidly. By the time he had reached his twentieth year Beethoven had produced a large number of works, though none that proclaimed the supreme genius of the master. But thereafter his compositions began to assume greater independence and significance. His first Trios (Op. 1) and the first piano Sonatas (Op. 2) were written in 1795; his first Symphony (Op. 21) in 1800.

Beethoven's life up to this time had been, aside from his hours of musical occupation, most unhappy and even wretched, partly, no doubt, by reason of the peculiarities of his disposition—an aggressive spirit of independence, self-assurance, contempt of shams and courtly subservience, besides no little personal eccentricity. But these attributes were also proofs of the sterling honesty of his nature; for at heart he was nobly generous and devoted to those whom he liked. Thus he made more friends than enemies, and was a welcome and honored guest in the highest circles, receiving material assistance from Princes Lichnowsky, Lobkowitz and Kinsky, and the nobles Archduke Rudolf, Count Waldstein, von Brunswick and others. Though anything but arrogant in a baser sense, Beethoven was so sure of his genius that he treated these nobles as his equals, if not his inferiors.

Already in 1800, symptoms of ear-trouble began to appear, and the malady became steadily more acute until, in 1822, Beethoven was totally deaf. The loss of hearing is commonly considered the most tragic affliction that can befall a musician, and that is probably true in many cases. But with Beethoven it may be adjudged a blessing in disguise; for it set up a benignant barrier against disturbing noises, and enabled him more easily to withdraw within himself, and to concentrate upon those problems and ideals which exist within the soul.

The years 1800—1815, popularly designated his "second period," brought forth rich treasures of priceless music, in which the true Beethoven, in all the glory of his rare genius, stands fully revealed. This period covers 8 of his Symphonies, 17 more piano Sonatas (up to No. 27, Op. 90), all 5 piano Concertos, the first 11 String-quartets, the Opera *Fidelio*, the C major *Mass*, all but one of his Overtures, and many more compositions of various styles.

His "third period," extending from 1815 to his death on March 26, 1827, was devoted to the production of his Ninth Symphony, the last 5 piano Sonatas, the last 5 String-quartets, the elaborate *Missa solemnis* in D, and smaller works.

It was the essential qualities of Beethoven's genius, as stupendous as it was original, that retarded the recognition of these culminating works; and this, coupled with other causes, again clouded an existence which during his second period had been one of greater satisfaction and happiness than he had ever before known. Today all misconception, all lack of comprehension, all doubts, have passed away, and we recognize in these latest works of Beethoven the most mighty creations that instrumental composition has ever yet, in its entire range, put forth.

"Beethoven's loftiest originality, and that whence the differences in formal construction naturally flowed, is the intensity and fervor of subjective emotion which pervades his works. It is this mood of profound subjectivity, of individual, powerful soul-expression which, most of all, differentiates Beethoven's music from that of Bach, or Haydn, or Mozart, and which opens the era of 'romantic' composition."*

*Theodore Baker, *Biographical Dictionary of Musicians*.

MASTERS OF THE SYMPHONY

BEETHOVEN'S FIRST SYMPHONY

The first of Beethoven's Symphonies, in C major, Op. 21, was written in Vienna in 1800—twelve years later than the three "great" Symphonies of Mozart, and six years after the last and best of those of Haydn.*

In this first symphonic work Beethoven is so completely dominated by his veneration of Mozart's music, that it manifests more of the distinctive traits of the latter than of those elements which characterize the later Beethoven and elevate him to a far loftier rank than Mozart was destined to reach.

Still, there are enough indications here of Beethoven's independence to make this Symphony interesting and important for its own sake.

It opens with an Introduction, the very first chord of which seems to menace the old order of things. The score agrees with the "full" orchestra of Mozart—quintet of strings, octet of wood-wind, two horns, two trumpets and two drums. The design of the First Movement is sonata-allegro, based upon these Themes:

Ex. 40. I. Introduction — BEETHOVEN (1800)

---

*The student should have at hand, and constantly refer to, the *Analytic Symphony Series*, No. 21.

The Introduction begins (like the Trio of the Minuet in Mozart's C major Symphony—Ex. 37) with a perfect cadence; not in the principal key, however, but in F major. No wonder that the staid old guardians of classic purity shook their heads! The chromatic progression in measures five and six of the principal Theme betrays the influence of Mozart. The Development is regular and finely proportioned; the Recapitulation an exact reproduction of the Exposition, with the necessary transpositions. A Coda of normal extent is added.

For the slow (second) Movement, Beethoven conceives a principal Theme that is reminiscent of the Finale of his piano Sonata in F (Op. 10, No. 2), but in slow tempo. This Theme and the others are as follows:

The design of this Movement is sonata-allegro, regular but very broad. In character it diverges somewhat from the manner of Mozart; it is less emotional, more reflective, and, though not ungraceful, exhibits some degree of that sterner quality which became typical of Beethoven. Note the striking iambic pulse of the drum in the second Codetta; also the alternating chords in the wood-wind.

Beethoven calls the third Movement a Menuetto, though it merits the title *Scherzo* quite as much as any of that type which Beethoven so delighted in.

It presents these Themes:

Ex.42. III Menuetto

The cunning "return," from the course of the second Part (principal Division), indicates more of the influence of Haydn than of Mozart; but the older Beethoven developed such "hints" as these in his own distinctive fashion.

In the gay, animated, conventional Finale Beethoven becomes again the close imitator and emulator of Mozart, in conception and manner. It is a sonata-allegro design, with this thematic material:

Ex. 43. IV Finale

In the introductory measures (there is no "Introduction" in the structural sense), Beethoven engages in a musical pleasantry that would probably have been uncongenial to Mozart. The structure is normal and conservative, and exhibits no significant traits.

* * *

Beethoven's melodies emerge straightway from the simple chords, and from the scale. For illustration, see the first phrase of the principal Theme in Ex. 44 (two measures of scale and two measures of the tonic chord); also the subordinate Theme in Ex. 47 (two measures of tonic, two of dominant chord); the same in the principal Theme in Ex. 48 (four measures of tonic chord); the same in Ex. 52, principal Theme (two measures of tonic, one of subdominant, one of dominant—and then the scale); also Ex. 53, principal Theme (three measures of almost unbroken scale)—and so forth. This is also the case, of course, with *all* classic composers; but when Beethoven makes such derivation, it sounds altogether different, and positively distinctive. He seems to possess some hidden knowledge of the respective inherent qualities of chord-root, third and fifth, and of the most convincing *rhythmic* placing of these chord-tones, or scale-tones. His melodic eloquence is due to the fact that he does not use the tones, as some writers use words, for their pleasant *sound,* but as one who has fathomed their *meaning,* and places them where they carry out the thought he has in mind.

Beethoven never juggles with tones. He has a fine sense of humor, surely, and goes out of his way at times to tickle the hearer's sense of the incongruous—see the whimsical fortissimo $c\sharp$ in measure eighteen of the Finale of his Eighth Symphony.

He employs the device of Repetition more than any other composer, for therein he recognizes a primary law of nature—and Nature was ever his most compelling inspiration and guide. The Creator places a leaf upon the tree, and next to it another leaf of the same pattern and kind, though no two leaves in all creation are absolutely alike. Never does He place a maple leaf upon an oak; neither was Beethoven ever guilty of any similar inconsistency. For he has an unerring perception of natural law; he is its staunchest advocate and defender; and the strongest expression of his personal, subjective impulses never contravenes this supreme law. This it is that carries such conviction to the listener's heart, and makes Beethoven's music so irresistible, so compelling, and so *enduring*.

Further, Beethoven did not repose blind trust in his first musical impressions. Always aware of the possibly false allure of such "inspirations," he trained his phenomenally keen and strong mind upon them and by tenacious *reflection* removed the weak spots, remodeled or rejected; never satisfied until he had brought his ideas and their development to the highest degree of perfection. It must again be emphasized, however, that all classic masters possessed these qualities in some degree, and that is why we call them classic; but with Beethoven the degree was superlative, exclusive.

The Second Symphony

This one, in D major, Op. 36, was written in 1802. It is of greater breadth than the First one, and though still exhibiting the influence of Haydn and Mozart to some extent, it contains far more originality, and a sort of "democratic" fearlessness, sharply differentiated from the courtly restraint of the foregoing masters. The score corresponds to that of the First Symphony.

It opens with a rather long, stately Introduction of great beauty and power, but suggestive of Mozart. The first Movement is in sonata-allegro form, employing these Themes:

The Exposition is regular; the Development lengthy, but finely proportioned, and ingenious. Of especial moment, as attesting the independence that was already asserting itself strongly in Beethoven's methods, is the manner in which he plans the return to the beginning—at the end of the Development: the last sixteen measures hold firmly the remote key of F♯, the dominant note of which (c♯) is the leading-tone of the original key (D major). The quiet transmutation of the chord through this c♯, in the bass, to the dominant chord of D, two measures before the opening of the Recapitulation, is extremely impressive. What is more, almost precisely the same modulatory device is employed again in the Trio of the third Movement, and again in the Finale. The first Movement is extended by a fairly lengthy Coda.*

In the second Movement Beethoven creates a lyric *Larghetto* of singular beauty, and of a more distinctive character, that plainly foreshadows the later Beethoven. Its Themes run thus:

The design is sonata-allegro, considerably spun out.

*Consult for details of all four Movements, the *Analytic Symphony Series*, No. 31.

The third Movement is confessedly a *Scherzo* with Trio (see the text beneath Ex. 32), upon the following Themes:

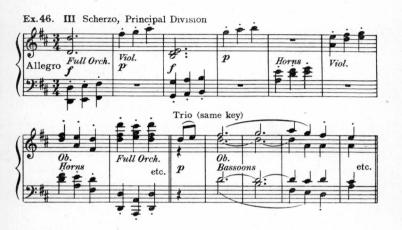

The principal Division is ingeniously extended, in its Third Part. A unique feature of the Trio, of genuine Beethoven complexion, is that its Second Part (fourteen measures long) is built entirely upon a single chord, intoned by the strings in unison; this chord is the tonic of F♯ major, and its Fifth ($c♯$) is made to serve—as in the first Movement—as leading-tone of the original key (D).

The Finale, a sonata-allegro of an extremely vigorous, animated, jovial character, as full of pranks as the wonderful Finale of Haydn's last Symphony (Ex. 21), betrays hereditary traces of Haydn, though none the less stoutly original at the core. Its thematic factors are as follows:

Ex. 47. IV Finale
Principal Theme

Observe the two staccato quarter-notes in measures two and six; and compare the comment below Ex. 27 (in small type). The Exposition has no defined cadence; its final Codetta is so "dissolved" as to lose itself in a returning passage that leads into the Development. Further, the Development *begins so exactly like the Exposition* that the design is rendered obscure.* This was not an infrequent occurrence with Beethoven and also with Brahms.

See Beethoven, piano Sonata, Op. 31, No. 1, first Movement; the first seven measures of the Development correspond literally to the first seven of the Exposition. Also Beethoven's Symphony No. 8, Finale. Also Brahms, Second Symphony, Op. 73, last Movement; Fourth Symphony, Op. 98, first Movement, and third Movement.

The tendency of this pseudo-return to the principal Theme is so to modify the sonata-allegro design that it approaches the *effect* of the Rondo forms.

*See the author's *Larger Forms of Musical Composition*, par. 162 (p. 186).

As stated above, the Recapitulation in this Finale is also entered in a novel and very striking manner: the last Section of the Development (twenty-six measures) is held without wavering in F♯ minor, whose dominant note, the c♯, is here again the prospective leading-tone of the original key, and finally very gently turns the harmony over into the opening tones of the principal Theme—almost exactly as in the first Movement. The entrance of the Coda (which is unusually long and elaborate) is likewise novel and effective.

* * *

The Third Symphony

By the time Beethoven was ready to undertake his third Symphony, the heritage of his great predecessors, Haydn and Mozart, had fulfilled its mission, and scarcely a vestige of its influence upon Beethoven's methods of expression is here outwardly recognizable. The contrast between this third Symphony and the two that preceded it is amazing—unparalleled in the history of musical progress. It is as if the youth had suddenly attained to full manhood, and was now asserting *himself*, the true Beethoven, with all the originality, independence, supreme vigor of mind and spirit that proclaims the mighty genius of tone. This great work is commonly assumed to inaugurate his second, most fecund and joyous period.

The Third Symphony, in E♭, Op. 55, written in 1804, was designed as a tribute to the life of a Hero, and Beethoven himself gave it the title *Eroica*. The hero foremost in his mind was Napoleon, whose remarkably victorious military career excited the admiration of Beethoven and made him appear a worthy object of Beethoven's musical plan. To Napoleon, therefore, the Symphony was originally dedicated; but his subsequent acceptance of the imperial crown impressed Beethoven as a sordid act of personal ambition, and the dedication was withdrawn.

It is not easy to trace a definite connection between Beethoven's heroic design and the music of the Symphony itself. The first Movement, it is true, is of that extremely vigorous, manly type that is associated with heroism, and it is also "heroic" in dimensions: with the exception of the Ninth Symphony, this is the longest of Beethoven's symphonic Movements. Also, its prime thematic phrase is a bugle-call. The second Movement is the only one of the four that refers explicitly to heroism: it bears the title *Funeral March, on the Death of a Hero*. The third Movement, a *Scherzo*, has been interpreted as depicting the bustle of a military camp; but it might quite as well be the commotion of a country fair—apart from the three-voiced bugle-call in the Trio. And in the Finale there is not a single episode that is specifically heroic; in fact, the gentle, winning Theme that runs through the whole Movement was conceived and used by Beethoven years before; it appears as concluding number in his early Ballet-music *Prometheus*, and is the subject of his piano Variations, Op. 35 (1802). But, for all that, this vital Symphony fits the definition "brave, vigorous, venturesome" sufficiently well, and is therefore truly *heroic* in spirit.

Here, for the first time in his symphonic work, Beethoven dispenses with an independent Introduction; after two peremptory tonic strokes he intonates the bugle-call (in the 'cello) in which the first Movement centres. The thematic material is as follows:

The Exposition is regular and unusually long; but its extreme length is matched by proportionate depth and breadth, so that, far from being a wearisome drawback, it is an essential, logical consequence; and the mighty plan unfolds with unfailing interest and unabated fascination through to the triumphant end. The preponderant heroic mood is softened by interspersed episodes of tender beauty —note the effective contrasts which the Themes and Codettas present. Note, also, the frequent assertion of 2/4 measure, which heightens the impetuous rhythmic effect by shifting (contracting) the accentuations. Despite its length, Beethoven insists upon the repetition of the Exposition. In the later course of the proportionately extended Development (in Section 8), after about thirty measures of this intensified 2/4 meter, culminating in four measures of fierce dissonance, he arrests the tumult and introduces a wholly new motive of great beauty.*

Four measures *before* the Recapitulation begins, the horn softly intonates the first measures of the principal Theme on the chord of E♭, *against the Dominant-Seventh chord* in the violins (*pp, tremolando*). This famous episode, so

---

*The most consistent scheme for a Development is a series of Sections. A "Section" is an indeterminate passage of optional length and optional contents—thus providing for the necessary freedom of Development. The Sections are expected to make use of the thematic factors of the Exposition, and this they very naturally and usually do; but since a Section is totally *optional* in contents, it has a right to present entirely *new* material, and not infrequently does so—in some rare instances to an almost exclusive extent: see the last Movement of Beethoven's first piano Sonata, Op. 2, No. 1. The justification for inserting a *new* feature in a Development of this length—in the Third Symphony—is obvious. Other examples may be seen in the first Movement, and also in the last, of Mendelssohn's *Italian* Symphony.

characteristic of Beethoven's daring, was at first regarded as a misprint!

The Recapitulation is nearly literal—with the customary transpositions. The Coda assumes proportions commensurate with the magnitude of the Movement as a whole.

The slow Movement, the *Funeral March*, is an irregular variety of the Second Rondo-form.* It is also very broad, profoundly moving, dramatic, filled with genuine pathos, throughout distinctive of the maturer Beethoven; and it is as replete with beauty as it is original. It presents these Themes:

This may appear to be a meagre showing, but it is an essential quality of Beethoven's genius that he prefers to evolve the most lengthy and finished products out of the simplest, smallest germs, and he possesses the faculty of so

*See the *Analytic Symphony Series*, No. 12, for details of all four Movements.

doing to an unparalleled extent—compare the first Movement of the Fifth Symphony; and of the Sixth; and Seventh.

In place of the Second subordinate Theme, prescribed in the legitimate Second Rondo, he inserts a genuine "Development," and therein lies the irregularity of the form. The first Section of this Development is a *fugato* in Triple-counterpoint—with three Themes, combined in various mutual inversions. There is an impressive Coda (thirty-nine measures), the last ten measures of which consist in a most remarkable presentation of the first Period (eight measures) of the principal Theme—absolutely literal in tone-succession but in curiously distorted rhythmic form, that suggests the broken utterance of a dying person. It will repay the student to make a minute comparison of the two forms.

For the third Movement Beethoven again adopts the term *Scherzo*, and here it is particularly appropriate; for this ebullient music, though thoroughly sound and earnest, fairly bubbles over with vivacity and good humor. Its two Divisions are thus represented:

Ex. 50. III Scherzo, Principal Division

The Finale is a miracle (to ordinary minds) of tonal treatment and development. No other word adequately describes this musical creation. In structure it approximates the Rondo-form, inasmuch as a constant principal Theme *alternates* regularly with contrasting episodes. This principal Theme is a lyric Three-Part Song-form, beautiful of course (since a Beethoven conceived it), and at each reappearance it is variated—at times in different keys. But quite equal, if not greater, importance attaches to the *Bass-part* upon which the harmonic accompaniment of this thematic melody rests. The Melody and Bass of the Theme are as follows:

Ex. 51. IV Finale
Principal Theme

(The student will find a playable version of this in Beethoven's piano Variations, Op. 35.) The episodes which alternate with this Theme consist of: (1) a *fugato* (in double-counterpoint) upon the first phrase of the *bass-theme*, with an important addition, in C minor; (2) a contrasting Two-Part Song-form of vigorous character, in G minor, built upon the first phrase of the bass-theme, again extended; (3) a recurrence of the *fugato*, this time in E♭ major. Between and around these episodes stand the variated forms of the principal Theme. The Movement ends with a fairly long Coda, devoted chiefly to the thematic melody, from which, oddly enough, the former ubiquitous bass-part entirely disappears.

Another, and unique, function is assigned to the thematic bass-part in the Introduction to the Finale. This Introduction is divided into four Sections: (1) a torrent of tone, three measures on the tonic of G minor, and eight measures on the dominant of E♭; (2) the bass-theme *alone*, full length; (3) the bass-theme, as inner voice, with one or two contrapuntal associates; (4) the bass-theme as upper voice, with three or four added melodies. Hereupon then follows the announcement of the actual Melodic (principal) Theme.*

It was at that time unprecedented to select the Variation style for the final Movement of a Symphony, and it occurs since in only one other classic instance—in the Finale of the Fifth Symphony of Brahms.

---

*A similar use of the bass-voice as Introduction to a set of Variations may be found in the piano *Impromptus*, Op. 5, of Schumann.

THE FOURTH SYMPHONY

In his Fourth Symphony, B♭ major, Op. 60, written in 1806, Beethoven returns to a more cheerful mood, as if enjoying a period of recreation after the storm and stress of his elaborate, intensely reflective Third Symphony. In its playful, joyous spirit it harks back to Mozart again, but evinces greater maturity, and is musically more significant in many respects than the creations of the latter. It pursues its happy, sunlit course without a shade of melancholy or dramatic inclination, and although distinctively "Beethoven," in conception and construction, it exhibits comparatively few outstanding features.

Beethoven reverts in this Symphony to the tradition of the Introduction, and nothing could be finer than the simple earnestness and serene loveliness that here prevail. The thematic material of the first Movement (sonata-allegro) is as follows:

Note the droll character of the subordinate Theme, emphasized by the instruments employed. The first Codetta is an octave-canon (eight measures, repeated). The final Sections of the Development execute the necessary return to the beginning (into the Recapitulation) in an astonishingly original and effective manner—far more so than in the Second Symphony: the harmony is led into the chord of F♯, as dominant-seventh of B major, and held there, *pianissimo*, for twenty-eight measures; the *a♯*, equivalent to *b♭*, is murmured intermittently by the kettledrum; then the harmony shifts suddenly into the tonic of B♭ major (the original key)—the drum continuing its roll upon the same tone, and increasing its volume with the rest of the orchestra until the Recapitulation opens, with a glorious volume of sound. It is an example of "pivotal" modulation—through a stationary tone—and this pivotal tone is here entrusted to the *drum*.

(Consult the *Analytic Symphony Series*, No. 34.)

The second Movement, *adagio*, is of a pronounced lyric quality and appealing beauty. The design is Third Rondo, in unusually concise form. The principal Theme is preceded, at every announcement, by a measure in marked rhythm, which, though introductory in effect, is nevertheless an integral part of the Theme, thus:

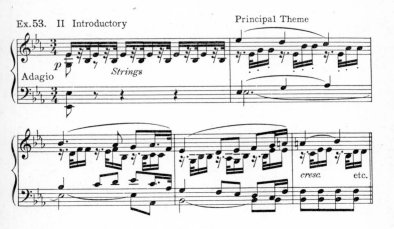

Ex. 53.

The other Theme (subordinate) and the Codetta are easily recognizable, and may be left to the student's search—or traced in the *Analytic Symphony Series*. Beethoven's valuation of the kettledrums, as an essential part of the orchestral apparatus, and his effective employment of them, are demonstrated throughout his Symphonies. So here: the rhythmic introductory measure is given repeatedly to the drums; once with the horns (just before the Recapitulation), and once *as solo*, two measures before the end.

For the third Movement Beethoven uses no other title than the tempo mark, *Allegro vivace;* but it is of course a *Scherzo*, with Trio, as usual, and utilizes these Themes:

Ex. 54. III Principal Division

Note the manner in which the phrasing creates the impression of 2/4 metre in the first Phrase, and also through a large portion of the Second Part of the principal Division. The form is enlarged by a second statement of the Trio, solely for the sake of broader dimensions. This recurrence of the Trio is literal, but the final *da capo* (the inevitable return of the principal Division) is reduced to its Third Part only.

The bubbling Finale—a *Humoresque* with delightfully contrasted Themes—is another instance of Beethoven's return to the earlier manner of Haydn and Mozart, the rollicking style that they adjudged most appropriate for the final Movement. It is cast in the sonata-allegro form, and is embodied out of these Themes:

Ex. 55. IV Finale
Principal Theme

The structure is perfectly regular, simple, and easy to follow. Note the humorous elongation (augmentation) of the principal phrase, eleven measures before the end: after a boisterous climax in the full orchestra, the violin (three measures), the bassoon (one measure), and the viola and 'cello (one measure), very softly and apologetically intonate the thematic melody in slower rhythm (eighth-notes), pausing most comically upon the last eighth-note, in each of the last three measures.

* * *

The Fifth Symphony

Again Beethoven's mood undergoes a complete change, in passing from his Fourth Symphony to the Fifth (C minor, Op. 67, finished in 1808). It is the first one of his Symphonies for which he chose the minor mode, and its spirit is correspondingly stern, sombre and passionate —in all but the final Movement. This is particularly true of the first and third Movements. But even the tender slow Movement has emotional moments that alternate like shadows with the prevailing brightness. The Finale is a monument of symphonic breadth and might.*

It is not easy to speak dispassionately and with beseeming moderation of this wonderful Symphony of Beethoven. Viewed calmly and fairly, from every angle, it cannot be called his *greatest* Symphony; for his genius matured steadily, and there are qualities in his last three Symphonies which pertain to a more elevated plane of artistic creation than does this Fifth one. What lends this one its irresistible appeal, is its elemental power, and its inherent simplicity; its architectural plan unfolds so naturally, so consistently, with such unfaltering logic, such clearness and sureness of purpose, and in such straightforward, powerful strokes, that the responsive hearer is thrilled with satisfaction and enjoyment from the first tone to the last.

The structural scheme of the first Movement (sonata-allegro form) is extremely concise; no time is wasted on

---

*See, again, Arthur Ware Locke's translation of E. T. A. Hoffmann's commentary upon the Fifth Symphony of Beethoven, in the *Musical Quarterly* of January, 1917, pages 129, 130.

gallant concessions.   There is no Introduction.   The harmonic basis is strikingly simple, consisting very largely of the plain tonic and dominant chords.   The modulations are of telling effect, but not extreme—the most striking appear in the series of remote keys near the end of the Development—in the "solid" rhythm of the subordinate Theme.

This first Movement is a miracle of motive-development, such as only a Beethoven could perform.* There is scarcely a single measure in the entire course of the Movement that does not owe its origin to, and is not derived directly from, the motive of the opening four measures—with chiefly rhythmic alterations. Thus, the subordinate Theme corresponds, at its outset, to this principal motive; the eighth-notes in its third measure are suppressed, with the result of a more solid rhythm of half-notes, and at the same time the intervals are widened, thus adding emphasis to the rhythmic change. The thematic material assumes therefore this astonishingly terse shape:

Ex. 56. I Principal Theme   BEETHOVEN (1807-8)

*Consult the *Analytic Symphony Series*, No. 3, for details of all four Movements.

For the second Movement—an indescribably beautiful Lyric of contemplative mood, with powerful contrasts—Beethoven chooses the First Rondo-form; at least, this most nearly indicates his structural intention. But it is treated with much latitude: the frequent repetitions and recurrences of the melodious principal Theme are variated—analogously to the scheme of the Finale of the *Eroica* Symphony; and there is no more than a barely recognizable intimation of a subordinate Theme. As an illustration of the discrepancy, sometimes slight but often very marked, between a musical idea as it was first engendered in Beethoven's mind, and the same idea after his rigorous testing had brought it to the perfected shape suited to its thematic purpose,* we give first the original form of the first Phrase of this *Andante,* and then its present shape. Also the fragmentary "subordinate Motive:"

*If the student will procure and consult Beethoven's Sketchbooks (edited by M. G. Nottebohm) he will discover many illuminating proofs of this remodeling and refining process of the master. Some of the original sketches of this Fifth Symphony reach back to the years 1800 and 1801.

Beethoven calls the third Movement a *Scherzo*; but it is of a deeply serious character, with a weird background of veiled apprehensiveness pierced at intervals with flashes of mysterious menace, later on hushed to a tense, broken, whispered utterance (see Ex. 58). The Themes are as follows:

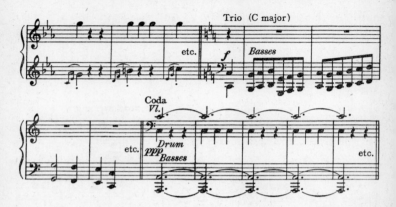

The principal Division is in Three-Part form—five Parts, with the repetition of Parts II and III. The first and second of these present two widely different but equally important thematic shapes, the first ominous, almost foreboding, the second oracular in tone. Note the rhythmic analogy between this oracular second Part, and the first motive of the first Movement. The Trio is sometimes cited as a specimen of Beethoven's humor; and there is doubtless a touch of the grotesque in the rapid passage for the lumbering double-basses, during the first Phrase, and still more later on. But it is hard to believe that his mind was at any moment, in this singularly serious work, accessible to any humorous suggestion. Even this unwieldy bass passage is to be taken seriously.

Out of the mysterious turmoil of this *Allegro* finally emerges, directly, almost suddenly, the magnificent Finale, like the triumph of Light over Darkness. For Beethoven joins the third Movement to the fourth (contrary to his habit in the symphonic form), and the transition displays his original genius in another aspect: the Coda (see the Example) begins with the A♭ major chord, the Third of which, *c*, is very softly tapped out by the kettledrum, in the rhythm of the "oracular" motive, while the strings hold the rest of the chord (*ppp*) for no fewer than fifteen measures—the drum meanwhile modifying its rhythmic tap as if endowed with human intelligence. Thereafter the first violins resume and retain the *first* thematic melody; the harmony sways around the *c,* with which the drum now keeps up an incessant tapping, until a final *crescendo,* through four measures of the dominant chord, leads into the Theme of the Finale (*ff*); the *c* is foreign to this chord, but that makes no difference to the drummer; he keeps right on beating his *c, crescendo,* until it "wins out" as emphatic keynote.

The thematic factors of the Finale are as follows:

The form of the Finale is a very broad sonata-allegro. The orchestra is increased by the addition of a piccolo, a contra-bassoon, and three trombones, for this Song of Triumph called for a larger, more resounding tone-apparatus. The final Sections of the Development revert, in an unusual manner, to the *Scherzo,* and consist in a recurrence of the "oracular" phrase of the second Part, in minor as before, and extended; and a dominant ending similar to that which preceded the Finale, and which here leads (with a few measures of the same drum-beat on *c*) into the Recapitulation. The Coda is quite lengthy, and its last Sections are in *presto* tempo, with motives from the Codetta and from the principal Theme.

* * *

The Sixth Symphony

It appears to have been a natural impulse, perhaps a conscious act, with Beethoven to alternate his moods from each Symphony to the next. For here again, as he turns from the Fifth to the Sixth Symphony, a complete change takes place, not only in his mood, but in his whole attitude. From a flight in lofty spiritual regions he returns to earth, and discourses of Nature herself, in the most intimate terms. If the inherent quality of the one in C minor may be defined as divine, that of the *Pastoral* is purely and whole-heartedly human.

These two so radically diverse Symphonies, it must be remembered, were written very nearly together (in 1807-8). Beethoven's mind had been occupied with thoughts of the C minor Symphony for a period of years; thematic fragments of it were jotted down in his notebook as early as 1800. But when he turned seriously to the composition of the Fifth, his attention seems to have been divided between it and the Sixth; and when these "twin" Symphonies were both first publicly performed, in December, 1808, at Vienna, the *Pastoral* occupied the first place and was called No. V, while the other was marked No. VI. This reverse order prevailed until as late as 1813, though Beethoven, upon their joint publication in 1809, insisted upon the order in which they stand today, and which therefore corroborates his intention: No. V, Op. 67, and No. VI, the *Pastoral*, Op. 68.

The motto of this entire Sixth Symphony is *Simplicity*— in melody, harmony, modulation and structure; and this frank, artless quality contributes directly to the appropriate "rustic" atmosphere that pervades the pastoral composition. Beethoven states explicitly that he aims at "*Mehr Ausdruck der Empfindung, als Malerey*"—"more an expression of the feelings, than painting;" and from this we infer that he harbored no intention of producing a specimen of descriptive (program) music—an aim that was decidedly prevalent during those earlier days when the art of tone was still immature, and its true spiritual mission so imperfectly understood,* but for which Beethoven, the imposing advocate of Absolute music, had but little sympathy. The first Movement contains no evidences whatever of a "descriptive" tendency; the second Movement, however, does *reflect* (not depict) the repose and the murmuring voices of the forest, chiefly, as the title shows, of the brook; the bird-trio near the end of this slow Movement was admittedly an innocent pleasantry—though some birds do emit musical tones of fairly definite pitch and rhythm; further, music offered Beethoven, especially in the orchestral body, convenient approximate means of imitating the roll of thunder, the wailing of the wind and the tumult of a storm. These means Beethoven did not hesitate to employ, in accentuating the elements concomitant with his total pastoral project; but therewith all descriptive tendencies cease; the rest, by far the greater mass of its measures, is all strictly and purely emotional suggestion, sufficiently characteristic to justify the title—*Pastoral* Symphony.

---

*Compare Ex. 3 and its context; also the titles given to some of Haydn's Symphonies. And see the article upon *Beethoven and Program Music* by R. W. S. Mendl in the *Musical Quarterly* of April, 1928.

BEETHOVEN

Since Beethoven inserted a "Storm" between the *Scherzo* and the Finale, this Symphony has five Movements, to which he himself affixed these titles:

I. *Allegro.*   "Pleasant feelings awakened upon arriving in the country."
II. *Andante.*   "Scene by the brook."
III. *Allegro.*   "Jovial gathering of country-folk."
IV. *Allegro.*   "Thunderstorm."
V. *Allegretto.*   "Shepherd's Song. Happy and grateful feelings after the storm."

There is no Introduction; the first Movement (sonata-allegro design) opens at once with the principal Theme.* This, and the other thematic components run thus:

Ex.60. I — BEETHOVEN (1808)

*See the *Analytic Symphony Series*, No. 25.

The whole first Movement actually seems to exhale the fresh, invigorating air of the countryside—meadows and forests, Nature's playground. Note the four different rhythmic figures, each one of which contributes an important quality to the moving scroll: (1) the order of eighths and sixteenths in the second measure; (2) the uniform eighths in the subordinate Theme (against heavy notes in the bass); (3) the lilt of the Codetta; and (4) this latter group reduced to uniform triplets. In the hands of this consummate master of subjective expression, these four rhythmic figures, so nearly alike and still so characteristically different, seem to mirror Nature's movements— ever changing yet ever the same — and are most vitally responsible for the indefinable "rural" atmosphere which the Movement creates and sustains.

Beethoven's estimate of the basic significance of Repetition, touched upon above, is nowhere more conspicuous than in this Symphony, and nowhere more obviously conditioned by the nature of his "pastoral" scheme. Compare, for one thing, measures sixteen to twenty-five of this first Movement; also the *six* successive presentations of the first Phrase of the subordinate Theme; also the second and fourth Sections of the Development, based upon the first of the four rhythmic figures just cited. In the subordinate Theme, the melody in the bass-part appears to have the greater thematic weight. It is noteworthy that Beethoven throughout this entire Symphony uses *no drums*, excepting in the Thunderstorm. Also, for the Storm, he adds to his score a piccolo and two trombones, retaining these latter during the Finale.

The second Movement, "At the Brook," is also cast in the sonata-allegro form, and is of unusual length. One is permitted to *imagine*, especially with the clue provided by the title, that one actually hears the murmur of the brook, the rustle of the forest, and—in the curious fragmentary form of the melodies—the tuneful call of birds; and one may imagine that one senses the soothing magic and odors of the woods. Beethoven would not have objected to that; but he would probably have fallen into one of his famous tantrums if anybody had offered him a narrative, describing every measure of the piece. For Beethoven, as clearly stated, aimed only at subjective emotional expression. At the same time, he did insert one realistic scene, with explicit designation, in the bird-trio (nightingale, quail and cuckoo) near the end of the Movement; he may have meant it as a joke, but he thought so well of it that he repeated it, right away, literally. The thematic material of this delightful slow Movement is as follows:

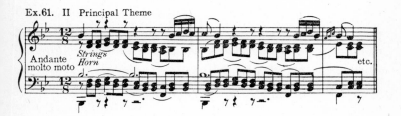

Ex. 61. II Principal Theme

The third Movement, a *Scherzo*, is frankly "descriptive" —but it must be borne in mind that it is an inherently *musical* subject, a rustic Dance; and the only touches of direct realism in it are Beethoven's deliciously comical allusions to the technical limitations of these amateur peasant-musicians. The form is larger than usual, comprising *two* different Trios in succession (in the same key), that are followed by an abbreviated *da capo* (Part I, only, of the principal Division), which is interrupted by the ominous rumbling of the impending Thunderstorm. The Themes of the *Scherzo* run thus:

Ex.62. III Principal Division

Having conceived the notion of including a thunderstorm in his symphonic scheme, Beethoven was compelled, for the time, to write purely realistic music. We are expected, here, to *imagine* the mutter and crash of thunder, the swishing of the rain, the howling of the wind, even quick lightning flashes (in the piccolo), the mighty tumult of the elements—alternately advancing and receding—all unfolded in masterly succession and proportions, and nowhere for an instant violating the normal sense of tonebeauty. This Movement, naturally, has no specific structural design; it consists in a series of Sections (thirteen in number),* many of which are recurrences of those that went before. There are a few brief "motives" but no "Themes," in the ordinary sense; hence no musical illustration is required.

*See, again, the *Analytic Symphony Series*, No. 25, for details of the entire work.

The storm gradually subsides; a shepherd's pipe is heard, like the *Ranz des vaches* of the Swiss Alps; this is answered by another, and then another call—which latter becomes the chief Theme of the hearty, good-natured, wholesome Finale. The design chosen for this is the Third Rondo-form, rather long drawn out, but of engaging *naïveté* and unalloyed beauty. Its Themes are as follows:

Note the resemblance of the First subordinate Theme to the subordinate Theme in the first Movement.

* * *

The Seventh Symphony

It will not have escaped the student's notice that Beethoven's mood, as we have intimated, alternates regularly from each Symphony to the next. Omitting the first Symphony from this generalization because it can hardly be regarded as a distinctive product of the great master's genius, it will be observed that the Symphonies whose serial numbers are even (II—IV—VI—VIII) are of a lighter, happier emotional quality; while those with odd numbers (III-V-VII-IX) are of a sterner, more serious character. Those with even numbers are all in the major mode; of the others, two (Nos. V and IX) are in minor, and correspondingly more profoundly earnest, dramatic, even tragic, in their subjective emotional expression.

Thus, the lighthearted, refreshingly unsophisticated, spontaneous Sixth (*Pastoral*) Symphony is succeeded by one of great conceptive gravity, momentous tendency, and a pulse of tremendous energy.

This does not imply that only those with odd numbers are "great;" it is always Beethoven, throughout, and each separate Symphony, even the first one, has its individual value, and lofty musical significance.

The Seventh Symphony, A major, Op. 92, was written in the early months of 1812, and first performed late in 1813, in Vienna. During the four years that had passed since the composition of the Sixth, Beethoven's genius had matured still further, and the advance he had made in freedom and sureness of touch, particularly in his command of tonal architecture, in the structural formation of his Movements, is strikingly apparent. In his Seventh, Beethoven manifests complete control of the elemental forces of musical speech, an amazing originality, and an inexhaustible fund of resources, that are not met with in such luxuriance and assurance in his foregoing Symphonies. The dictum: "The Seventh Symphony is the apotheosis of Rhythm," is attributed to Liszt; Wagner is said to have called it "the apotheosis of the Dance." The former simile befits the work with quite sufficient accuracy, since it is the element of Rhythm which seems chiefly answerable for the singular vivacity and irresistible urge of all but the *Allegretto* Movement; furthermore, each of its Movements has a distinctive and persistent rhythmic motive, or prosodic metre. For illustration:

Ex. 64.

Beethoven reverts here again to the tradition of the Introduction; and this Introduction is so lengthy, so impressive, and so independent in contents and character, that it may be regarded as a separate Movement, wherefore the Seventh Symphony, like the Sixth, actually comprises five Movements.

The structural design of this wonderfully beautiful Introduction is a very broad Two-Part form, the Second Part of which—a truly exquisite sentence—assumes the appearance and importance of a subordinate Theme, placed at first in C major. This whole "Exposition" is then recapitulated, with transpositions, and thus the whole Movement (Introduction) approximates the sonatine-allegro form. The "subordinate Theme" is placed, the second time, in F major, whose tonic, f, is the lowered (or minor) sixth scale-step of A, the original key, and therefore tends naturally and urgently toward the tone e, the dominant, and portal, of the opening harmony of the *Allegro*. This discloses Beethoven's modulatory purpose, and it is faithfully carried out in an exceedingly striking manner, characteristic of Beethoven and no other master—thus: when the e is finally reached and rooted (ten measures before the Theme begins), it is reiterated alone, alternately in the wood-wind and violins no fewer than *sixty* times!*

The thematic contents of the *Allegro* (First) Movement are as follows:

*See the *Analytic Symphony Series*, No. 26.

The Development is the most masterly, fascinating, logically and structurally perfect model of what a Development may and should be, that even Beethoven ever consummated. The Recapitulation is nearly exact, with the prescribed transpositions. There occurs, in the Coda, one of those daring episodes which confirm Beethoven's occasional unconventional methods, and which for a time caused some consternation even in the Beethoven ranks, viz.: some fifty measures before the end of the Movement, the basses softly intonate a figure of two measures (derived with quaint modifications from the first measures of the principal Theme), and repeat this drone, waxing into a growl, eleven times—as ground-motive or *basso ostinato*—against an almost absurdly primitive "yodel" in the violins. See the Example, and note the relation of the bass-motive to the principal Theme.

The second (slow) Movement is the world-famous, apparently imperishable *Allegretto*, always sure of its profoundly moving appeal to every music-loving soul. Its design approximates the Second Rondo-form, akin to that chosen by Beethoven for the Finale of his Third Symphony, and the slow Movement of his Fifth; also, later, for the slow Movement of his Ninth—inasmuch as the numerous restatements of the principal Theme convey the impression of Variations.

The Themes run thus:

It begins with two introductory measures on the 6-4 chord of the tonic—a chord without "support," hovering, as if wafted in from some ethereal region. The principal Theme is stated four times, at full length, with heavy *crescendo,* before the soothing, touching First subordinate Theme enters. As a matter of fact, there is no other (second) subordinate Theme, but the place reserved for it in the design is filled—exactly as in the *Adagio* of the Third Symphony—by a *fugato* in triple-counterpoint, the Subject marked A being drawn from one of the phrases of the principal Theme. The Coda begins with a portion of the First subordinate Theme, precisely as before, and this is followed by another complete Variation of the principal Theme.

For the vivacious third Movement, with its majestic Trio, Beethoven uses no other titles than the tempo-marks; but it tallies in every respect with his customary *Scherzo* and Trio. As in the Fourth Symphony, it is expanded to imposing dimensions by an additional complete statement of the Trio, and subsequent *da capo*. It presents these Themes:

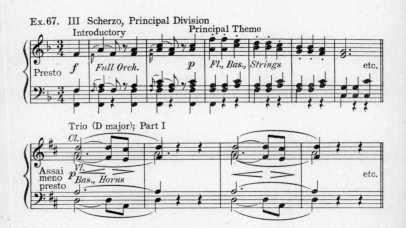

Note the singular choice of keys—F major and D major, in an A major Symphony. The Trio is remarkably simple in its harmonic material—nothing but the tonic and dominant chords of the chosen key. The violins hold the tone *a*, in octaves, with very brief digressions, throughout Parts I and II of the Trio. Note the striking use of the horn in the second Part; this horn-figure (derived from the first two measures of the chief melody) is reiterated nine times, then quickened into a 2/4 metre, *crescendo*, culminating in a magnificent recurrence of Part I (as Part III).

The last Movement is a riot of tone and rhythm. In its vivacity, audacity, splendid vitality and rollicking humor, it transcends any and every Finale elsewhere recorded in classic symphonic literature. The form is sonata-allegro, with these Themes:

Ex. 68. IV Finale, Introduction

The most serious, almost sinister, episode occurs in the third Section of the Coda: the basses ramble through a tragico-comical, chromatically wavering, descending spiral sequence of considerable length, against sustained chords in the wood-wind and the first measure of the principal Theme in the violins, until they (the basses) have groped their way to the low dominant-note (*e*), where they sway in alternation with *d♯* for twenty-one measures, while the rest of the orchestra asserts the home-key. Beethoven evidently took this very seriously; and it is one of the finest, most ingenious and original passages to be found anywhere in his Symphonies.

* * *

THE EIGHTH SYMPHONY

Beethoven's Eighth Symphony, in F, Op. 93, was also written in 1812—in its later months. Therefore, this and the Seventh form another set of "twin" Symphonies, as do the Fifth and Sixth. Again he adopts, in this Eighth, a lighter and somewhat simpler style, particularly in the first Movements; but despite its humor and good nature, it nowhere sacrifices its symphonic dignity. It is shorter, more concise, than its fellow-symphonies; for Beethoven was ever more deeply concerned with quality than with quantity, and here he has committed himself to brevity because he possessed the rare faculty of fitting the vessel to the contents, and had mastered the art of "much in little." This need not veil an implication that the extreme length of some of his Movements is a weakness; when a work is large in portent, a broad expanse of canvas is imperative: compare the first Movement of his Third, and of his Ninth Symphonies; also of the First and Fourth Symphonies of Brahms; and the entire colossal C major Symphony of Schubert. The Finale of this Eighth Symphony seems to be conceived in this wider sense, and is therefore of unusual length, especially in its extraordinary Coda.

There is no Introduction—not a single preliminary note. The thematic factors of the first Movement (concise sonata-allegro form) are as follows:

Beethoven experiments here with the modulatory location of the subordinate Theme, in *each* of its two presentations: in the Exposition, its first Period is placed in D major (too high) and then restated in the "right" key, C major; and in the Recapitulation it is first set in B♭ (too low) and then, as before, restated in the "right" key, F major. This wonderfully sunny Movement abounds in Beethoven's pet device of Repetition, especially in the Development and Coda.

(Consult the *Analytic Symphony Series*, No. 37.)

The second Movement stands for the *slow* one, but it is not of the conventional lyric, sustained type. Its daintiness and genuine good humor fully compensate, however, for the expected change of mood. It is in reality a musical pleasantry, originating in Beethoven's interest in the metronome, and other mechanical contrivances, upon which Maelzel was at that time experimenting, and which Beethoven seems to have regarded with favor. The Movement—like the *Allegretto* of the Seventh Symphony—begins with a 6/4 chord, but for a vastly different reason; there, it was portentous; here, it immediately reveals itself as a part of the musical jest. The design is amazingly compact, and represents a miniature sonatine-allegro form. Its brief motives run thus:

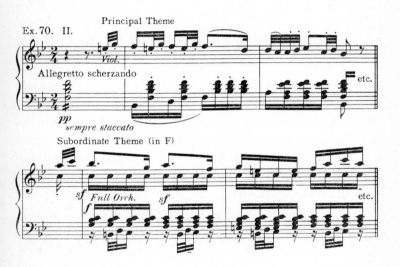

Beethoven heightens the delightfully genial, intimate effect of his "little" Eighth Symphony (as he fondly called it) by repressing his predilection for the *Scherzo* as third Movement, and returning to the leisurely, graceful Minuet of former days. Both Divisions are surpassingly lovely. Their thematic contents are as follows:

The Finale is anything but "little." In the sprightliness of its chief motive, the wonderful grace and richness of its subordinate Theme, its strong contrasts, and the marvellous formation of its Development and of its unusually long Coda, this Finale ranks very high among the most imposing of the great master's orchestral creations. It is built upon these Themes:

There are two strokes of humor in the Movement that are worthy of special mention. One is the sudden, explosive, wholly unanticipated *c*♯ in the seventeenth measure. Theoretically it is *d*♭, the lowered (or minor) sixth scale-step of the key—the same harmonic interval as the *d*♭ in the thirtieth measure. But to Beethoven's keen musical discrimination there is a difference between *c*♯ and *d*♭, and it was *c*♯, and nothing else, that he wanted; for precisely therein lies the incongruity and genuine humor of the situation. Later, in the sixth Section of the Coda, he gives it first the correct notation, *d*♭, and then changes it to a *legitimate c*♯. The other bit of drollery is his use of the drums (tuned in the tonic *octave* instead of the usual tonic and dominant), twice with the bassoon alone, ostensibly as solo, and again, beginning thirty-four measures before the end, as accompaniment to the wood-wind and then to the violins, until the full orchestra masses itself together.

It is further noteworthy that precisely the same experiments with the modulatory location of the subordinate Theme take place here, as in the first Movement: the first Period is placed in a remote key, and then restated in the "right" key. This occurs likewise in the Recapitulation.

Among the Sections of the Coda (whose contents, it will be borne in mind, are *wholly optional*) there is a nearly complete reappearance of the principal Theme, and also of the subordinate one, in their proper keys. This is misleading, but no one will question Beethoven's musical judgment.*

*See, again, the *Analytic Symphony Series*, No. 37.

The resemblance of the principal motive in this Finale to the second Codetta of the first Movement may be an accidental coincidence, though foremost among Beethoven's salient qualities are his concentration and unfailing logic.

* * *

The Ninth Symphony

Ten years elapsed after Beethoven had written his Seventh and Eighth Symphonies, before he again turned to this highest type of musical conception, and created his last, the Ninth, Symphony. During these ten years he was by no means idle, but composed a number of his finest works. Still, it was a comparatively less fruitful period than any other of his life. It was a period of relaxation and recreation, in which his great spirit was more active than his pen; as if he were collecting and strengthening his forces for the four supreme efforts of his final years: the last piano Sonatas, all of the last five String-quartets, the *Missa solemnis,* and the *Choral* (Ninth) Symphony.

This, in D minor, Op. 125, was conceived as early as 1817, but not finished until 1824. Its first three Movements are of the conventional symphonic type, though they transcend in scope, breadth of design, proportions, and depth of spiritual significance—to say nothing of their surpassing technical richness and perfection — anything ever brought into being in the sphere of symphonic creation. But for the Finale Beethoven conceived the idea of adding the ultimate "instrument"—*the human voice*—to the score, and thus magnifying the Movement into a comprehensive Hymn of Joy, for which he selected the *Ode to Joy* of Schiller. It was the final realization of a plan that had been slumbering in his mind for many years; away back in his youthful days—in 1793—the project of setting music to this wonderful poem challenged his creative spirit, and in 1811 fragments begin to appear in his sketchbooks bearing on the subject.

The Ninth Symphony was ordered by, written for, and dedicated to, the Philharmonic Society of London, and the agreement made embraced *two* Symphonies. From some yet unexplained cause, however, the Ninth was ultimately dedicated to King Frederick William III, and received its initial performance, not in London, but in Vienna, in May, 1824.*

The first Movement opens with an introductory passage of sixteen measures (not an independent Introduction) on the dominant, leading thence naturally into the imposing principal Theme. This, and the other thematic components of the Movement are as follows:

*See *Beethoven's Nine Symphonies* by Sir George Grove, for further interesting details.

To this, two brief Codettas are added. The whole Movement is a very regular, though extremely broad, sonata-allegro form. The Development is a marvel of consistent and logical thematic manipulation, unusually elaborate, and at a first hearing apparently abstruse. Uncommon prominence is given to the third measure (often joined by the fourth) of the principal Theme. The Recapitulation is nearly exact, with the expected transpositions. The Coda is also uncommonly long, and exhibits a notable feature in its eighth Section (about thirty-five measures from the end): the basses carry a ground-motive (*basso con-*

tinuo) of two measures, with descending chromatics and ascending scale, gradually reënforced by the whole body of strings, and repeated seven times.

(See the *Analytic Symphony Series*, No. 38.)

In this Symphony Beethoven locates the *Scherzo* as *second* Movement, contrary to his custom. It is likewise of extraordinary length; so much so that the principal Division is amplified to a full sonata-allegro design. Its Themes, and the Trio, present this appearance:

The principal Theme is preceded by eight introductory measures, all derived from the first measure. Here again Beethoven assigns a striking function to the kettledrums— tuned exactly as in the Finale of the Eighth Symphony, in the octave *f*: the fifth measure of the introductory passage is taken by the drums, *solo;* and in the fourth Section of the Development he gives to the drums alone the first measure of the three-measure thematic phrase, four times in succession.

The Trio manifests Beethoven's faith in Repetition: nearly the whole of it is built upon a four-measure Phrase, always placed in the same key (with one exception)—similar in general effect to the *basso ostinato*. The design of the Trio is also expanded, into a Five-Part form.

The third Movement, a very broad *Adagio*, is probably the most impressive slow Movement that Beethoven ever created, and he was particularly noted for the great beauty and appropriate expression that he always imparted to this important division of the symphonic form. The structure is fundamentally a First-Rondo, since it presents two alternating Themes; but it diverges somewhat from the orthodox arrangement: the subordinate Theme is stated *twice*, in different keys, and consequently the principal Theme appears three times—at each recurrence so elaborately embellished that it gives to the Movement the general character of a Variation-form. In reality it is analogous to the design adopted by Beethoven in the Finale of his Third, and in the slow Movements of his Fifth and Seventh Symphonies. Another noteworthy feature is the formation of the Retransition (returning passage) to the last presentation of the principal Theme (three-flat signature); it is in effect a brief "Development."

The principal Theme is preceded by two introductory measures. The two Themes are as follows:

As to the Finale: it was Beethoven's original intention to make the Ninth Symphony a purely instrumental work, and it was not until he had sketched an instrumental fourth Movement that he decided to gratify his lifelong desire to set Schiller's *Ode to Joy* (written in 1785) to music, as a Finale to the three preceding Movements. The original fourth Movement, already sketched, was therefore set aside for the time, but was utilized later as the Finale to his String-quartet in A minor, Op. 132.

Thus the present Finale became a sort of Cantata, consisting in a series of successive related, though clearly individualized *Episodes* — thirteen in number, including a distinctive Introduction, a principal Theme, a kind of Attendant Theme (in the ninth Episode), and a Coda.*

Beethoven selected only certain verses from Schiller's *Ode*, and even altered the order of these, thus affirming his

---

*The details are all fully recorded in the *Analytic Symphony Series*, No. 38.

right to exercise his own judgment and single out only that which suited his artistic purpose.

The principal Theme and Attendant Theme have these melodic and rhythmic shapes:

The first and second Episodes are introductory: after a tumultuous passage in the orchestra, a Leader seems to appear (represented by the string-basses, *declamato*) and invite suggestions for a final Subject; the Themes of the first, second and third Movements pass successively in review, but are rejected; whereupon a new motive is intimated, found acceptable, and developed into the principal Theme of the whole Cantata. The third Episode is an Exposition of this Theme, in the orchestra; the fourth Episode is a recurrence of the turbulent first Episode, which, as before, is checked by the Leader—now a vocal baritone; in the fifth Episode, the Theme is given out in its full scope by the chorus and orchestra; the sixth Episode is another presentation of the entire principal Theme, transformed in rhythm, metre and character into a stirring martial scene (in keeping with another of the verses of the *Ode*), in which the chorus later joins; Episode seven is an orchestral *fugato* with two Themes, that of Episode six combined with a new contrapuntal phrase; in Episode eight this same idea is carried out with chorus and orchestra; the ninth Episode presents the "Attendant" Theme, extended by other material of an austere dramatic character; in Episode ten the principal and Attendant Themes are combined, with some necessary modification, for chorus and orchestra; Episode eleven reverts to one of the dramatic sentences of Episode nine; the twelfth Episode is a new setting of the first lines of the *Ode*, with stronger emphasis on the attribute of Joy, and here a Solo-quartet is added to the tonal mass.

What follows, from this to the end, is a mighty Coda—three Sections—in which the central emotional idea, Joy, reaches its fullest consummation, and most jubilant and spirited expression.

As stated above, the agreement between Beethoven and the Philharmonic Society of London was to include *two* Symphonies, so that a Tenth was expected to succeed his Ninth. It was not to be; but Beethoven's general plan, and some sketches of the projected Tenth Symphony (dating from 1826) have been preserved.

* * *

Regarded from every artistic point of view, and in every esthetic sense, the nine Symphonies of Beethoven stand, in their fundamental simplicity and spiritual grandeur, unparalleled in the whole range of symphonic production. They emanated from a master-mind whose great genius seems to have fully grasped and comprehended the eloquent, impressive Language of tone, and who interpreted this Language in a strongly subjective, vitally emotional, convincing way, with a perfection of structural proportion and detail that gave a lucent, unobstructed sense of reality to the rare messages that it carried.

* * *

QUESTIONS FOR REVIEW

1. What poetic simile defines in a general way the distinctive musical conceptions of Haydn, Mozart, and Beethoven?
2. Outline the biography of Beethoven, emphasizing dates of birth and death.
3. After whose muse did Beethoven model his First Symphony?
4. What technical device does Beethoven persistently employ?
5. Between which two of his Symphonies did Beethoven's distinctive genius evince the greatest progress?

BEETHOVEN

6. Why is the Third Symphony called the *Eroica?*
7. In what manner is the succession of moods from each Symphony to the next manifested?
8. What type did Beethoven substitute for the conventional Minuet?
9. Which of his Symphonies are in minor?
10. Which have an independent Introduction?
11. In which Symphony is there a Funeral March?
12. In which one does the famous *Allegretto* occur?
13. What light do Beethoven's sketchbooks throw upon his attitude toward his tasks?
14. In which symphonic *Allegro* is the entire Movement developed out of one short motive?
15. Which two of his Symphonies have practically five Movements?
16. In which of the Third Movements (*Scherzi*) is the form enlarged, and in what manner?
17. In which of his Movements is the form apparently that of the Variation?
18. Which Symphony was called the "Apotheosis of Rhythm," and why?
19. Which of the Symphonies are called "twins," and why?
20. Which important orchestral instrument is almost wholly absent from the score of his Sixth Symphony?
21. Mention some of Beethoven's characteristic uses of the kettle-drums.
22. Between which two of his Symphonies did Beethoven make the longest pause?
23. Which is the *Choral* Symphony, and why is it so called?

* * *

References

MASON	Beethoven and his Forerunners.
THOMAS AND STOCK	Talks on Beethoven's Symphonies.
GROVE	Beethoven and his Nine Symphonies.
EVANS	Beethoven's Nine Symphonies.
BERLIOZ	A Critical Study of Beethoven's Symphonies.
WEINGARTNER	On the Performance of Beethoven's Symphonies.
MIES	The Importance of Beethoven's Sketches for the understanding of his Style.
BEKKER	Beethoven.
CROWEST	Beethoven.
FISCHER	Beethoven.
D'INDY	Beethoven.
NEWMAN	The Unconscious Beethoven.
ROLLAND	Beethoven.
SONNECK	Beethoven: Impressions of Contemporaries.
SULLIVAN	Beethoven: his Spiritual Development.
THAYER	Life of Beethoven.
TURNER	Beethoven, the Search for Reality.
WALKER	Beethoven.
KALISCHER	A Selection of Beethoven's Letters.
SHEDLOCK	Beethoven's Letters (complete).

ILLUSTRATIVE RECORDS AND ROLLS

Records: B—Brunswick; C—Columbia; E—Edison; H—His Master's Voice; O—Odeon; Pa—Parlophone; Po—Polydor; V—Victor; Vo—Vocalion.

Rolls: A—Ampico; D—Duo-Art; M—Melodee; Pl—Pleyela; Q—QRS; U—Universal; W—Welte-Mignon.

Music Mentioned in Chapter III:

Beethoven Symphonies
    No. 1, in C major   C, Pa, Po, V, O; M, Pl, Q, U.
    No. 2, in D major   C, Pa, Po, V, O; M, Pl, U.
    No. 3, in E♭ major (*Eroica*)   C, Pa, Po, V, O; A, M, Pl, Q, U.
    No. 4, in B♭ major   C, Pa, Po, V, O; M, Pl, Q, U.
    No. 5, in C minor   C, Pa, Po, V, O; M, Pl, Q, U.
    No. 6, in F major (*Pastoral*)   C, Pa, Po, V, O; M, Pl, Q, U.
    No. 7, in A major   C, Pa, Po, V, O; M, Pl, Q, U.
    No. 8, in F major   C, Pa, Po, V, O; M, Pl, Q, U.
    No. 9, in D minor (*Choral*)   C, Pa, Po, V, O; M, Pl, Q, U.

Chapter IV

SCHUBERT AND MENDELSSOHN

THE two giants of symphonic production are Beethoven and Schubert — the Schubert of the *Unfinished* (Eighth), and of the great *C major* Symphony (No. 10). Subsequent days brought forth some writers who attained to towering heights in the chain of musical mountain peaks, but probably no one who has quite reached the supreme altitude of these two giants. We shall see, in the coming chapters, how these compare.

Both Beethoven and Schubert did their most important symphonic work in the same span of years, the third decade of the nineteenth century. But Schubert was by twenty-seven years the younger of the two, and this difference in their ages indicates a singular superiority on Schubert's part. When Schubert wrote his first Symphony, in 1813 (at the age of sixteen), Beethoven had already completed his seventh and eighth; and the difference in the quality of their work *at that date* was enormous beyond all comparison, that of the boy Schubert being vastly inferior to that of the maturer master. That Schubert should have caught up with Beethoven in the succeeding ten or twelve years speaks volumes for the rapidity of Schubert's development, and the power and richness of his genius. But we must take into account the significant fact that Schubert enjoyed the benefits of Beethoven's wonderful artistic achievements, the vitalizing influence of his mighty compositions, with which he (Schubert) was thoroughly familiar, which he venerated beyond measure, and studied with consuming ardor. Beethoven, on the other hand, could not profit by any means to an equal extent from the creations of his predecessors, Haydn and Mozart, because these were not of a kind calculated to stimulate him, in the same degree in which his infinitely maturer creations aroused the enthusiasm and ripened the genius of Schubert. This accounts, no doubt best, for Schubert's extraordinary progress during so brief a span of years, and invites the regretful question: What might Schubert not have accomplished, had he lived beyond the less than thirty-two years that measured his brief life?

Franz Peter Schubert was born on the 31st of January, 1797, in a small town not far from Vienna. His father was a schoolmaster there, and was musical enough to give the lad his first instruction in violin playing, while the choirmaster, Holzer, taught him piano, organ, singing and a little harmony. In 1808 he was admitted to the court choir, and received further instructions from Rucziska and the famous Salieri. Among numerous early experiments in composition, his song *Hagar's Klage* (1811) has survived, and bears witness to his extraordinary natural gifts.

In 1813 his voice changed and he was obliged to leave the training-school; in that year, also, he composed his first Symphony. During the ensuing three years he wrote three more Symphonies, 4 Masses, 2 Operettas, 3 *Singspiele*, and over 140 songs, many of which are still appraised as rare lyric gems, and all of which attested the phenomenally rapid evolution of his genius, the quality of which was now completely manifest.

In 1817, Vienna became his permanent home, only excepting two summers (1818 and 1824) spent as music teacher in Count Esterhazy's family, in Hungary. At this time he was so fortunate as to gain the sympathy of the then famous tenor singer, Michael Vogl, who was one of the first, and always the greatest, of the interpreters of Schubert's songs. But while he received general recognition—even Beethoven spoke highly of his songs—Schubert was infamously imposed upon by his publishers, and excepting occasional transient periods of good fortune, his life was a continual struggle for the means of subsistence. His greatest compositions were almost wholly ignored; but he fared better with his wonderful songs and with his dramatic productions (comprising 18 Operas, Operettas and *Singspiele*) some of which remained fragments, it is true, while others still rank as masterly examples of dramatic art.

From 1817 until 1828, the year of his death, Schubert created an incredibly large quantity of works, in every form and style of composition, a complete list of which has never been definitely compiled. Very many were not discovered until long after his death, and to this day an occasional authenticated piece is brought to light. Schumann unearthed the great C major Symphony (No. 10) in 1838, at which time only seven Symphonies of Schubert were supposed to exist.

Early in 1828 Schubert's health began to fail, and all efforts to arrest his illness proved futile; he died on the 19th of November, 1828, having not quite completed his 32nd year.

Beethoven and Schubert both lived in Vienna, not far from each other, and it is certain that they must have met often upon the street, and have known each other well. And yet music history is strangely reticent in regard to their companionship;

some authorities declare that they actually met and spoke together but twice; others place such closer encounters at six or seven times. It is certain that Schubert was one of the torch-bearers at Beethoven's burial, and quite as certain that no one appreciated the loss to himself and all humanity, or mourned more sincerely than Schubert did.

Such deplorable lack of intercourse between these two kindred geniuses may be accounted for, partly by Beethoven's deafness, his absorbing preoccupation in his creative labors, and his generally seclusive disposition and habits; also partly, on the other hand, by Schubert's diffidence, and reluctance to approach a person so exalted in his (Schubert's) esteem; also by the radical difference in their dispositions. Beethoven moved in aristocratic circles, when he moved in any; though a warm-hearted, generous friend, he was outwardly uncompromising, retiring, and not easily accessible. Schubert, however, was of a jovial, light-spirited, companionable nature; he loved to spend his time, especially evenings, with the half-dozen youths whom he regarded as his social equals, in comfortable gatherings in some cosy inn, playing, singing, improvising, discussing esthetic matters with his chums, and not disdaining the cheering cup—or mug—though never indulging beyond moderation.*

Schubert's ruling passion was *Melody*. Merely touch his emotional constitution at any point, and a stream of Melody gushed forth, delightful, pure, straight from the fountainhead of Nature herself, and in rhythmic motions that are irresistibly captivating. In this regard, Schubert and Mozart were close of kin. Yet, while the melodies

*The reader should complement this imperfect sketch by a thoughtful reading of *Schubert's Fame*, by Carl Engel; *Beethoven's and Schubert's Personal Relations*, by Walter Nohl; *The Epic of the "Unfinished,"* by Herbert F. Peyser—and other admirable Schubertiana, all contained in the *Musical Quarterly* of October, 1928.

of Mozart are inherently individual and unmistakable, it is nevertheless possible to confound them, at times, with those of his contemporaries; but those of Schubert are so original, so absolutely typical, so exuberant, that they discourse of *Schubert* and no one else.

Not that his overwhelming melodic musical disposition made him indifferent to harmony. He performs feats of harmonic succession, and particularly of modulation, that are staggering—though always normal, impeccably clean and "correct." But he draws the melodic line so boldly and strongly that one seems to forget that the harmony is there, as substratum and indispensable source. To such an extent is this the case, so completely does his melody embody the harmony, that it appears to bear the musical message fully, in itself alone; and that is one reason why Schubert can and does often state his most important (thematic) melodies without harmonic accompaniment — note the beginning of the *Unfinished* Symphony, and the horn solo with which the one in C major opens.

Early Symphonies

Schubert's First Symphony, in D, was composed in 1813, shortly after Beethoven had completed his Seventh and Eighth, and when Mendelssohn and Schumann, who were to become the next bright stars in the symphonic firmament, were very small boys, unconscious of the power they were destined to exert.

This First Symphony is in no wise remarkable, save in that it is the product of a boy of sixteen. Schubert's uncontrollable flood of melody overruns it—as yet in rivulets only—but otherwise it gives but little recognizable promise of what was to succeed it. Then came a second, in B♭, and a third, in D (both in 1815). These record remarkable progress; but it was the next following Symphony, No. IV, known as the *Tragic* (C minor, 1816), which first revealed some of the qualities of Schubert's outstanding genius in this larger sphere of tone-expression.

There has always been much confusion in regard to the number and order of his Symphonies. This was a natural consequence of the comparative indifference of the public, though most largely owing to Schubert's own indifference. A "little thing" like a Symphony, floating on the immense current of his productive flood, did not mean much to him; it was written, shoved to one side, buried under piles of manuscript, stowed away after his death, in dusty drawers, until some eager, appreciative hand drew it forth and gave it back to the musical world. Schumann knew of only seven, and when he discovered the great C major one (in 1838), obviously the last, he called it "No. VII." Others still insist on limiting the number to eight. But it seems to be the tradition that there were ten—though his biographer Kreissle appears (in 1860) to have known of only eight; all but one of the ten are accessible, though not all are published. The list is as follows:

No. I (D, finished in October, 1813); No. II (B♭, March, 1815); No. III (D, May, 1815); No. IV (the *Tragic*, C minor, April, 1816); No. V (B♭, October, 1816); No. VI (C,

February, 1818), which Schubert spoke of as a "grand" (large) Symphony; No. VII (in E, begun in August, 1821, left in partly sketched form—not completed); No. VIII (the *Unfinished,* B minor, begun October 30, 1822); No. IX (the *Gasteiner,* C, 1825); and No. X (the great C major, March, 1828). Of these, No. IX, though persistently cited, seems to be irretrievably lost; some authorities have ventured the conjecture that it may have been merely a revision of the one in C, No. VI, and neglected or destroyed by Schubert himself, as of insufficient novelty.

The "Tragic" Symphony

This one, No. IV, in C minor, composed early in 1816, is the first of Schubert's Symphonies which challenges attention, since, as already stated, it presents features of more than transient interest, and manifests, already, the distinctive, typical Schubert idiom. But the title "Tragic" is inaccurate, pompous, and a bit pretentious. For no youth of nineteen summers really knows what tragedy signifies— at least, Schubert did not; he bases his conception of it upon what he has read or heard, but not upon what he has *felt* and known. Therefore there is to be found in this Symphony no more than a general, artificially emphasized dramatic strain (in the first and last Movements only), and a few pathetic touches, but no genuine tragic outbursts.

The forms are regular, but disclose Schubert's characteristic treatment of modulation, particularly in the placing of his subordinate Themes, and in the Recapitulation, where he indulges in transpositions that modify the traditional scheme, though they cannot be charged with impairing the structural impression. Thus, in the first Movement (C minor) he sets the subordinate Theme in A♭, instead of the conventional E♭, and ends the Exposition in that key; and the Recapitulation begins in G minor, instead of C, with the subordinate Theme in E♭. The Coda is in C major—which is normal.

The second Movement is a lovely Lyric, of friendly character, in sonatine-allegro form (i.e., without a Development), and here are encountered episodes of touching pathos.

The third Movement is called a *Menuetto*, but it is in reality a *Scherzo*, quite after Beethoven's heart, and decidedly effective. Its Trio is a beautiful specimen of Schubert's typical conception.

The Finale is again a sonata-allegro design; the principal Theme is inferior—scarcely more than a boyish imitation of pseudo-dramatic opera; but the subordinate Theme (here again in A♭) is a truly beautiful, redeeming feature. The Recapitulation is in C *major,* the subordinate Theme placed at first in F.

Schubert was almost as inveterate a devotee of the device of Repetition as was Beethoven. But when Beethoven repeats, the effect is quite a different thing; like so many of Beethoven's creative processes, which, being controlled by serious mental effort, profound reflection and untiring comparison and pruning, turn out results that are unique and firm. Beethoven's repetitions always strengthen the structure, while those of Schubert (and others) often weaken it; those of Beethoven make for unity—those of Schubert are apt to produce the impression of monotony. The comparison may be somewhat unfair, since this refers mainly to Schubert's *earlier* works, composed during a period in which Beethoven had already attained to maturity. At any rate, the student will find that it does not apply to Schubert's last two *great* Symphonies, wherein we would not willingly dispense with a single tone.

The Fifth Symphony

This Fifth Symphony, in B♭, though written in the same year as the *Tragic* (September—October, 1816) is greatly superior to the latter, and evinces such an advance in freedom and power of original expression that it may be accepted as the actual beginning of Schubert's significant symphonic career. While it frankly adopts and sustains the simple, comparatively primitive style of Haydn, or, more correctly, of Mozart, it possesses an attractive physiognomy of its own; and it is permeated with the buoyant, joyous spirit of this amazingly gifted spendthrift of spontaneous melody. The score is that of the small orchestra of former days, comprising *one* flute, two each of oboes, bassoons and horns, and the quintet of strings—but no clarinets, *no drums*, and no trumpets throughout. This reduction of the instrumental apparatus augments the brightness and lucidity of the charming music.

The first Movement, a concise sonata-allegro design, with this thematic material:

opens with an introductory phrase of four measures, preceding the principal Theme, but with no thematic reference to the latter. The structure is extremely regular; the fundamental four-measure pattern is employed almost without exception in its phrases, though an occasional Extension checks the menace of monotony. This well-nigh obstinate regularity of form (and of cadence) testifies to the rapid spontaneous flow of Schubert's melody; he was not given to critical reflection, at least not yet, and he felt no need of exciting the hearer's interest by rhythmic shifting, or any similar device. This simplicity of conception is further attested by his constant use of Repetition, in which respect, as stated above, he almost outrivalled Beethoven himself. In this Movement Schubert again gratifies his characteristic inclination to alter the traditional modulatory scheme, by setting his Themes in unexpected keys—a trait pointed out in connection with the *Tragic* Symphony, and a prevalent impulse, peculiarly distinctive of Schubert: thus, he begins the Recapitulation in the "wrong" key—E♭ instead of B♭.

(Consult the *Analytic Symphony Series*, No. 14.)

The second Movement is a complaisant Lyric of semi-serious quality, vitalized with fine contrasts. It is in sonatine-form (without a Development) and is enlarged by an additional (partial) statement of the principal Theme, in lieu of a Coda. Its Themes are as follows:

Schubert calls the third Movement a Minuet; its tempo and character, however, proclaim it a *Scherzo*. It has these thematic factors:

The Trio is one of those ingratiating tuneful sentences in which Schubert gives free vent to his irresistible melodic fancy—a type which he developed, in part, in writing his songs, and which for unadulterated loveliness has probably never been surpassed.

The Finale is a perfectly regular sonata-allegro design, masterly in conception and formulation, whose vivacity is held in effective restraint by episodes of considerable dramatic power and eloquence. It utilizes these Themes:

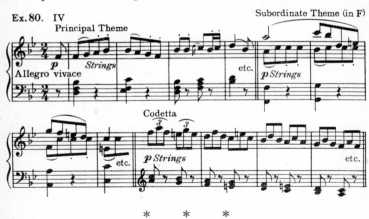

* * *

Schubert was not a typically studious musician. He was endowed with an *intuition* of unheard-of alertness, opulence and infallibility; and this usually precarious, and very often evanescent quality served him stedfastly all his life; he instinctively depended upon it, and therefore never felt the impulse to engage in serious theoretical study (at least not in his earlier years), or to apply his exceptional mental forces in a reflective and selective way. It would be unfair, however, to conclude that he was in the slightest degree superficial, or indifferent to the obviously essential laws of his art. Such sketches of his works as have been discovered, and notably his later creations themselves, reveal a measure of earnestness at times scarcely inferior to that of Beethoven. Schubert was simply averse to the dry, mathematical routine of textbooks and "methods," and found it more congenial and fruitful to study *music itself*, as he found it supplied in ample quantity by the great classic masters; and this he did, with absorbing conscientiousness. At the same time, it is undeniable that his lack of technical drill, coupled with the impetuosity of his musical conception, resulted at times in certain lapses in his formal structure, a lack of that strong, unfaltering, convincing logic, and the fine balance of architectural detail in which Beethoven excelled so greatly.

* * *

The Unfinished (Eighth) Symphony

Six years intervened between the composition of the Fifth Symphony and that of the Eighth—the *Unfinished*, as it is called—and during these years Schubert's spirit made such incredible progress toward maturity that with this Eighth Symphony he may be said to have reached the pinnacle of his musical genius. The two Symphonies that preceded this one (the Sixth, in C, and the Seventh, in E), though of positive historic interest, do not warrant detailed demonstration here; they were chiefly important as stepping-stones. It was with the *Unfinished* that Schubert's symphonic genius seemed to burst all at once into flame.

Beethoven was more profound, more scholarly, undeniably a spirit of far larger calibre and wider outlook; but in none of his works has Beethoven surpassed the tremendous primitive vitality, the mighty dramatic surge, the inescapable appeal of the *Unfinished* Symphony of Schubert. And surely no other than Schubert has ever produced so unique a masterwork at the age of twenty-five!

This Eighth Symphony (in B minor) was written the latter part of 1822. It consists of two Movements only, whence the title: *Unfinished*. Just why Schubert should have left it in this so-called "unfinished" condition, it is not easy to determine. There are two facts which appear to indicate that he intended, originally, to write a complete four-Movement Symphony: (1) The second (slow) Movement is in E major, and closes in that key, which does not provide an orthodox ending for a B minor composition; and, notwithstanding his noted modulatory freedom, Schubert was very particular about asserting a central tonality, and closing every work in the key in which it began; (2) Schubert actually started a third Movement (a *Scherzo*) and sketched no less than 130 measures of it.* This, however, is so inferior in quality, so obviously alien and inadequate, that no one will question why Schubert abandoned it. Then there are other conjectures: Schubert may have mistrusted his ability to sustain consistently so lofty an emotional flight; or he may have wearied of the task—a not uncommon habit with him; or—and this brings us to the probable crux of the matter—his unfailing instinct may have informed him that the message was *complete,* so perfect and so final that any addition would be worse than useless. In reality, then, this marvellous Symphony is no more "unfinished," in the highest esthetic sense, than are the four piano Sonatas of Beethoven which contain only two Movements each (Op. 54, 78, 90, 111).

* * *

The orchestral score of both Movements includes, besides the ordinary contingent, three trombones.

The first Movement is in strict sonata-allegro form, and presents the following Themes:

*The interested reader will find a facsimile of the first nine measures, in score, in the above-cited article, in the *Musical Quarterly* of October, 1928, opposite page 645.

It will be seen that the principal Theme consists of two separate and widely different members. Such division of the chief Theme, which is almost tantamount to *two* distinct Themes, was a favorite practice with Schubert; his fertility of invention was so active that he was never at a loss for a new idea. Herein he was unlike the more reflective Beethoven, who preferred to evolve his structure out of one brief, fruitful Theme. In point of fact, this two-fold physiognomy of the theme is not new. In ordinary cases, as has repeatedly been seen, the theme is almost invariably a Two-Part form (at least), and each of these two Parts constitutes a *somewhat* independent thematic member; but they are only the related "Parts" of one and the same thematic factor. The novelty in the former case, attributable to Schubert, consists in the *widely different* character of the two members, which actually increases the sum of thematic factors.

Of the above two members in the *Unfinished,* the first one is the *real* thematic basis of the Movement, albeit it occurs, strangely enough, only once during the entire Exposition; but, on the other hand, it dominates the Development and the Coda almost exclusively. The other member is of very little consequence; the subordinate Theme is the factor which greatly predominates and distinguishes the Exposition, and, naturally, the Recapitulation. Schubert here again indulges in his apparently whimsical choice of keys: in the Exposition the subordinate Theme is placed in G major (instead of the conventional D), and in the Recapitulation it appears at first in D, but finally swings over into the expected B major.

(See the *Analytic Symphony Series,* No. 4.)

The second Movement is cast in the sonatine-form (without a Development). Its thematic material is as follows:

Here again the principal Theme separates into two essential members. The first one has the quality of an Introduction, but it recurs constantly, before and between the other phrases after the manner of a ritornelle or Refrain, and is of vital thematic importance.

It would be futile to undertake to point out all the many masterly and beautiful episodes in these two wondrous Movements. The student will discover, in both of them, passages of intense dramatic stress, tempered by the contrast of cheerful moments of supreme loveliness.

The Tenth Symphony

The "Great" C major Symphony was written in the early months of 1828, a short time before Schubert's divine voice was stilled forever. And here again there had been a lapse of six years between this and the preceding (Eighth) Symphony. As stated, a supposable Ninth Symphony presents a puzzling problem to the historian; possibly it never existed, though history persists in mentioning and numbering it.

The salient characteristic of this entire stupendous creation is Breadth. It is large in every respect — large in conception, in spirit, broad in proportions and structural plan. The many welcome repetitions, the "heavenly lengths" (as Schumann called them), the irrepressible joyous pulse of the music necessitated a canvas of very unusual dimensions. And its prevailing tone is Joy; in the slow Movement, only, is this joyous spirit of a serener type, tinged with melancholy, and yielding here and there to bursts of passion.

Its breadth of purpose demanded an Introduction, and Schubert conceived one which in extent, independence and impressiveness, forms an analogy to that of Beethoven's Seventh Symphony. The Themes of this, and of the entire first Movement are as follows:

The design is sonata-allegro, orthodox and regular but extremely long. The Introduction is a Three-Part Song-form, enlarged to five Parts by the addition of an extra (fourth) Part, which is followed by another recurrence of the First Part, thus: I—IIA—III—IIB—III. One of the figures of this Introduction enters quite frequently and fearlessly into the texture of the *Allegro;* and the culmination of the whole first Movement is a jubilant intonation of the entire first Phrase of the Introduction.

(See the *Analytic Symphony Series*, No. 15.)

The second Movement is a lyric creation of indescribable beauty, and at the same time powerful dramatic contrasts; no music could be lovelier than the two melodic Themes, and the Codetta to the first Period, with its wonderfully soothing change to the major mode; and the dramatic climax before the second recurrence of the principal Theme has rarely been equalled in intensity anywhere else in symphonic literature.

Further, this Movement (and in truth, the whole Symphony) displays mental acumen, superb mastery over *structure* in every respect, scarcely excelled by any other great master. Schubert may not have been a profoundly learned musical scholar, and surely he never wasted his precious time over abstruse musical problems; but his marvellous intuition, and a splendidly healthy mind, more than compensated for any fruits of sheer calculation.

The thematic components of this slow Movement are as follows:

An introductory phrase of seven measures precedes the principal Theme. The third measure of the latter Theme is of overruling thematic significance: the repeated *e* in the melody is the *thematic Germ*, so to speak, of the entire Movement. It appears most frequently in the rhythm of quarter-notes, but is modified at times to eighth-notes (as in the introductory measures), to sixteenths, and even thirty-second notes, as shown in the above example. It occurs upon different scale-steps, but is most persistently *e-e*. In various incisive rhythmic forms, and doubled in thirds, it provides the tremendous pounding throbs of the dramatic climax alluded to above. The insistent pulse of this motive also underlies the fascinating dialog between the horn and the strings, during the twelve measures which precede the first recurrence of the principal Theme.

The third Movement is a *Scherzo* of unusual breadth; its principal Division is enlarged to a complete sonata-allegro form, with two definite Themes—as in Beethoven's Ninth Symphony, which is the only other example of such form-dimensions (as *Scherzo*) in the literature of the symphony. Its Themes run thus:

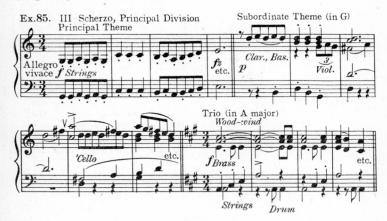

Between the principal Division and the Trio an Interlude is inserted which serves as an introduction to the Trio. This introduction consists of twenty-four successive *e's*, chiefly by the horns and trombones, and is therefore reminiscent of the famous sixty *e's* leading into the principal Theme of Beethoven's Seventh Symphony. The melody of the Trio is one of those unforgettable lyric outbursts, in folk-song style—to which no one ever gave readier and more captivating voice than Schubert did.

The Finale, a sonata-allegro of extraordinary breadth and extent, is a revel of gladness, a genuine exuberant *Ode to Joy*, more jubilant and convincing than the Finale of Beethoven's Ninth Symphony, and of that fundamental simplicity that is synonymous with true greatness. It comprises these thematic factors:

The principal Theme is here again divided into two "Parts," as shown, but these are not so essentially differentiated as are the thematic "members" in the *Unfinished*

Symphony. The four reiterated half-notes which distinguish the subordinate Theme constitute an analogy with the thematic germ of the slow Movement—a sort of echo of the latter, which may have been subconscious, or possibly intentional. The Exposition includes three Codettas, of which only the second one is cited in the example. The Development opens with an apparently *new* melodic phrase, but it is a derivative of this second Codetta; the arresting feature of this melody is its close resemblance to the principal Theme of the Finale of Beethoven's Ninth Symphony: reverse the order of the first three tones, and the parallelism is complete (compare the above example with Ex. 76, third Episode). Surely Schubert stood in no need of "borrowing" melodic ideas from anyone, nor was he ever known to do so. If this coincidence has any special meaning, it serves only to indicate how deeply Beethoven's musical spirit impressed that of Schubert.

The Recapitulation is transposed (to E♭), extended, and considerably modified.

* * *

Felix Mendelssohn-Bartholdy

With Mendelssohn the Symphony evinced a decisive inclination to enter a new sphere of musical conception, and to respond more freely and fully to the promptings of the Romantic muse. This does not by any means imply that the Classic domain was being abandoned; these two spheres, the classic and the romantic, overlap so widely, and foster such cordial interrelations, that the composer's attitude toward them is rather relative than absolute, and signifies often no more than a general personal preference; that is, he may be classically-minded but with a leaning toward romantic ideals, or *vice versa*.

The distinction, in its broadest aspect, is easily defined: the Classic school places its first and strongest dependence upon the Laws which govern the art, and subordinates all personal, emotional promptings to this authority; whereas in the Romantic school, subjective emotional impulses, and freedom of imagination claim precedence over any binding or cramping considerations. The romantic composer is not an iconoclast; he does not ignore, or deny the validity of natural law and order, in its bearing upon tone-organization; he knows that universal Law is immutable, a manifestation of the divine Creative Spirit, which is not to be defied with impunity. But he may question the degree to which his "rules" actually corroborate the universal law, and he claims the right to modify or set aside these rules when they interfere with his personal judgment, his *feeling*, and his personal fancy, which are doubtless just as divine in origin as is "universal Law." In a word, the Classic method is orthodox, objective, reflective; the Romantic method is free, subjective, imaginative.

Evidences of this romantic incentive are quite clearly recognizable far back in music history, for no classic composer has ever been wholly indifferent to the call of his own individual, human ideas, yearnings and emotions.

SCHUBERT AND MENDELSSOHN

The first name associated definitely with this incentive is that of *Carl Maria von Weber* (1786-1826), who is called the founder of the German Romantic School. Weber wrote two Symphonies (both in C), of which history takes no special notice—his claims to romantic precedence resting upon his justly famous Operas. Thereafter, this new conception of the mission and the potentiality of music became more and more conscious in its nature, and grew steadily in definiteness of purpose, and in popular favor. Beethoven was surely classic to the core; but we have seen how imperiously he brushed "rules" aside when he had something of personal importance to proclaim. And Schubert, though no less instinctively loyal to the essential traditions of classic methods than was Beethoven, was still more free to express his own proper feelings in music.

The next after Schubert to emphasize strongly the subjective inclination was Berlioz (1803-1869), of whom we shall speak later; and he was followed closely by Mendelssohn, (Chopin), Schumann, Liszt and Wagner.

Mendelssohn was at heart a faithful disciple of the classic school, and his music is chiefly distinguished for the purity of its spirit and the refinement of its workmanship. But Mendelssohn (and the rest) lived in an age when the romantic tendency in literature and music had already gained considerable momentum, especially in Mendelssohn's surroundings, and he could not wholly escape its influence. Hence he is spoken of as a Classic composer with marked Romantic inclinations.

Felix Mendelssohn-Bartholdy, was born February 3, 1809, in Hamburg, of a distinguished family. His grandfather was the eminent philosopher Moses Mendelssohn; his father, Abraham Mendelssohn, a successful banker. The wealth, social distinction and high intelligence of the family provided for Felix the most favorable environment for the rapid and healthy development of his rare musical talent, and of his no less admirable and thoroughly genial qualities of heart and mind. Like Mozart, he was exceptionally precocious; at the age of ten he set music to the 19th Psalm which was publicly performed and warmly applauded; and in the following year he produced more than fifty works, including a Cantata, a piano Trio, two piano Sonatas, a Sonata for piano and violin, and many Songs. As early as 1818 he made his first appearance in public as a pianist, and was then already noted for his remarkable gift of improvisation. In 1826, at the age of seventeen, he wrote the Overture to Shakespeare's *A Midsummer-Night's Dream*; it is a composition of such originality, unique beauty, mature conception and technical mastership, that it is still valued as one of the finest gems in the treasury of musical achievement; one whose perennial charm and refreshing vigor seem to be imperishable.

His first Symphony was composed in 1824, and its initial performance in London, in 1829, was conducted by himself. In that same year he rescued from threatened oblivion, and succeeded despite no little opposition in reviving and producing, Bach's stupendous *St. Matthew Passion*. In 1836 Mendelssohn's Oratorio *St. Paul* was brought out in Düsseldorf. In 1842 he organized the Conservatory of Music in Leipsic; it was opened in January, 1843, with a distinguished staff of teachers, and soon became a unique centre of musical education. In 1846, upon his last visit to London, he conducted the memorable first performance of his Oratorio *Elijah*.

SCHUBERT AND MENDELSSOHN

Mendelssohn's life was one of great activity, and he was frequently subjected to a physical and nervous strain that was too severe for his none too robust constitution. This gradually undermined his health; and the shock he sustained upon the death of his beloved sister Fanny (four years his senior) hastened the end; he passed away on November 4, 1847, at Leipsic, to the profound grief of the whole musical world.

Mendelssohn was not destined to attain to the supreme rank of his classic predecessors, Mozart, Beethoven and Schubert. He fell short of them in intellectual magnitude and power, in wideness of vision and gravity of aim; but in sincerity, fine discrimination and absolute command of structural and technical resources, he was their equal. His gentle, refined, amiable nature is reflected in his music; its genial, charming, irresistibly appealing quality was instantly appreciated and enthusiastically admired, and he soon became, and remained all his life, the idol of the musical public. The immense popularity of the man, as well as of his music, resulted, during his lifetime and for years afterward, in an unfair overestimation of Mendelssohn's importance in the history of musical progress; and the inevitable reaction led to an equally inaccurate prejudice and lack of just esteem.

On the whole, Mendelssohn's career was not strikingly progressive—possibly it was slightly retrogressive; his later compositions do not exhibit the superiority over his early ones that a normal growth would naturally achieve. The uniform amiability of his expression, original though it is, tends to become wearisome; a certain default of pungent contrasts, the absence of ever-widening scope and increasing virility, may account for the reaction. At the present day, Mendelssohn's true significance, his incalculably beneficent influence upon musical culture, the enduring quality of very many of his creations, are clearly recognized, and he is assigned an honorable place among the Masters of the Symphony, by all fair-minded critics, without question.*

Mendelssohn's Early Symphonies

Besides many boyish experiments in symphonic composition (some dozen or more) which have not been preserved, Mendelssohn wrote five Symphonies. These are usually numbered in the order of their publication, but they are here taken up according to the dates of their composition.

The first Symphony, in C minor, Op. 11, was written in 1824, at wh'ch time Mendelssohn was only fifteen years of age. Quite aside from the interest which attaches to it as the symphonic product of so youthful a composer, it discloses qualities of undeniable intrinsic value; it was at once publicly performed, published, and listed as a welcome and permanent number on Symphony programs for many years, and even in our day it is still occasionally encountered. It is not strikingly original: the whole is patterned closely after Mozart, in general style and mode of treatment. But it is not barren of features that fore-

*See the Introduction, by Daniel Gregory Mason, to the author's Analytic Edition of Mendelssohn's *Songs Without Words*.

shadow the maturer Mendelssohn. Perhaps the most independent factor is a passage that occurs in the subordinate Theme of the final Movement: here a twelve-measure phrase-group is intonated by the strings, in staccato chords, on uniform beats, tracing an unpretentious melodic thread; this is then exactly repeated, and is unexpectedly joined, with charming effect, by an expressive sustained melody in the clarinet—somewhat after the manner in which César Franck opens the slow Movement of his Symphony in D. This device is used occasionally by Mendelssohn in later works.

Mendelssohn's second Symphony bears the title *Reformation*. It is in D, was written in 1830, and was published as Op. 107.* Nothing appears to have been farther from his mind than the creation of a "Tone-poem," or of program music, descriptive of the events, or of any particular event or personality, connected with this momentous upheaval in ecclesiastical history; and therefore the music reflects in a general way, only, the impulses, the ominous atmosphere, the heroic figures involved, and the victorious issue of the revolutionary religious movement. The most obvious connection between the title and the music itself, is the employment of the German chorale *Ein' feste Burg* (attributed to Martin Luther), in the Finale. Less relevant, though of some weight, are: the warlike motive at the beginning of the first *Allegro*, and the spirit of

---

*The works of Mendelssohn, published during his lifetime, run through to Op. 72 only; all the rest, up to Op. 118, were issued after his death, and these embrace many early compositions which he possibly had no intention of making public.

agitation which pervades the Movement; also the repeated insertion of the *Dresden Amen*, at the end of the Introduction (the same phrase that Wagner employs in his *Parsifal*). For the entire second and third Movements, however, any other, far different, title would be just as appropriate.

The Italian Symphony

The third of Mendelssohn's Symphonies (in the order of their composition—but published as *No. IV*), in A major, Op. 90, was written during his long journey through Italy, and finished in 1833. This affords the best explanation of the title; for the work as a whole is not specifically Italian—except the Finale, which is a distinctive Italian dance, the *Saltarello*, and is so named. The score embraces the instruments of the ordinary full orchestra: two each of flutes, oboes, clarinets, bassoons, horns, trumpets and drums; and the quintet of strings. There is no independent Introduction; the first Movement (in regular sonata-allegro form) begins at once with a joyous burst of melody, and an invigorating rhythmic pulse, and this bright, sunny atmosphere envelops the whole Movement. Its thematic material is as follows:

Only the second Codetta is here noted; the first one is derived directly from the principal Theme, with enlargement of the first figure. The persistent similarity of melodic and rhythmic formation throughout this first Movement is wisely modified, with fine structural instinct, by the insertion and extended manipulation of a *new* thematic phrase, in the Development, and again in the Coda. This somewhat irregular, though fully justifiable and not uncommon practice, is commented upon in the footnote following Ex. 48 (Beethoven's Third Symphony), and may there be reviewed. A similar thematic addition occurs also in the Finale of this Symphony.

(See the *Analytic Symphony Series*, No. 13.)

The slow Movement is a sort of Chant, and its stately rhythmic tread suggests a Procession. Mendelssohn is said to have had here an old Bohemian folk-song in mind. The Movement is based upon these Themes:

It is beautifully conceived, and is executed with the utmost technical refinement. The design is sonatine-allegro (i.e. there is no Development). Considerable importance attaches to the brief Prelude, which, though obviously introductory in purpose, is drawn upon for the Codetta to the principal Theme, and recurs as Interlude before the Recapitulation. In the latter, the principal Theme is transposed, and otherwise modified.

For the third Movement no other title is indicated than the tempo-mark; it would have been consistent to call it a *Menuetto,* for its elegance and grace of line, its winning melody, and its suave, serenely lovely mood, conjure up the vision of this courtly dance. Its design is the usual Song-form with Trio, using these Themes:

SCHUBERT AND MENDELSSOHN

Ex. 89. III Principal Division

The opening of the Trio, in horns and bassoons—an incipient fanfare with cunningly rounded edges, is one of the most original and delightful conceits to be found anywhere in Mendelssohn's music. And its reverberation in the Coda is a master-touch.

The Finale is a whirling, vertiginous *Saltarello*.* Its Themes are as follows:

Ex. 90. IV Finale
Principal Theme

*Consult Pratt's *New Encyclopedia of Music and Musicians*.

The principal Theme is preceded by six measures of related introductory matter. Of the three Codettas, only the second one is here given; the first one closely resembles the principal Theme, and the third one is brief. In two respects this Finale is noteworthy: the first is the choice of the *minor mode*. It is not at all unusual to end a minor composition in the *major* mode (see the Fifth and Ninth Symphonies of Beethoven, the First of Brahms, the *Scotch* Symphony of Mendelssohn—and very many others); but contrary to all tradition and usage, and with an apparent reversal of the finer and truer psychologic consequence—*per aspera ad astra*—Mendelssohn rounds out this singularly joyous (major) Symphony, in the sombre minor mode. Incidentally, he does the same thing, with almost weird effect, in one of his earliest piano pieces (Op. 7, No. 7). The other exceptional feature of the Finale is its unusual structural design: it is ostensibly a sonata-allegro form, states a perfectly regular Exposition, and a long and legitimate Development (in which, as in the first Movement, a *new* motive is inserted), but there is *no Recapitulation;* true to nature, the progressive whirl of the turbulent dance gradually, and naturally, undermines the later structural parts, so that finally the expected Recapitulation is engulfed—nothing remains but a Coda, which is more normal, less orgiastic than might be awaited.

The Hymn of Praise

This extensive work, in B♭, Op. 52, was finished in 1840, and first called a *Symphony-Cantata,* consisting as it does of three preliminary orchestral Movements, and seven vocal numbers, Solos and Choruses. The plan of the work is therefore similar to that of Beethoven's Ninth Symphony, and it is quite possible that the idea may been inspired by the latter, albeit Mendelssohn lays particular stress upon the vocal numbers, and contemplated calling the work simply *Cantata*. The chief motive, at the opening of the whole, runs thus:

Ex. 91. MENDELSSOHN (1840)

Al - les was O - dem hat,   lo - be den Herrn.

It is more specifically a musical Motto than a Theme, and it does not dominate the entire composition.

While not the most impressive or significant of Mendelssohn's creations, it exhibits many traits of great beauty and vigor, and testifies in its own way to the originality and power of his genius. The three instrumental numbers which precede the Cantata scarcely attain to the dignity of the symphonic ideal. The first Movement is a sonata-allegro form with independent Introduction. The second (connected with the preceding) is an *Allegretto* of touching melodic beauty, suggestive of the *Songs Without Words;* it is a Song-form with Trio, and the Trio is an original chorale-melody, quaintly interwoven with fragments of the principal Division. An atmosphere of melancholy, not altogether consistent with the character of a Hymn of Praise, pervades this Movement, and also the next, which is an *Adagio religioso* that does not at any point rise above the level of a *Song Without Words*.

The Scotch Symphony

The last of Mendelssohn's Symphonies (No. V in the order of composition, but known as the *Third*), in A minor, Op. 56, was composed in 1842. The designation *Scotch*, which he himself gave to the Symphony, may be explained in the same way as the title of the *Italian* Symphony is accounted for: it owes its inception to impressions received during a journey—this time through Scotland, as early as 1829. These impressions naturally gave color to the work, but merely in a general way; only the second Movement has the rhythmic lilt of some Scottish dance; and the five-tone scale upon which its chief melodic Theme is built gives it a decided Caledonian flavor. Some commentators recognize many other Scottish allusions—among others, the Harp of Ossian in the third Movement, and the sound of echoes over Scotland's hills and lakes. But such deductions are apt to mislead the listener, and to becloud, rather than to confirm, the intrinsic, abstract musical purpose. Certain it is that Mendelssohn executed the actual composition of this Symphony in the radically un-Scotch atmosphere of Berlin, some thirteen years after gathering his Scottish impressions.

It is Mendelssohn's most masterly symphonic creation, and it manifests the finest, most enduring qualities of his genius.

The first Movement opens with a lengthy Introduction (*Andante*, Three-Part Song-form), the initial melodic phrase of which is an amplified, and otherwise modified, version of the principal Theme of the *Allegro*. These, and the other Themes of the first Movement, are as follows:

The design is sonata-allegro form, normal and regular in construction. The melodic relation between the introductory phrase and the principal Theme is clearly recognizable. The subordinate Theme is a new melody, counterpointed against the first figure of the principal Theme. Such parallelism between the two chief Themes, often amounting to indirect or even direct identity of the subordinate Theme with the Principal one, has been repeatedly alluded to (see the footnote below Ex. 21). The ingenious coalescence of the two, in the above example, where the new Theme is a counterpointed companion to the principal one —at least for a time—may be witnessed again in the slow Movement of the First Symphony of Brahms.

Mendelssohn conceived the idea of making this Symphony a unit, by running the Movements together; thus, after an effective recurrence of the first Period of the Introduction, at the end of the *Allegro*, the word *attacca* indicates that the following Movement shall begin at once, without interruption. The same direction appears at the close of the second and third Movements. He may have adopted the idea from Schumann, whose D-minor Symphony (*in einem Satz*), with connected Movements, was first performed in December, 1841, while Mendelssohn was busy with this *Scotch* Symphony. One a single instance of such continuity appears in Beethoven's nine Symphonies: in the Fifth, the third Movement leads into the Finale without a break.* Such continuity may serve some lofty artistic purpose, but in lengthy compositions its wearisome effect upon the listener is likely to frustrate the good intention.

(See the *Analytic Symphony Series*, No. 8.)

The title of the second Movement is limited to the tempo-mark, *Vivace;* in spirit it is a *Scherzo*, though it has no Trio (its design is sonata-allegro). Its Themes run thus:

It is one of those exquisitely delicate, airy, sparkling musical creations which so faithfully reflect the genial, vivacious quality of Mendelssohn's spirit, and are admirably

*There is, to be sure, a parallel instance in the *Pastoral* Symphony of Beethoven, the last three Movements of which constitute a continuous unit. But the case here is different: this connection was as inevitable as in the Episodes of the Finale of the Ninth.

characteristic of a predominating phase of his musical conception.

An introductory passage of eight measures precedes the principal Theme. In the Recapitulation the Theme is greatly reduced—only its first Phrase is presented.

The slow Movement, located here as third, instead of in its usual place as second, is of exceptional beauty. Its principal Theme is a lyric melody of rich, mature, mellow quality, with harp-like accompaniment; alternating with a subordinate Theme of serious character and march-like tread, which provides an effective and impressive contrast. The design is sonatine-allegro form, with an introductory Period of nine measures, and it exhibits the following thematic contents:

A coalition of the two Themes, like that in the first Movement, but of a totally different kind, takes place here in the following manner: the second Part of the subordinate Theme corresponds almost exactly to the second Period of the principal Theme. This unusual structural arrangement lends extra prominence to the lyric element of the Movement.

The Finale is a Movement of tremendous vitality and rhythmic strength; and is as near an approach to genuine dramatic utterance as Mendelssohn's gentle, self-restrained disposition was capable of. The Themes are as follows:

The motive of the Transition (from the principal Theme into the subordinate) is new, as it has a right to be, and assumes special importance in the Development, where (in Section 3) it becomes the theme of a Fugue-exposition.*

The design is sonata-allegro, broad but admirably proportioned. The Coda is a masterly culmination of the Movement; its first and second Sections utilize foregoing motives; the third Section, however, is entirely new: it turns to the major mode, alters the metre and the tempo, and intonates a hymn of serene, dignified, mildly majestic character, and very genuine beauty. Such a totally new ending is called an Independent Coda.

* * *

QUESTIONS FOR REVIEW

1. What reason is given for the rapidity of Schubert's artistic development?
2. Outline Schubert's biography, emphasizing dates of birth and death.
3. What is the outstanding element in the music of Schubert?

---

*See the *Analytic Symphony Series*, No. 8, for a detailed demonstration of this and many other essential traits.

SCHUBERT AND MENDELSSOHN

4. What is the comparative quality of his early Symphonies, and which was the first to challenge attention?
5. What caused confusion in the numbering of his Symphonies, and what enumeration is now accepted?
6. Are there good reasons for naming No. IV the *Tragic?*
7. What opposite effects may result from Repetition?
8. What is the character and quality of Schubert's Fifth Symphony?
9. What attribute compensated for Schubert's lack of theoretical training, and how did it operate?
10. What facts seem to intimate his intention of completing the *Unfinished* Symphony?
11. What unusual formation of the principal Theme is exhibited in this Eighth Symphony?
12. Which of Schubert's Symphonies is mysteriously untraceable?
13. What is the distinctive character of his Tenth Symphony?
14. Define the thematic germ of its second Movement.
15. What change of conception becomes evident in the Symphonies of Mendelssohn?
16. Define the distinction between the Classic and Romantic schools.
17. Which name is earliest associated with the Romantic impulse?
18. What was Mendelssohn's artistic attitude?
19. Outline the biography of Mendelssohn, emphasizing dates of birth and death.
20. Outline Mendelssohn's comparative position among the Masters of the Symphony.

21. At what age did Mendelssohn compose his first important Symphony, and what are its qualities?
22. What is the title of his second Symphony, and what justifies it?
23. What is the name of his A major Symphony, and why is it so called?
24. Where, and in what manner, is the thematic material of its first and last Movements increased?
25. What peculiarity of mode does its Finale exhibit?
26. What happens to the structural design of this Finale?
27. Give a general outline of the *Hymn of Praise*.
28. What is the title of his A minor Symphony, and why is it so called?
29. How is the subordinate Theme in its first Movement conceived?
30. What peculiarity in the formation of the subordinate Theme in the slow Movement is noted?

References

Bie	Schubert the Man.
Duncan	Schubert.
Flower	Franz Schubert; the Man and his Circle.
Grove	Dictionary of Music (article by Grove)
Kobald	Franz Schubert and his Time.
Mason	The Romantic Composers.
Whitaker-Wilson	Life of Schubert.
Deutsch	Franz Schubert's Letters and other writings.
Brent-Smith	Schubert—the Symphonies.
Weingartner	Symphony Writers since Beethoven.

SCHUBERT AND MENDELSSOHN

Rockstro   Mendelssohn.
Stratton   Mendelssohn.
Runciman   Mendelssohn.
Lampadius   Life of Mendelssohn.

ILLUSTRATIVE RECORDS AND ROLLS

Records: B—Brunswick; C—Columbia; E—Edison; H—His Master's Voice; O—Odeon; Pa—Parlophone; Po—Polydor; V—Victor; Vo—Vocalion.

Rolls: A—Ampico; D—Duo-Art; M—Melodee; Pl—Pleyela; Q—QRS; U—Universal; W—Welte-Mignon.

Music Mentioned in Chapter IV:

Schubert Symphonies

    No. 5, in B♭ major   M, U.
    No. 7 (8*), in B minor (*Unfinished*)   C, Po, V, O; M, Q, U, A, D.
    No. 10, in C major   C; M, U.

Mendelssohn Symphonies

    No. 3, in A minor (*Scotch*)   M, Pl, Q, U.
    No. 4, in A minor (*Italian*)   V; M, Pl, U.
    No. 5 (2*), in D (*Reformation*)   Pl, U.

*The number in parenthesis is the one by which this Symphony is known in this book.

Chapter V

SCHUMANN AND BRAHMS

SCHUMANN'S Symphonies stand squarely upon Romantic ground. For this master was endowed with an extraordinary, no doubt slightly abnormal imagination, and his impulse to set forth his individual, subjective musical views and feelings was irrepressible. He was enthusiastically interested in new musical products, gave support to them whole-heartedly, and his own startlingly original conceptions led him into such sharp conflict with traditional methods, that his music was for a long time viewed with mistrust by conservative critics, and this impeded the recognition that he deserved, and ultimately won.

Schumann possessed an extremely keen, though somewhat erratic mentality, and an equally forceful, unbending perseverance, which enabled him to carry out his musical ideas against all obstacles. He seems, however, to have lacked some of that breadth of vision that enables its possessor to hold firmly all the branching details of a large problem, and so to control their direction as to produce a well-proportioned, logically consistent, centralized, strongly-knit whole. And for this reason his Symphonies betray weaknesses of *structure*. But these structural defects are so richly offset by the fascination of every measure, the very striking and engaging *beauty* of every phrase, of every essentially musical detail, that the hearer's attention is absorbed by these allurements, and he gives scarcely a thought to the structural result as a whole.

It would surely be unjust to infer from this that Schumann was recklessly revolutionary, rebellious, or even indifferent to the higher law of classic art. His reverence for the great classic masters, Mozart, Beethoven and Schubert, was unlimited; and while he explored new harmonic, modulatory and rhythmic realms, and recorded his findings fearlessly, he obeyed the "rules" faithfully, and never sacrificed the ideals, or violated the essential conditions of true tonal beauty.* While Schubert's conception was dominated by Melody, that of Schumann was centered in Harmony and Modulation; and the products of his genius in this field are replete with interest and charm, and are punctuated by novel rhythms that vitalize all of his creations.

Robert Schumann was born in Zwickau, Saxony, on the 8th of June, 1810 — but little over a year later than Mendelssohn. Though not so precocious as the latter, Schumann's musical bent impelled him to attempts at composition as early as his seventh year; and when eleven, he already produced, without instruction, works in larger form. From 1820 on, he attended the schools of his native town, and in 1828 entered the University of Leipsic as a student of law, but he was then already deeply engrossed in philosophic studies also, and ardently fostered his romantic tendencies. In 1830 he overcame family objections, and turned his

*See, further, the Critical Note to the first Symphony of Schumann, in the *Analytic Symphony Series* (No. 5).

attention to the exclusive study of music. His piano teacher was Friedrich Wieck, with whom he lived, and whose daughter Clara he married, after much opposition, in 1840. Up to that year his compositions were all for the piano, to Op. 23, inclusive, but thereupon he began to exercise his lyric inclination in Song-writing, a sphere in which he rivalled Schubert, and attained to almost unparalleled eminence.

Meanwhile he asserted himself as exponent and defender of liberal and progressive musical thought and action; he established the famous *Neue Zeitschrift für Musik* (1834), and wrote very numerous powerful essays and criticisms (under characteristic fictitious names—Eusebius, Florestan, Master Raro), and through them exercised an immense influence for good. The unselfishness of his thoroughly noble disposition manifested itself in his enthusiastic championship of many promising young composers, among them Chopin, and (later—1853) Brahms.

In 1841 he wrote his first two Symphonies (B♭, and D minor). In 1843 he joined the Faculty of the Leipsic Conservatory, founded by Mendelssohn. In 1847 he became conductor of the *Liedertafel* in Dresden. In 1850 he succeeded Ferdinand Hiller in Düsseldorf, as musical director, and remained there until, in 1853, the mental disorder that had haunted him for many years (since 1833) became so menacing that he was obliged to discontinue his public activities. This tragic affliction came to a climax in February, 1854, when he suddenly attempted suicide in the Rhine. He passed his remaining days in an asylum in Endenich until death called him, July 29, 1856.

Schumann's orchestral compositions include four Symphonies, and a work of allied character to which he gave the name *Overture, Scherzo and Finale,* Op. 52, written in 1841, between his first and second Symphonies. His reluctance to call this latter work (a creation of unique beauty) a Symphony, may be explained by the fact that it has only three Movements—the slow Movement, the "kernel" of the true symphonic type, being omitted; and further, that it lacks some of the dignity inseparable from the genuine Symphony. It is therefore in reality an orchestral Suite.

The First Symphony

Of Schumann's Symphonies, the first one, in B♭, Op. 38, was written early in 1841, and it is said that he himself called it the *Spring* Symphony. Whether this is the case, or whether the name was suggested and applied to it by some poetically-minded admirer, is not positive. But certain it is that this title is singularly appropriate, for the whole work exhales the fresh, crisp, now exhilarating, and again balmy, breath of springtide. It is scored for large orchestra, including trombones. In point of structure it is the most nearly perfect of his Symphonies.

The first Movement has a fairly extended Introduction, devoted to more or less pointed allusions to the chief Theme of the *Allegro*. In its present form it opens with an intonation of the thematic phrase (by the trumpets and horns), but pitched a third higher than in the *original* draft. Schumann was constrained to alter the pitch in this manner, because of the decidedly awkward effect of the original tones upon the "natural" brass instruments then in vogue — not yet supplied with the valves that equalized the entire scale. The change in pitch is generally regarded as deplorable, and nowadays can easily be rectified.

The thematic factors are as follows:

The form (sonata-allegro) is regular; the Recapitulation begins with a magnified version of the first thematic phrase, with thrilling effect. But the greater part of the Coda consists in a wholly new motive, in quieter rhythm, of fine harmonic and melodic character, distinctly Schumannesque in conception. There is no conceivable *structural* justification for this new factor; it is due to a purely romantic impulse; in a Beethoven Symphony it would be unthinkable. But in itself it is lovely enough to supply its own excuse.

Note that the principal Theme of the *Allegro* begins upon the *original* pitch of the introductory phrase.

(See the *Analytic Symphony Series*, No. 5.)

The second Movement is an exceedingly beautiful lyric creation, serene but impressive. The design is concise, and resembles a miniature Second Rondo-form. Each of the two alternating subordinate Themes is scarcely more than a melodic fragment, though enough to indicate a Digression. The principal Theme has this form:

Ex.97. II Principal Theme

Upon its first recurrence, the principal Theme is transposed. The first subordinate Motive extends from measure twenty-five to forty; the second subordinate Motive from measure fifty-five to seventy-four. To the Coda an extra Section is appended, which (in trombones and bassoons) anticipates the chief motive of the following Movement; thus, the second and third Movements are connected.

For the third Movement, Schumann follows Beethoven's lead and adopts the *Scherzo* type. It is an extremely broad Movement, and is further enlarged by the addition of a second Trio and another (this last time abbreviated) *da capo*. The first Trio provides an unusual degree of contrast, in its altered metre and its buoyant swing, to the splendid vigor of the rest. The Themes of this *Scherzo* run thus:

Ex.98. III Scherzo, Principal Division

The Finale is one of the most exultant, irresistibly cheery, vivacious Movements in symphonic literature; and the design (sonata-allegro) is finely drawn. It opens with an introductory Phrase, apparently independent, but later interwoven with the rest in a most significant manner: it becomes the second Phrase of the subordinate Theme, and its rhythmic form gives birth to the first Codetta, besides dominating the Development and the entire Coda. The thematic factors are as follows:

Ex.99. IV Finale, Introduction

There is a noteworthy parallelism between the two chief Themes, somewhat similar to the plan of the slow Movement in the *Scotch* Symphony of Mendelssohn; i.e., the Second Part of the subordinate Theme is derived almost literally from the First Part of the principal one.

THE SECOND SYMPHONY

Schumann's Second Symphony, in D minor, was first written in the later months of 1841, and performed in December of that year in Leipsic. It was not altogether to his liking, and he laid it aside until 1851, when he revised the instrumentation of it, and published it as Op. 120. Consequently, it is known as *No. IV*, although it was the second in order of composition. He called it at first a Symphony-Fantasia, with the sub-title *Symphony in One Movement*—for its five tempo-Divisions are all connected without interruptions, and certain thematic factors are carried through the entire work. It is widely esteemed as his most attractive symphonic creation, and in truth nothing could be more winning and impressively beautiful than the Introduction, the *Romanze,* and every one of its thematic melodies; a wonderfully alluring atmosphere envelops the whole, and the fine rhythmic pulse of the two *Allegros* is exhilarating. Nevertheless, this work betrays some of Schumann's undeniable shortcomings, particularly as concerns the structure and the orchestration; and the listener's impressions waver between fascination and disappointment. It is a genuine specimen of Romantic musical expression: original, intensely subjective, emotional, free—at times somewhat regardless of the regulations so essential to classic art. The Introduction, and the first Allegro, present these thematic factors:

Note the relation of the subordinate Theme to the principal one. The structural plan of the *Allegro* is irregular, consisting as it does in a normal Exposition, a Development which trails off into a series of related Sections that "develop" nothing vital, and *no Recapitulation* — a jubilant Coda taking its place.

(See the *Analytic Symphony Series*, No. 35.)

The truly lovely lyric *Romanze* is a Three-Part Song-form with Trio, the *da capo* transposed and reduced to one Part only. The Second Part of the principal Division is borrowed from the Introduction, and the Trio (in D major), in which a Solo-violin gracefully embellishes the principal violin part, also contains thematic allusions to it.

This Movement is followed by a vigorous *Scherzo*, in the usual form. The Trio contrasts most effectively with the principal Division, and is strongly reminiscent of the exquisite Trio in the preceding Movement (with the Solo-violin part). After the *da capo*, the Trio is restated, with ingenious dynamic alterations—its last Part "fading away," dissolving into a brief Coda, that serves to connect this Movement with the next.

The succeeding Finale begins with a transitional Interlude (or Introduction), based upon the chief thematic figure of the first *Allegro*.   The Finale utilizes the following thematic material:

Ex. 101. Finale

The form is sonata-allegro, slightly abbreviated. The principal Theme (or, rather, Motive only) is derived from the third Section of the Development in the first Movement. The second Codetta, related to the principal Motive, furnishes the main contents of the Development in this Finale; the Recapitulation begins with the subordinate Theme (the principal Motive being omitted); the Coda ends brilliantly with new, though very similar motives.

The C major Symphony

The third of Schumann's Symphonies, in C major, Op. 61, was finished in 1846, five years after the composition of the first and second. For reasons pointed out above, this C major Symphony is listed as the *Second*.

It is the longest of his Symphonies—large in conception and dimensions. The hearer is enveloped in an atmosphere of grandeur; and he is also confronted at every turn by musical images of delightful originality and beauty. The Themes are magnificent, imposing in melody, harmony and rhythm.

The first Movement opens with an impressive Introduction, based at first upon an independent motive which in conception is akin to the Introduction to his D minor Symphony, but assumes a radically different character through the incisive bugle-calls of the brass that set the lines of the form; the later Sections of the Introduction allude to Themes of the coming *Allegro*, and lead into the latter. The Themes of the *Allegro* are as follows:

The design is sonata-allegro; the Exposition is exceptionally concise. The Development is long, and diffuse, but is thematically consistent and interesting in every detail; its third Section is derived from Part Two of the principal Theme, and contains an effective reference to the first measure of the Introduction (but without the bugle-calls); and the final Section, leading back to the beginning (over an obstinate Dominant organ-point) is finely delineated, and, at its climax, tremendously powerful and stirring. But, as a whole, this Development, and likewise the long-drawn Coda, lacks that gathering momentum which can result from nothing less than a straightforward, clearly defined, unwavering structural *purpose*—in the manner so gloriously accomplished by Beethoven. The cause of this defect may be inferred from a remark of Schumann's in reference to this Symphony: "I sketched it while still physically very ill . . . ." But the student is no doubt more concerned with simple facts than with causes.

The succeeding *Scherzo* here appears as *second* Movement. It is uncommonly long, containing two Trios. The principal Division is a brilliant *perpetuum mobile* in the first violins—that is, the violins run in an uninterrupted rhythm (of sixteenth-notes) throughout. In the vivacious first Trio the metre is changed to 6/8 measure (in effect, though not so marked), while the second Trio falls back upon a quiet rhythm of quarter-notes, and is more subdued and lyric in quality; thus both Trios stand out in marked contrast to the principal Division. The Coda is a rushing, impetuous continuation of the sixteenth-note rhythm.

The third Movement is an *Adagio;* an inspiration of profoundly moving character and indescribable beauty, doubtless the most masterly and impressive of Schumann's symphonic slow Movements. The design is sonata-allegro; but in place of the conventional "Development" an entirely new Motive (in staccato sixteenths) is inserted and treated briefly in polyphonic Imitations, as *fugato;* this same staccato motive is then carried along through the first Period of the principal Theme which follows as Recapitulation, thus vindicating its presence in the Movement. Particularly noteworthy is the Codetta—the last fourteen measures of the Exposition—which rises to a climax of thrilling power, restrained at its peak and turned back into a gentle cadence. The Themes of this wonderful *Adagio* are as follows:

Subordinate Theme (E♭)

The Finale is a tremendously vigorous, resplendent hymn of Triumph; at least, it is chiefly this, but relieved by a few episodes of quieter, more sustained melodious character. From the classic point of view this Movement is "formless;" there is but little in the nature of tangible, distinguishable "Themes" in it; the general structural impression seems to be effected by a number of affiliated thematic fragments, into which, however, the opening melodic figure of the preceding *Adagio*-Movement is most ingeniously and effectively interwoven, quite extensively. Hence the design can be defined no more accurately than as an arbitrary, fantastic series of *Episodes*, twelve in number.* The more essential thematic phrases occur at the outset, and run thus:

Ex. 104. IV Finale, Introductory phrase — First Episode ("Principal Motive")

*See the *Analytic Symphony Series*, No. 17.

There was one technical element that Schumann never quite mastered, and that was the *scoring* of his concept; his orchestration is for the greater part too thick, opaque, and very often ineffective. For this reason the student will, in many cases, obtain a clearer impression of the musical conception, and derive more satisfaction and enjoyment from it through the medium of a good piano arrangement (preferably for four hands), than from an orchestral performance.

The E♭ Symphony

Schumann's last Symphony, in E♭ major, Op. 97, was written in the later months of 1850, and first performed at Düsseldorf in February, 1851. Although, as explained above, it was the fourth of his Symphonies, it is known as *Number III*. There is no doubt that Schumann received the incentive to this work from visits in Cologne, and the prospect of the mighty Cathedral of that city, which produced a deep and inspiring impression upon his profoundly romantic, susceptible artistic nature. It is therefore generally designated the *Rhenish,* or Cologne, Symphony, and no one will question the appropriateness of this title: the broad curving lines of the magnificent Theme with which it opens, are inescapably suggestive of the wide arches of a Gothic structure; and the majestic solemnity of the fourth Movement, the medieval pattern of its sonorous tones (as of an organ), its echoes, and the suggestion of swinging censers, unmistakably reflect some impressive ceremony within the sacred, vaulted edifice.

Four years had passed since the composition of his C major Symphony under the cloud of physical and mental depression, and during this period the deplorable handicap had not been completely removed; the cerebral disorder haunted him constantly. And yet this last Symphony of Schumann's is more lucid in structure, richer in melodic beauty, and more concise in formulation than the one which preceded it, although all but the first of its five Movements are strikingly unconventional or downright irregular. The first Movement is a sonata-allegro without Introduction, built upon these themes:

The Exposition is regular and clear; the Development is very long, out of proportion to the rest; and it is to some degree impaired in its ultimate Sections by several premature onsets of the principal motive *in the original key*, which anticipate and weaken the actual Recapitulation, robbing it of its freshness.*

In this Symphony, again, Schumann alters the traditional order of the Movements, and places the *Scherzo* immediately after the first *Allegro*. And one may wonder why this second Movement should be called a *Scherzo*, for neither in its character nor in its tempo does it conform to that type. Its design is very unusual, consisting in a group of Song-forms, all finely interrelated, but strung together arbitrarily, in a fashion quite distinctive with Schumann. One condition of satisfactory form is fulfilled, however, by a final return to, and literal restatement of the principal Part—to which is then added a lengthy and beautiful Coda. Of this Movement, with its warm-hearted, good-natured musical sentiment, Schumann said: "it seemed necessary to give prominence to popular (folk-song) elements, and I believe that I succeeded in doing so." This surely applies also to the third and last Movements, which are as "popular" in character as it was possible for Schumann's music to be. The thematic lines of this Scherzo are as follows:

---

*To be sure, Brahms does precisely the same thing in the slow Movement of his Second Symphony, and again in the slow Movement of the Third. All depends, obviously, upon the manner in which such novel and hazardous experiments are made.

Ex. 106.

The third Movement, a lovely lyric tone-poem, in moderate tempo, is also unconventional in structural design—best definable as a "group-form," without clear-cut thematic outlines.*

The fourth Movement, likewise, is a genuinely Schumannesque series of thematic sentences—another "group-form," the purport of which is demonstrated above. Schumann placed in the original score the superscription: "In the character of an adjunct to a solemn ceremony," but later erased it, with the remark: "One must not bare one's heart to the people; a general impression of the work of art is better for them, for then at least they make no faulty comparisons."

The prevailing thematic figure is as follows:

*See the *Analytic Symphony Series*, No. 32, for more specific details.

The Finale, an *Allegro*, in which Schumann's aim to emphasize the folk-idiom is clearly evident, is likewise irregular in structural design, but approximates the sonatine-allegro form. The Themes are as follows:

The irregularity concerns chiefly the subordinate Theme, which, in defiance of all precedent, recurs (for the greater part) in the *same key* as before; and it is a disproportionately lengthy chain of related Sections—wisely abbreviated in the Recapitulation. Brief allusions to the motive of the fourth Movement occur here and there.

* * *

JOHANNES BRAHMS

The attitude of Brahms toward music was reactionary. In all of his works, from first to last, he places himself unflinchingly on classic ground, and sternly rejects any concessions to the rapidly spreading romantic—or rather, hyper-romantic and wilful modern tendencies. With serious mien and unmistakable gesture he points back to the ideals and methods of the classic era. Not that this was a preconceived, intentional purpose with him; it was his true nature. Brahms was serious in spirit, supremely conscientious in his conception and practice of the tone-art; thoroughly imbued with the conviction that perfect and legitimate musical unfolding is identical with all natural evolution; that the problem of an artistic tone-product can consist of nothing else than the origination of a responsive, wholesome, fruitful *Subject* (or Theme), and the progressive development of this Subject in a logical, well-ordered, perfectly balanced, accurately and firmly adjusted architectural structure. In this conception he was closest of kin to the great Bach—whose whole musical being centered in thematic evolution; but also akin to Beethoven—whose unity of purpose held him unswervingly "to his text," and who responded (in his greater works) to no other artistic or spiritual impulse than the unfolding of its concealed meanings. This was the dominating artistic aim of Brahms likewise; he was absolutely unmoved by the preferences and demands of the superficial music-lover, who is notoriously as ignorant as an infant of the *divine essence* and real power of music, and who is usually satisfied with infantile musical playthings. This sounds severe; but it is true; and with this particular popular attitude

Brahms had no patience. His music is therefore at times abstruse, in its exterior apparently more intellectual than emotional; and this quality, coupled with its originality, renders it difficult to follow. But each separate hearing discloses new meanings and new beauties, and ever increasing appreciation is certain to reward the sincere student.

Had this lofty classic pursuit by Brahms been carried on in a purely mathematical fashion, with narrow-minded consideration for "correct" delineation only, the results would of course have been lifeless and spiritually valueless. But this was not the case: an ardent soul, cognizant of every phase of human emotion, and pulsing with Life, vitalizes the whole product. His technical method is unique: he leads the hearer from one display of thematic evolution to another, always with absolutely flawless technical setting, and with unerring instinct for rare and appealing tonal beauty, so that the intelligent listener experiences sheer joy all the way along. And not only the brighter moods are present; Brahms loves the light, but he seems almost to prefer the sombre hues, and his music glows at times with deep emotional passion, and tragic earnestness; his climaxes are overwhelming. In common with all truly great spirits, Brahms knew the value, and heeded the call of Simplicity; very many of his Themes possess a decided folk-song quality, and there are countless passages, in his works, of exquisite lucidity and genuinely primitive charm.

Brahms has been accused of "mannerisms." Which master has not had his typical traits? Critics who stress this would seem to deny to a genius the right to possess and to show his own distinctive features in preference to the vacant stare of a plaster mask, stroked smooth with a classic trowel. The bare mention of such physiognomic trifles, in the presence of such stupendous spiritual might and genius as Brahms possessed, seems childish.

Johannes Brahms was born on the 7th of May, 1833, in Hamburg, Germany. His father played the double-bass in the City Theatre, and was musical enough to direct the boy's early studies. Later, Edward Marxsen became his teacher. Johannes made his first bow to the public as a pianist in 1847; and in 1858 he undertook a concert tour with the violinist Remenyi; in Göttingen he came in contact with Josef Joachim, who urged him to visit Schumann. The latter was so deeply impressed with Brahms' extraordinary musical talent, that he gave vent (in his journal *Die Neue Zeitschrift für Musik*) to his famous enthusiastic prophecy of the future of Brahms.

In these years (1853-4) he produced a number of works in larger form: three piano Sonatas, the B-minor Trio. Also several other piano pieces, and Songs, remarkable for their originality, power, scholarly finish and striking beauty, though not all of that ingratiating character that compels immediate recognition and favor with the community of music lovers.

In 1862 Brahms went to Vienna, and became conductor of the *Singakademie* there the following year, holding that position for two years. The next five years were spent in various tours and on concert trips; he returned to Vienna in 1869 and lived there until 1875 as conductor of the *Gesellschaft der Musikfreunde*. After another absence from Vienna he returned thither in 1878, and that city then became his permanent home.

Up to this time Brahms had written a large number of compositions, among them many that bore witness to his unusual genius, and gradually overcame the inertia of a musical public that for a time was held aloof by the uncompromising, often austere quality of his style, until he finally won the appreciation that his significant creations merited. His *German Requiem*, a work of unsurpassed sincerity and profundity, thoroughly classic in spirit and in technical perfection, was written in 1868. His First Symphony was completed in 1876. His very numerous Songs place him worthily upon the eminent plane of lyric conception occupied by Schubert and Schumann, if indeed he may not be said to surpass them in intensity of feeling and marvellous technical finish.

Brahms' life was, for the greater part, one of contentment, and crowned with honor. His disposition was genial and affectionate, and his companionship with friends and intimates of his own spiritual rank was cordial and mutually beneficial. With some people he was, at times, impatient and even brusque, for he was stoutly inimical to superficiality or insincerity, and he detested flattery. His last years were sadly clouded by the disease which caused his death, April 3, 1897, in Vienna.

" . . . . he chose, unmoved by praise or blame, to be a standard-bearer of the traditions of a glorious past . . . . Brahms was an idealist of the highest and purest type. The fine fibre of his musicianly feeling vibrates in his humblest song as in his proudest symphonic Movement."*

THE FIRST SYMPHONY

Unlike Mozart, whose first Symphony was written at the age of eight; or Schubert, who attacked that formidable type when sixteen; or Mendelssohn, who did the same when fifteen, — Brahms withheld his hand from the exacting, supreme effort of symphonic creation until he had reached

*Dr. Theodore Baker, *Biographical Dictionary of Musicians.*

his forty-third year. It is true, this elaborate and impressive First Symphony had occupied his attention during the preceding ten years, but this again confirms his reluctance to plunge prematurely and self-confidently into a task of such magnitude and serious artistic spirit.

Despite its often abstruse style, the music of Brahms presented enough of striking, spontaneous, instantly prepossessing and frankly beautiful features to win him a host of enthusiastic friends; and upon the appearance of his First Symphony, these ranks re-echoed with the cry "The *Tenth* Symphony!"—implying that this was the full-blooded successor of Beethoven's Ninth; it was an imprudent burst of enthusiasm that did more harm than good to the reputation of the sufficiently great and accredited master. The "Tenth" has never been written, and perhaps never will be; it is as unlikely as the prospect of an equivalent successor to Shakespeare's dramas. It is sufficient to affirm that the First Symphony of Brahms is a creation of superlative significance, which holds its place worthily beside (not beyond) the "immortal nine" of Beethoven.

This First Symphony, in C minor, Op. 68, completed in 1876, is the only one of the four of Brahms in which he adopts the venerable tradition of a separate Introduction, in *sostenuto* tempo. It foreshadows the thematic components and the dramatic character of the *Allegro;* and the final allusion to it, as Independent Coda, rounds out the Movement in a most effective and impressive manner. The design of the first Movement is sonata-allegro, evolved with such superb logic, unswayed purpose, perfection of proportion, such masterly provision for well-placed and well-balanced contrasts, and such monumental dramatic vitality, as only so great a genius could achieve; and the music is, in its every measure, harmonious and truly beautiful.

The most significant structural feature, and one that is unquestionably original with Brahms, is the adoption of a brief but striking phrase which precedes the Exposition, and for which the term *Basic Motive* seems most fitting, since it *underlies* the entire Movement, either as generative or as a component factor. The Themes are all based upon it, or derived from it.* The Themes are as follows:

*See the *Analytic Symphony Series*, No. 20, for further details of this trait, and others.

The subordinate Theme is, for a few measures, identical with the principal one: such similarity between the chief Themes has been repeatedly seen—beginning with Haydn—and is recognized as one of the conditions of the early symphonic Movement. The first Codetta also displays remarkable likeness to the principal Theme; the Basic Motive is set forth in the uppermost tones, while the principal Theme is given to the basses, "upside down."

It would be impossible in the narrow limits of this book to point out every masterly trait of the music. The student may, and should, trace for himself the course of thematic manipulation, as far as he can perceive it. The chromatic form of the Basic Motive renders it everywhere easily recognizable.

The second (slow) Movement, in the unexpected key of E major, is a sustained, serene lyric conception, of a richer and more eloquent romantic quality. Its design is the First Rondo-form, with these Themes:

Ex. 110. II Principal Theme

Note, here again, the close relation of the subordinate Theme to its principal one; its melody is counterpointed against the first two measures of the latter, as shown.

The third Movement is neither a *Scherzo* nor of any of the dance-types; but it fits admirably into the psychologic scheme of the Symphony. It is one of those graceful, intimate, delightfully smooth conceptions, that were as essential and precious a part of Brahms' musical spirit as were the surges of passion, and the sombre, deeply earnest pathos that characterize his more serious moods. The design is Second-Rondo, the Themes of which have this form:

An Introduction in *Adagio* tempo, of extremely impressive, grave character, precedes the final *Allegro,* and refers thematically to it in every detail. Of its three Sections, the first and second employ motives of the *Allegro,* while the much longer third Section, in more animated tempo, presents an apparently new, wonderfully beautiful Song of Hope, which falls like a ray of sunshine athwart the sombre, ominous background of the opening Phrases. A brief quartet of trombones and bassoons (the "Second Part" of the Song) seems to add assurance to the message of comfort. A recurrence of the first melody (as "Third Part") leads over into the Finale proper. This begins with the principal Theme, a melody of folk-song simplicity and quiet power, in conception akin to the principal Theme of the Finale in Beethoven's Ninth Symphony—emphatically *not* a blundering imitation, but the natural coincidence of kindred genius. The Themes of the Finale are as follows:

Ex.112. IV Finale Sec.3 of Introduction

The subordinate Theme is traced as counterpoint against a *Ground Motive* (a brief figure repeated several times, as *basso ostinato*—persistent bass); and this Ground Motive corresponds to the first four accented beats (first, third, fifth and seventh beats) of the principal Theme.

The design of the Allegro exhibits a noteworthy digression from the traditional form, which is wholly original with Brahms: there is no separate Development, in the specific sense; the Recapitulation follows the Exposition immediately (as in the sonatine-allegro form); but this Recapitulation is systematically and very broadly extended by *"developing" each successive factor* in unaltered order, during ten masterly Sections—that is, up to the announcement of the subordinate Theme. The latter then appears, in its proper key (transposed to C major), and from there on, the Recapitulation agrees literally with the Exposition.* The form is therefore, strictly speaking, sonatine-allegro, enriched by thus fusing the process of Recapitulation with that of Development. Exactly this

*See, again, the *Analytic Symphony Series*, No. 20.

same scheme will be met again in the Finale of the Third Symphony.

THE SECOND SYMPHONY

Having exercised wise discretion in undertaking his first symphonic effort without precipitation, Brahms proceeded almost immediately, no doubt with greater assurance, to create a companion to it: his Second Symphony, D major, Op. 73, was written the following year (1877). This truly beautiful work is almost throughout of a brighter, happier mood than its predecessor; the first and third Movements, especially, are simpler in melodic character, more cordial, spontaneous and engaging, and, in their presentation, less involved and abstruse.

The first Movement (in sonata-allegro form) has no Introduction, but also opens with a *Basic Motive* (as the First Symphony does) of two measures in the bass, over the final tone of which the principal Theme sets in. This Basic Motive assumes many different rhythmic shapes, and is shifted to other beats in the measure; and thus it pervades the Movement, always tangible though not unduly obtrusive, *unifying* the whole splendid design in a most admirable manner.*

The thematic components of this first Movement have the following form:

*See the *Analytic Symphony Series*, No. 6, for annotations of all these thematic details.

The second Codetta is built upon a Ground Motive with Imitation in the upper part, and a curiously syncopated rhythmic accompaniment.

The following episodes have become famous for their peculiar beauty: the first sixteen measures of the Development (beginning five measures after the double-bar); the last twenty measures (or forty, for that matter) before the Recapitulation; the horn-passage in the first Section of the Coda—and the rest of the Coda.

The second Movement (*Adagio*) is of an uncommonly serious romantic character, original in melodic conception, and refined in sentiment throughout. It is also somewhat involved in its construction and in the method of its presentation, so that one hearing scarcely suffices for penetrating its profound spiritual purport, and apprehending its very rare and beautiful qualities. The design is First Rondo-form, with these Themes:

The Retransition (from the subordinate Theme back into the principal one—signature of two sharps) is unusually elaborate, and exhibits the traits of a "Development;" it also contains an allusion to the Basic Motive of the first Movement.

For the third Movement Brahms has indicated no other title than the tempo-mark *Allegretto grazioso*, but it resembles the graceful old Minuet, though far more masterly in its formulation, and of greater warmth and charm of contents. Its design is the traditional dance-form, but with two Trios; and these two Trios differ in character radically from that which tradition would lead us to expect, i.e.: instead of being entirely independent of their principal Division in contents, each is a unique *Variation* of the latter, contrasting in metre and in tempo. The Theme of the principal Division begins thus:

The first *da capo* is abbreviated to its first Phrase, which is repeated. Upon reaching the fourth measure, the period halts there, unexpectedly, and proceeds to spin out that measure as a Ground Motive (eleven measures) up to the cadence before the second Trio. The second *da capo* is partly transposed, and the modulation back to the original key (in the fourteenth measure) offers a lesson of supreme value to the student.

In the Finale, Brahms yields to an impulse of unusual vivacity, vigor, and spontaneous gaiety; and the craftsmanship is as superb as it is transparent. The joy and abandon in it are inspiring. Its thematic factors are as follows:

Ex. 116. IV Finale. Principal Theme

Note the brief Ground Motive which, in the bass, underlies the first Phrase of the principal Theme; also the manner in which the first figure of this Theme is interwoven in the subordinate Theme; further, the adoption of this figure, in widening intervals, for the first Codetta; and the very striking (possibly intentional) similarity of the jolly lilt of the second Codetta, to the first Codetta in the Finale of Haydn's *London* Symphony.

(See the *Analytic Symphony Series*, No. 22.)

The design is sonata-allegro, very regular, and splendidly proportioned and balanced, but with this somewhat uncommon feature: the Development begins exactly as the Exposition does, thus depriving the hearer, for a moment, of one of his most necessary bearings. (Compare the context to Ex. 47.) In this restatement of the principal Phrase, the Ground Motive in the bass is carried on to the length of fifteen measures—in augmented form in the last six of these. Note the effective transformation of the principal motive into triplet-rhythm in the fourth Section of the Development.

The Third Symphony

Six years elapsed after the completion of his Second Symphony, before Brahms again applied himself to the symphonic task. These six years were by no means idle ones, for during that period he created many of his most imposing works. The Third Symphony, in F major, Op. 90, finished in 1883, differs notably from the two which preceded it; it offers "more" than the latter, in several respects: it is more *scholarly*—the first Movement presents an array of extremely ingenious rhythmic metamorphoses, and the last Movement is a marvel of thematic manipulation; further, it is more *dramatic*—the Finale, especially, contains passages of fierce passion, that seem even more gripping than the dramatic outbursts in the first Movement of the First Symphony; and it is more *beautiful*—the subordinate Theme of the first Movement is one of the most exquisite musical sentences ever conceived, and many episodes in the second and third Movements are of rare originality and artistic grace.

The first Movement, precisely as in the First and Second Symphonies, opens with a *Basic Motive*. To this, placed in different voices (first in the bass) and in altered rhythms, the melody of the principal Theme is counterpointed—with autocratic indifference to the "cross-relation" in the first mating. Thus the Motive constitutes the essential *Basis* of the Movement; but it is also used independently, with wonderful effect. The structural design is sonata-allegro, and the thematic material is as follows:

Two brief Codettas are added. The form is perfectly normal, and its treatment masterly in the highest degree. The final two Sections of the Development (leading into the Recapitulation) are of impressive beauty; and there is a climax of tremendous power in the second Section of the Coda, followed by gradual relaxation in the remaining Sections.*

The second (slow) Movement conveys the impression of a Hymn, of four Lines of varying length, though rather of a secular than of a religious type. It is simple, and sedately graceful, but immeasurably remote from the commonplace; replete with ingenious touches that are as beautiful as they are original—a thoroughly lovable but also thoroughly aristocratic Movement. It is cast in the mold of the First Rondo-form, with these Themes:

*Consult the *Analytic Symphony Series*, No. 33.

Note how each cadence-measure of the principal Theme is filled out ("bridged over") with a sort of echo of the preceding phrase-member; also the very great beauty of each one of the three Sections of the Coda.

To the third Movement Brahms affixes no title. His strong predilection for the Absolute qualities of musical expression kept him aloof from any descriptive experiments, and from the use of music as anything but a language that has its own intrinsic meanings. And though he wrote a very large number of Songs that are wonderfully apt in their blending of the musical with the poetic ideas, they remain genuinely "absolute" music.

This third Movement is not a Minuet, much less a *Scherzo*, nor a "dance-form" in any sense of the term. It might answer to the title of *Romanza*, or Song Without Words. The lovely melody, with its quaint rhythms, has a tinge of that gloomy, pathetic mood which Brahms seems to have loved. The design is First-Rondo (or perhaps more correctly Song with Trio—the difference being often scarcely recognizable); its Themes run thus:

Ex. 119.   III   Principal Division (or Theme)

The last Movement is another of those exceedingly rare examples of a *minor* Finale to a *major* Symphony, as seen in the *Italian* Symphony of Mendelssohn (compare the context to Ex. 90). Here, however, the Coda returns to, and ends in, the major mode.

This Finale is long, many-hued, and of unparalleled mastership in conception and formulation. The preponderant mood is lofty passion; now subdued, and again almost unbridled in its wide and mighty sweep. But other moods temper this, in wise alteration: after the mysterious monody and weird duet in the opening measures, there follows (measures eighteen to twenty-nine) a heavy, ominous proclamation, led by the trombones, like a prophetic warning of the storm that breaks loose — lulls — bursts forth again, and seems to whip the elements into fury; then the amazingly jovial, almost roistering subordinate Theme, during which the preceding stormy motive grumbles on, much subdued, in the bass; and finally, in the extremely beautiful Coda, the broad (rhythmically augmented) intonation of the first Phrase of the principal Theme, in major, rounded out, in the seventh and eighth measures, with the *Basic Motive* of the first Movement, and joined ultimately (as a direct consequence of the Basic Motive) by the principal motive of the first Movement, in such natural sequence that this Finale closes almost precisely as did the opening Movement. All this is recorded, with astounding ingenuity, and equally astounding technical mastery, in the Finale—and much more than this, which the observant student may ferret out for himself. The structural design corresponds very nearly to that of the Finale of the First Symphony: there is no *separate* Development; the Recapitulation follows the Exposition immediately, and *each one of its successive factors* is "developed" in the corresponding order—up to the reappearance of the subordinate Theme, whereupon the "recapitulation" continues almost literally.

(Compare the context to Ex. 112; and see the author's *Larger Forms of Musical Composition*, page 189.)

The themes are as follows:

The opening melody is not ingratiating, nor even inviting, on a first hearing; but the choice of that aspect for a theme is one test of Genius—the rough, forbidding, uncut diamond is skilfully fashioned into a resplendent gem.

The Fourth Symphony

The Third of Brahms' Symphonies was followed very soon by the Fourth—in E minor, Op. 98, completed in 1885. This Fourth Symphony is unquestionably the most mature and the most forcefully dramatic of them all; the Coda of the first Movement surges to an intensity of white-hot passion quite without an equal in any other of Brahms' symphonic creations. The choice of key is unusual: E minor seems to have been strangely unappealing to the early Masters of the Symphony (compare Ex. 10 and context), for some reason not easily fathomable. The temper of the entire Symphony, excepting only the third Movement, is severe, sombre, though not in the least pessimistic; flashes of genial radiance soften its austere lines in many places, and phrases of surpassing loveliness emphatically confute the opinion of some commentators that this Symphony is chiefly a product of intellectual ardor, more reflective than emotional. Brahms possessed—and used—that "cerebral power which is the necessary concomitant of the highest artistic achievements," as Mr. Cecil Gray so happily expresses a momentous fundamental principle. The probability remains, be it admitted, that the Fourth is not likely to become the most popular and beloved of the Symphonies of Brahms.

There is no Introduction, and here no Basic Motive. The thematic factors of the first Movement are as follows:

Ex. 121.
I Principal Theme
BRAHMS (1884-5)

The form is sonata-allegro, broad, but conventional; the only uncommon trait is the beginning of the Development *exactly* like the Exposition. This somewhat misleading procedure has already been encountered in other instances: see the context to Ex. 116.*

The second (slow) Movement is austere in its general bearing, and possibly more impressive through its masterly

---

*Consult the *Analytic Symphony Series*, No. 36, for ample details of this Movement, and of the others.

construction than notable for its unclouded beauty—though it surely contains very many moments of transcendent loveliness. The four-measure Prelude has a "modal" flavor, and might pass as a specimen of the Phrygian Mode.* But it is extremely doubtful that Brahms conceived it with such an intention. Critics are prone to hunt for subtle and remote causes, overlooking the real, simple explanation which lies close at hand. Here the keynote of the Movement, *e*, is used as Dominant note of A minor in its descending melodic form—hence the *g*♮ and *c*♮; and the ultimate transformation of this *e* into the proper keynote is singularly effective and beautiful.

The design is sonatine-allegro form (i.e., without a Development), with these Themes:

The *c*♮ on the third beat is a "lowered sixth Scale-step"— an item of expressive tone-color which all the classic

---

*See the *Dictionary of Musical Terms* by Dr. Baker or *The New Encyclopedia of Music and Musicians* by Waldo S. Pratt.

masters (especially Beethoven and Brahms) prized very highly and used with remarkable frequency; and the *d*♮ on the sixth beat is the "lowered seventh Scale-step," required under normal conditions (both in minor *and in major*) when passing downward to the lowered sixth step. The six-measure Postlude (at the end of the Movement) corresponds to the Prelude, and for ten beats confirms our assumption of A minor; the next ten beats are in C major (the *b*♭ and *a*♭ corresponding to the former *d*♮ and *c*♮ in E major); the rest appears to be in A minor again, so that the final cadence becomes "plagal."

Brahms calls the third Movement a *Jocose Allegro*, and of course it pertains to the *Scherzo* family. Brahms' warm-hearted, genial disposition is well known, and his jovial bent was pronounced; but music was to him so serious and sacred an object that he evidently considered humor an inappropriate adjunct, and examples of it in his compositions are exceedingly rare. Here, however, in this *Allegro giocoso*, he abandoned himself whole-heartedly to a veritable frolic of riotous humor and jollity. The Themes run thus:

Note the droll "stumbling" effect of the thematic melody—landing with a thud in a pit at the side of the road! The form is sonata-allegro; and the manner in which the Recapitulation begins (in D♭, thirteen measures before the *poco meno presto*) introduces a most effective respite in the turmoil of gaiety.

The Finale is a *Chaconne*. Brahms gave it no title, and some writers have called it a *Passacaglia*. The distinction is of small concern, since these two old Dances were very nearly identical, and the names are therefore practically interchangeable. There are three traits here, however, that seem to indicate a preference for the former term: (1) the Theme is not a *basso continuo*, but is embodied rather in the melody and harmony; (2) the texture of the Variations is purely homophonic—not polyphonic; (3) the endings of the Theme (the cadences) are often altered, and other changes occur which are rather foreign to the tradition of the genuine *Passacaglia*. Further, a comparison with two authoritative examples by the great Bach: the famous *Chaconne* for solo-violin, and the magnificent *Passacaglia* in C minor for the organ, reveals far closer resemblance here to the former.

The Theme, of which the uppermost melodic line is the essential part, runs thus:

Ex.124. IV Finale
Theme (upper voice)

The design is, of course, the Variation-form, consisting in the Theme, thirty Variations, and a Coda. But it is not a haphazard series of alterations, nor a progressively evolved unit. The Variations are divided into four groups, in approximate analogy to the four psychologic moods (Movements) of a complete Symphony, thus: Division One, from Variation I (after the initial statement of the Theme) to Variation XI, with the thematic melody chiefly in the bass, and with steadily increasing rhythmic animation; Division Two, from Variations XII to XV, in which the Theme is augmented (to notes of double time-value) and the mode altered to major; Division Three, from Variation XVI to XXIII, back to minor, and exhibiting greater rhythmic diversity; and Division Four, from Variations XXIV to XXX, in which there is a distinct return to the beginning—Variations XXIV, XXV and XXVI closely resembling Variations I, II and III. The Coda which follows is in more rapid tempo, deals mostly with fragments of the Theme, and forms an extremely brilliant climax to the whole.

* * *

Pioneers of the Romantic School

Carl Maria von Weber (1786-1826) has already been cited, and is generally regarded by historians as the founder of the Romantic school of musical expression; and he was undoubtedly the earliest distinguished forerunner of the great master minds who have illumined our fourth and fifth chapters. The most important and popular of his two Symphonies was the second, in C.

But there were a number of other pioneers who did significant work, and paved the way for coming achievements; they were not "Masters" of the Symphony in the broader historic sense, but they were Masters in their day and generation, as compared with a host of less renowned composers; and they richly merit honorable mention here.

Nor were they the very first: the workings of a Romantic spirit may be recognized as far back as history reaches. There probably never was a human being who, in trying to express something in tones, did not vaguely essay to express *himself*. Thus we conclude that there is no incompatability between the Romantic and Classic spirits, nor is there any overt antagonism there; those with romantic incentives have always admitted and respected the necessity of law and order, and, *per contra*, the classically-minded surely always claimed the right to say, in tones, under surveillance of the law, what they *felt*. Schumann and his adherents called themselves Neo-Romanticists, and were a bit more clamorous in their call for freedom. And these were succeeded by the Futurists, Polytonalists, Atonalists, and in our day by the Ultra-Futurists and Cacophonists, who simply go still farther in their disregard of the older conventions.

Just where these will land us, Heaven no doubt knows, but no mortal can foretell what Music (?) will be, a thousand years hence. The present storm will clear up — as surely as the sun emerges after devastating turmoil of the elements; and the results will mean real Progress, to the joy and benefaction of humanity.

It may be harking too far back to include *G. J. (Abt) Vogler* (1749-1814) in this list, but he was the author of at least one Symphony (in C) which was exceedingly popular; and he exerted a powerful influence as a teacher— Weber and Meyerbeer were among his many pupils; furthermore, he outlived both Haydn and Mozart.

Then came *Peter von Winter* (1754-1825) author of nine Symphonies, one of which, *The Battle* (with Chorus) appeared in 1814.

Ignaz J. Pleyel (1757-1831), who produced twenty-nine Symphonies, much admired for their grace.

Next followed, in chronological order:

Luigi Cherubini (1760-1842), an illustrious master of dramatic music, in France, and celebrated also for his contrapuntal erudition. On a visit to London in 1815 he wrote a Symphony for the Philharmonic Society, his only work of that type, and one that has historic interest alone.

Étienne Méhul (1763-1817), another outstanding representative of the dramatic side of musical art in France, author of many popular Operas, and four excellent Symphonies.

Then the cousins, *Andreas Romberg* (1767-1821), the composer of ten Symphonies, the best of which is one in D; and *Bernard Romberg* (1767-1841), who wrote at least one noteworthy Symphony—a tribute "Upon the death of Queen Louise."

Sigismund Neukomm (1778-1858), pupil of Haydn, an enormously prolific and popular composer, among whose works was a *Heroic* Symphony, written 1818—thirteen years after the creation of Beethoven's *Eroica*.

George Onslow (1784-1852), composer of four Symphonies, one of which, in A major, possesses positive merit.

Ludwig Spohr (1784-1859), famous violinist, author of nine noteworthy Romantic Symphonies, the best known and most admired, though not the most distinguished of which is the celebrated Fourth, in F (1834), *The Consecration of Tone* (or *Tones*); it is an example of straightforward program music, mirroring in succession: "Chaos, without Tone; Awakening; Cradle song; Dance; Serenade; Martial music; Funeral music; and Comfort in Tears"—a work of no little originality, and melodic and harmonic charm, but wholly wanting (in consequence of its descriptive purpose) in symphonic compactness and structural logic. In its day it was sure of a place on orchestral programs, and was everywhere heartily applauded; but, in company with many another meritorious production of the above-listed symphonists, it is now overshadowed and eclipsed by the

254   *MASTERS OF THE SYMPHONY*

preëminent creations of true, genuine Masters of the Symphony, from Haydn to Brahms—and of later time.

Finally, *Johann W. Kalliwoda* (1801-1866), who produced seven Symphonies, the third of which, written in 1831, exhibits qualities of substantial worth, deserving of sincere recognition. Like the others, it is now forgotten.

*   *   *

QUESTIONS FOR REVIEW

1. To which School of musical conception did Schumann belong?
2. What weakness do Schumann's larger forms betray, and what qualities offset these shortcomings?
3. Outline the biography of Schumann.
4. How many symphonic works did Schumann produce?
5. What name is sometimes given to his First Symphony?
6. What incident is connected with the opening Phrase of its first Movement?
7. When was Schumann's Second Symphony written, and why is it listed as Number IV?
8. What was it first called, and why?
9. What are the characteristics of Schumann's C major Symphony?
10. What apologetic remark did Schumann make in regard to this work?
11. What technical name is applied to the style of the principal Division of the second Movement?
12. Define the outstanding features of the Finale.
13. How is Schumann's E♭ Symphony designated, and why?

SCHUMANN AND BRAHMS

14. How many Movements has it?
15. What did Schumann say of its second Movement, and what of its fourth Movement?
16. What was the attitude of Brahms toward music, and how did it determine his conception and his dominant artistic aims?
17. How does this affect the character of his music?
18. Outline the biography of Brahms.
19. At what age did Brahms compose his first Symphony?
20. With what cry was it greeted?
21. What original and significant structural feature appears at the outset of the First, Second, and Third Symphonies of Brahms?
22. Define the technical traits of the subordinate Theme in the Finale of his First Symphony.
23. In what structural manner, original with Brahms, does the design of this Finale differ from the conventional form?
24. In which other of Brahms' symphonic Movements does this same exceptional design appear?
25. What is the predominating character of the Second Symphony of Brahms?
26. What unusual relation exists between the principal Division and the two Trios, in its third Movement?
27. How does the Third Symphony compare with the foregoing two?
28. What is the quality of the Fourth Symphony, and what is its prevailing mood?
29. How did Brahms mark the third Movement of the latter, and what is its character?
30. What is the type of the Finale, and what is the design?

31. Outline the subdivisions of the series of Variations in this Finale.
32. Name some of the earlier pioneers of the Romantic School.

* * *

REFERENCES

MAITLAND	Schumann.
MASON	The Romantic Composers.
NIECKS	Schumann.
PATTERSON	Schumann.
REISSMANN	The Life and Works of Robert Schumann.
SCHUMANN, EUGENIE	The Schumanns and Johannes Brahms.
LITZMANN	Letters of Clara Schumann and Johannes Brahms.
ANTCLIFFE	Brahms.
DEITERS	Johannes Brahms.
ERB	Brahms.
LEE	Brahms.
MAITLAND	Brahms.
MASON	From Grieg to Brahms.
MAY	The Life of Johannes Brahms.
HERZOGENBERG	Johannes Brahms: the Herzogenberg Correspondence.
PULVER	Johannes Brahms.

ILLUSTRATIVE RECORDS AND ROLLS

Records: B—Brunswick; C—Columbia; E—Edison; H—His Master's Voice; O—Odeon; Pa—Parlophone; Po—Polydor; V—Victor; Vo—Vocalion.

Rolls: A—Ampico; D—Duo-Art; M—Melodee; Pl—Pleyela; Q—QRS; U—Universal; W—Welte-Mignon.

SCHUMANN AND BRAHMS

Music Mentioned in Chapter V:

Schumann Symphonies
No. 1, in B♭ major (*Spring*)   Po; M, U.
No. 2, in C major   M, U.
No. 3, in E♭ major (*Rhenish*)   U.
No. 4, in D minor   B, C, Po.

Brahms Symphonies
No. 1, in C minor   C, Pa, V; M, Q, U.
No. 2, in D major   B, C, Pa, V; M, Q.
No. 3, in F major   V; Q.
No. 4, in E minor   H, V; M.

Chapter VI
LISZT, TCHAIKOVSKY, DVOŘÁK, SIBELIUS

OUR scroll of musical history has recorded, up to the present point, names of symphonic Masters who were exclusively of German, or Teutonic, origin. And to this race belonged, also, not only all, or nearly all, of the Pioneers mentioned at the close of the preceding chapter, but a goodly number of distinguished symphonists of the succeeding era, contemporaneous with the last two supreme Masters of the Symphony whose works were expounded in Chapter V. To these we shall return later on.

But interest in this most eminent type of musical expression was not to be monopolized by the Teutonic race to the end of time. Their supremacy appears to wane, after the days of Schumann and Brahms; for earnest musical minds of other nationalities were turning their attention to the Symphony, and were embracing it with ardor as a vehicle well-adapted for the realization of their best and loftiest artistic ideals.

Franz Liszt

With the single exception of Berlioz (who will be considered in connection with his Gallic compatriots in Chapter VII), the earliest non-Teutonic genius to adopt the symphonic medium of expression was *Franz Liszt* (1811-1886). To be sure, what he adopted and cultivated in an extraordinary manner, and to an epoch-making degree, may well be called the symphonic *medium* only; Liszt never wrote a genuine "Symphony" in the classic, or even romantic sense, but, actuated by the impetuous originality and independence of his musical nature, he applied the traditional medium in such a wholly novel way as to transform its spirit completely; and for the new types which he produced he originated the name *Symphonic-Poem*. His intensely romantic spirit recognized emotional possibilities in the voices of the symphonic orchestra that had never been essayed (save by Berlioz), and he envisaged a sphere of poetic and passionate experiences to which music, and music only, could give utterance.

Franz Liszt was born October 22, 1811, in the Hungarian town of Raiding. His father, a musician of talent, was his first teacher, and so rapid was the lad's progress that already at the age of nine he gave a public concert with complete success; this was followed by a second, which made so profound an impression that a number of Hungarian noblemen engaged to provide for six years of further study. The family therefore repaired to Vienna, and here Franz became the pupil of Czerny and Salieri, incidentally gaining the approbation of Beethoven. In 1823 he gave his first concert in Vienna, the results of which induced his father to take him to the Conservatory in Paris. Its Director, Cherubini, objected to his admission, however, because of Liszt's foreign birth, whereupon Franz continued his studies alone, with some assistance from Paer and Reicha. There he composed a one-act Operetta. He had already become extremely popular as pianist and as teacher. In

1831 he first heard Paganini, and this phenomenal violin virtuoso inspired Liszt to develop the resources of the piano in a similar unprecedented way. During the succeeding years his fame as the greatest living pianist spread over the civilized world.

In 1849 he accepted a position in Weimar as Court *Kapellmeister* upon the express condition that he was to be free to further his novel musical ideas, which were aligned with the New German school, fostered by Schumann and other progressive enthusiasts. Meanwhile he had evolved the form of the Tone-Poem, and become as famous for his remarkable compositions, as he had been as a pianist of unrivalled technical and interpretative proficiency. In Weimar he vigorously promoted the aspirations of Wagner and many other struggling young composers, displaying a large measure of that magnanimity and generosity which were the ruling attributes of his noble character.

In 1859 he went to Rome, where he took minor religious orders, culminating in the rank of Abbé in 1865. In 1870 he returned to Weimar, and the rest of his life was divided between that city, Rome, and Pest. He was followed everywhere by a throng of pupils, to whom he dispensed the treasures of his advice and guidance with unstinting hand; and among these were many who ranked eminently high in the pianistic sphere. Liszt's death occurred July 31, 1886, in Bayreuth.

Everyone who is familiar with Hungarian music, who has heard it in its genuine, strikingly original utterance, who has been deeply moved by the weird, irresistible appeal of its distinctive melodies and rhythms, now steeped in almost tragic melancholy, and again pulsing with the gypsy spirit of wild passion and joy;—everyone who knows the wonderful primitive beauty and fire of Magyar music, will recognize the heritage and the environment that were the foundation of Liszt's musical being. In him these native qualities were, however, modified and controlled by an exceptionally active and penetrating mind, and an exquisitely refined poetic spirit. It was the fusion of his very pronounced romantic nature with the preponderant musical quality of his genius, that determined his attitude toward the Symphony and orchestral music in general, and impelled him to substitute the idea, and title, of *Tone-Poem*, in his instrumental compositions in larger form. Of this novel type, Liszt created no fewer than fifteen. Two of them: the *Dante* Symphony and the *Faust* Symphony, consist each of three distinct Divisions or Movements, and are therefore analogous to the genuine Symphony in dimensions; but there all resemblance ends, for in conception and structure they diverge widely from the classic model.

These novel compositions, to which the name *Symphonic Poem* has been applied, are program-music in the best sense of the word—not descriptive in the narrow, inartistic pictorial manner of superficial composers, but music which is engendered and guided by the fluctuating emotional or dramatic phases of an epic poem, or of some suggestive, fruitful poetic idea. Liszt, in pursuing this romantic aim, originated the *Leit-motif*, or Leading Motive, which Wagner promptly adopted and developed to so supreme a degree in his operas. The Leading Motive corresponds technically to the principal Theme of the true Symphony, but is employed chiefly as an index, and not manipulated as thematic source of the "absolute" musical evolution.

The three Divisions of the *Dante* Symphony are: *The Infernal Regions, Purgatory*, and a Finale of considerable length entitled *Magnificat*—an angelic hymn, assigned to a female chorus.

The *Faust* Symphony is similarly, though more sharply divided into three Episodes: *Faust, Gretchen*, and *Mephistopheles*—the last containing a male chorus.

Both of these extensive works exhibit Liszt's originality, his extremely fine sense of tonal charm, and his amazing ingenuity, especially in certain constructive details, and in orchestration. It is generally conceded, however, that the melodic invention, the essential logical momentum and structural firmness of his works do not measure up to the skill he possessed in arranging and accentuating the emotional effects.

Of Liszt's smaller Tone-Poems, thirteen in number, No. III, *Les Préludes*, is probably the best known and most popular, as it is in many respects the one most characteristic of Liszt's original methods. Its origin is traceable to the *Poetic Meditations* of Lamartine, though the actual undercurrent of the work is defined by Liszt in a "preface" of his own, the first lines of which: "What is our Life but a series of Preludes to that unknown chant, the first solemn note of which is sounded by Death?" supply the title of the Tone-Poem. The composition is a continuous unit, divided into four Episodes, remotely analogous to the four Movements of the Traditional Symphony. These Episodes are called: (1) Dawn of Existence; Love; (2) Storms of Life; (3) Refuge and Consolation in Rural life; (4)

Strife and Conquest. The structural plan does not—with its poetic, realistic aim it could not—conform to any of the classic designs. But it presents two clearly defined, well-contrasted, effective and extremely engaging Themes, treated with superlative skill, and alternating in a fairly regular manner, suggestive of a Rondo-form. These Themes, with some of their rhythmic transformations, are as follows:

Ex.125. Theme A (Introduction) (C major)   A (Episodes 1 and 4)   FRANZ LISZT (1854)

The Motive which accompanies Theme B in the third Episode assumes almost the importance of a third Theme, since it constitutes the proper basis of that entire Episode.

The nature of the other Tone-Poems of Liszt may be inferred by the student from this one (*Les Préludes*). They all contain passages of great beauty, and all bear witness to the refined manner of their genial author. The complete list of them may be found in the musical dictionaries.

* * *

Richard Wagner (1813-1883) is a name that may not be omitted from any treatise upon music in its noblest and highest aspects. Wagner was the most opulently gifted tone-master of his century; endowed with an extraordinary, fertile imagination, a mighty, all-embracing intellect, and all the other qualities that sum up the outstanding genius of his era. Although his fame rests upon his stupendous dramatic creations, because his musical spirit was most in sympathy with the vividly emotional, realistic conception and application of the tone-language, his mind had been seriously occupied, during the earlier years of his life, with the Absolute phase of music, and he composed, besides eight Overtures, at least one complete Symphony, in C (in 1832, brought out in 1833 in Leipsic), and began another, in E, in 1834, which, however, remained a fragment. This Symphony in C, in common with the majority of Wagner's early creations (he was then nineteen) is in no other sense remarkable than that it represents the tentative, almost commonplace expression of a musical consciousness, oddly belated in its self-discovery. As with the oak, the progress of Wagner's early growth was slow, because—like the oak—he was destined to become a strong, enduring "monarch of the forest."

It is of historic and psychological interest to the student to scan the chief Themes of this Symphony of Wagner's, which, in the first and second Movements, run as follows:

There is a rather lengthy *sostenuto* Introduction, after the traditional manner. It would be unjust to assert that the work has no individual merit. It is a youthful witness of Wagner's unbounded reverence for Beethoven's genius; and while the first Movement is unimportant, the second one is a kind of *Ballade* of very real beauty and a certain measure of indisputable significance. The third Movement

(*Scherzo*) is decidedly commonplace, and the Finale can arouse no especial interest.

* * *

TCHAIKOVSKY

This master was of Russian descent, and his music, while in its broadest expression *absolute* and universal rather than narrowly national, is deeply impregnated with Slav characteristics: the persistent reiterations of brief melodic figures, like unwearying bird-calls; the quaint and vivacious rhythms; the vivid poetic imagination; the sweet, touching melancholy; and again the wild outbursts of passion, wrested at intervals from this highly intelligent but to some extent oppressed people, stirred and spurred by visions of a higher destiny, of a finer and better life than they, in their subjugation, could reach. These attributes pervade Tchaikovsky's music from first to last, and are fused with unyielding regard for harmonious beauty, with vitality of imagination, sureness and force of expression, a refinement of technical and structural skill, and a perfection and firmness of texture, that assure him an eminent place among the Masters of the Symphony.

Peter Ilyitch Tchaikovsky was born May 7, 1840 in Votkinsk, Ural district, Russia. Like Schumann, with whom Tchaikovsky has many qualities in common, he was expected to study law, and did so for a while, also entering the service of the government. In time, however, his strong musical inclination prevailed, and he turned to its serious cultivation. In 1862 he entered the St. Petersburg Conservatory (founded shortly before by Anton

Rubinstein), as a pupil of Zaremba in composition and of Rubinstein in piano. In 1866 he became a teacher of composition at the Moscow Conservatory, established by Nicolas Rubinstein, remaining in that capacity until 1877, after which he devoted himself exclusively to his own creative activity, producing a large number of works that have made him justly renowned as foremost among the eminent exponents of Russian music, and, at the same time, as one of the most serious, scholarly, most spontaneous and richly endowed masters of legitimate art in music history—romantic in expression, but solidly grounded in the principles of classic structure. In 1887 he began to visit many European cities as conductor of his own works, and in 1891 came to New York on the same artistic errand. Death overtook him with tragic suddenness on November 6, 1893.

Tchaikovsky was of a highly sensitive, poetic nature; and his musical utterances were inclined to oscillate between strongly contrasted moods, though with a somewhat pronounced bent toward melancholic expression. He differed from the majority of great composers in his very strong predilection for the theoretical side of his art; he wrote and published two remarkable *Manuals of Harmony*, besides translating into Russian Gevaert's famous *Instrumentation* and Lobe's *Katechismus der Musik*. This throws light upon the sources of the meticulousness and perfection of his musical craftsmanship, and the refinement and invariable effectiveness of his orchestration.

The development of Tchaikovsky's musical genius was thoroughly normal and steady. Each succeeding work appears to excel its forerunners in maturity, command of structure, eloquence of melody, and in accuracy and intensity of expression. His first Symphony, in G minor, Op. 13 (*Winter-Storms*), was composed in 1868; his second, in C minor, Op. 17 (*Little Russia*), in 1873; the third, in D, Op. 29 (*Polish*), in 1875. These first three all manifest many traits of superior beauty and originality, and confirm the earnestness with which he pursued his serious artistic ideals and aims. But they scarcely succeeded in passing beyond the frontiers of Russia, and, wherever they are known, they are overshadowed by the splendor of his other three, the fourth, fifth and sixth Symphonies, in which his genius is proclaimed in tones that resound throughout the civilized musical world.

The Fourth Symphony

The Fourth Symphony, in F minor, Op. 36, was composed in 1877; first performed in Moscow, February 22, 1878, under Nicolas Rubinstein's direction.

Tchaikovsky admitted that the first Movement was "very complicated and long," and music critics generally concur in his estimate of it "as also the most important." The Symphony opens with a powerful, oracular Introduction in the horns and bassoons (afterward joined by trombones), later in the trumpets and wood-wind; it is not thematically related to the first Movement, but later it enters vitally into the texture of the Movement, and bursts forth again near the end of the Finale, with thrilling, and superbly unifying effect. This Introduction, and the Themes of the first Movement are as follows:

LISZT, TCHAIKOVSKY, DVOŘÁK, SIBELIUS

Ex. 127. TCHAIKOVSKY (1877)

Tchaikovsky's own words are: "The Introduction is the kernel, the chief thought of the whole Symphony."* This first Movement is based solidly upon the classic sonata-allegro design, but contains one noteworthy digression: the structurally vital return of the principal Theme, at the beginning of the Recapitulation, is placed in a different

---

*For a full account of the interpretation which Tchaikovsky himself gives of the entire work, see the Program-book of the *Boston Symphony Orchestra* (by Philip Hale) for the season 1927-1928, pages 294—300.

key (D minor), and so shortened that this "keystone" of the form is reduced to but little more than an intimation of its presence. The Ground Motive in the drum, in the Second Part of the subordinate Theme, is extended unaltered through twenty-two measures.*

The second (slow) Movement is an exquisite *Canzona*, tinged with sadness, but brightened with finely tempered contrasts. The form is First-Rondo, and its Themes run thus:

The third Movement (*Scherzo*) is an original experiment that never fails of its fine effect and hearty appeal. The three chief instrumental groups (Strings, Wood-wind, and Brass) appear separately, alternating in distinct sections, somewhat after the arrangement of a Triple-choir, until near the end, where they unite. The strings are *pizzicato* (plucked) throughout, hence the superscription "*piz-*

---

*See the *Analytic Symphony Series*, No. 16, elucidating the details of all four Movements.

zicato ostinato." The form is Song with Trio; the latter being so radically contrasted in its Fourth Part (in the Brass-choir) that one is tempted to infer a "Second Trio." The Themes are as follows:

This Fourth Part of the Trio, it will be noted, is practically identical with the beginning of the principal Division—but in augmented rhythm.

The Finale is a tumult of vivacious gaiety—as Tchaikovsky himself designates it: "the joy of seeing others happy and jolly." It offsets the tragedy of the first Movement and the sadness of the second; but the terrific intrusion of the fateful motive of the Introduction turns the mortal's thought to his own misery, if only for a brief moment. The thematic material is thus conceived:

Ex.130. IV Finale
Principal Theme

The Russian folk-melody, though introduced very near the beginning, in the course of the principal Theme itself, is sufficiently individual to serve as a subordinate Theme. The rhythmic treatment of this popular tune is ingenious.

The student will note the interesting similarity in the formation of the first melodic member of the chief Themes: every one of the four principal Themes (Exs. 127, 128, 129 and 130) begins with a descending scale-line of four (or five) tones—likewise the subordinate Theme of the second and last Movements. It is unlikely that this was intentional, but the coincidence is unmistakable, and not without psychological movement.

The Fifth Symphony

The first four Symphonies of Tchaikovsky were written in reasonably close succession, during the years 1868 to 1877; but then he paused in his symphonic occupation (devoting his genius meanwhile chiefly to the creation of four of his great operas), for eleven years. His Fifth Symphony, in the unusual key of E minor, Op. 64, was composed in 1888. The progress in the steady maturing course of its author's genius is confirmed by two qualities which place this Symphony above all his preceding ones, namely: greater warmth, firmness of line, richness and depth of sentiment in the conception of the melodies; and greater command of the formal structure, which is here of genuine symphonic dignity and perfection.

The Symphony opens, like the Fourth, with a portentous, oracular Introduction, that appears to be thematically foreign to the purpose of the first Movement; but it is inserted twice, unexpectedly and with tremendous emphasis, in the second Movement (to which, also, it is wholly foreign in mood and character); appears again, greatly subdued, near the end of the third Movement; and then—at last asserting its true thematic quality and importance, it becomes (in a considerably extended form, and changed from minor to major) not only the introductory section of the Finale, but an essential thematic factor of the entire last Movement.* This significant Introductory sentence, and the chief thematic members of the first Movement (sonata-allegro form) are as follows:

*See the *Analytic Symphony Series*, No. 30.

The second Movement, in the First-Rondo form, is a lyric conception of rich, glowing melodic quality and very great tonal beauty.

The third Movement, is in one of the customary dance-forms, but it bears the somewhat surprising title *Waltz*, and one wonders how so plebeian a style can hold its own in aristocratic symphonic company. But it does so, with quiet dignity and individual charm. Besides, the *"Waltz"* is no more foreign to the traditional Minuet, than is the very common *"Scherzo,"* which no less a master than Beethoven introduced into this company.

The Finale is, in keeping with convention, a vigorous *Allegro*, more distinguished for forcefulness than for vivacity, and splendidly effective. The allusion to the chief Theme of the first Movement, at the end, in *major*, rounds out this imposing Symphony in a masterly manner.

(See the *Analytic Symphony Series*, No. 30.)

The Pathetic Symphony

Tchaikovsky wrote his Sixth, and last, Symphony (Op. 74, in B minor) in 1893, very shortly before his sudden death. He himself called it the *Pathetic*, and the impression became quite general that he had been laboring under the premonition of his approaching end. Nothing could be farther from the truth; moreover, only the brief final Movement is genuinely pathetic, and that but part of the time, this pathetic mood being brightened by contrasting episodes of decidedly hopeful and consoling quality. The first Movement is tragic rather than pathetic, yet here again frequent gleams of light and warmth fall across the background of passion—in this way, to be sure, accentuating the tragic pulses by their contrast.

The Themes of the first Movement (in regular, but broad sonata-allegro form) are as follows:

A brief Introduction (*Adagio*) precedes the principal Theme, based entirely upon the opening motive; and two Codettas follow the subordinate Theme. This first Movement contains a number of stirring climaxes, carried out with that logical force and sureness of aim in which Tchaikovsky was an adept.*

There is no authentic slow Movement, or, more correctly stated, the slow Movement is shifted to the last place in the Symphony — as Finale. The second Movement has, however, the lyric tone due at this point; it is a graceful, charmingly melodious song, or dance, in swaying 5/4 metre; its complacent, happy countenance is slightly clouded with a veil of melancholy in the Trio. Its Themes run thus:

Ex.133. II Principal Division

The third Movement represents the *Scherzo*, though it carries no title. It is anything but "pathetic," and it has

*See the *Analytic Symphony Series*, No. 7.

a unique structural plan: an apparently unimportant motive, in striking rhythmic form, creeps in (in the ninth measure) quite incidentally—later turns out to be the index of the subordinate Theme—and then advances steadily into overpowering prominence; its ultimate complete supremacy is recorded in crashing blasts of the brass instruments, in a climax that is almost without a parallel in legitimate symphonic literature. The design is sonatine-allegro (there is no Development), with these Themes:

The Finale, contrary to all precedent, is a slow Movement, *Adagio lamentoso,* that is no doubt chiefly responsible for the designation of the Symphony as a whole. Its principal Theme is profoundly "pathetic;" but the subordinate Theme is a lyric melody (in Song-form) of rich, trustful quality, that breathes hope and solace: some music lovers may regret the return to deep sadness at the end.*

---

*See again the *Analytic Symphony Series,* No. 7.

Besides these genuine Symphonies, classic in their ideal purpose and scholarly structure, Tchaikovsky composed five Symphonic-Poems, among which the music to Byron's *Manfred,* Op. 58, often called the Manfred Symphony, is worthy of particular note. It follows the dramatic program, in four Scenes, the first one of which, "Manfred," is the most impressive.*

* * *

Dvořák

This master represents the Bohemian national musical element, which, though absolutely distinctive by itself, is akin to the Hungarian. Its melodic movements and contents, its quaint and stirring rhythms, which strike the ordinary music lover as odd, foreign—now weird, and again sentimental, have also a degree of similarity to the Russian, especially in their fragmentary form and the persistency of repetition which both of these national types favor.

All of Dvořák's creations are permeated with his ardent Bohemian temperament. His rare genius for melody (not altogether unlike that of Schubert), rhythm, unusual and always effective harmonic successions, his absolute technical command, and his brilliant orchestration, assure for him an eminent rank among the masters of musical expression. Moreover, his utterances are as sincere as they are vigorous.

---

*For a fine general characterization of the man and his art, see the article *The Unvanquishable Tchaikovsky* by Chas. L. Buchanan, in the *Musical Quarterly* of July, 1919.

Antonín Dvořák was born September 8, 1841, in Mühlhausen, in Bohemia. His origin was humble, and his opportunities limited, but his musical gifts were so pronounced that he soon learned to play the organ and violin, and busied himself with experiments in composition. In his sixteenth year he undertook systematic study at Prague, profiting greatly by contact with Smetana and Bendl, and struggling heroically onward until, in 1875, he gained financial assistance from the Viennese government. In 1878 he brought forth his celebrated *Slavic Dances*, and thereafter his fame spread rapidly and steadily. From 1892 to 1895 he was the Artistic Director of the National Conservatory of Music in New York City; in 1895 he became a professor at the Conservatory in Prague, and in 1901 its Director. He died in that city, May 1, 1904.

Dvořák's imagination was romantic, intense, and exceedingly active, inclining rather to the passionate and pathetic moods; but he was at times infinitely tender and winning in his musical utterance, notwithstanding the characteristic vigor and ofttimes startling wildness of his musical disposition. The indulgence of his ready invention tended to weaken the sustained structural development of his ideas, but at the same time compensated agreeably for it. His designs generally accord with classic tradition.

Dvořák produced five Symphonies that were published during his lifetime, all of which testify to his superior genius. Two others (in E♭, written in 1872; and D minor, 1874) were issued posthumously, but they have not been brought to public notice, and possess no special importance.

His First Symphony, in D major, Op. 60, contains an admirable *Scherzo*, suggestive of his "Slavic Dances."

The Second Symphony, in D minor, Op. 70, is not strikingly original, in the best sense, but is none the less fascinating in its warm and lively emotional character, and the clarity of its presentation.

The Third Symphony, in F, Op. 76, is of a pronounced Pastoral quality—an attractive reflection of joyous Youth.

The Fourth Symphony, G minor, Op. 88, depends more upon fertility and richness of melodic invention than upon firmly-knit structure and thematic evolution; for this reason it is not genuinely "symphonic" in effect. The second (slow) Movement is its most successful and engaging one.

The "New World" Symphony

Dvořák composed his Fifth Symphony, E minor, Op. 95, in 1893, during his sojourn in America, and he himself gave it the title *From the New World*. His natural disposition, always in most intimate sympathy with the primitive, guileless musical speech of the people, turned his thoughts to the Negro and Indian melodies he heard here, doubtless for the first time in his life, and these he observed and absorbed with keen interest. That such popular strains should find their way into the fabric of his *New World* Symphony was inevitable. But it was not a selection of the actual folk-songs themselves that he employed; according to his own creed: "It is the duty of composers to reflect in their music the spirit of the folk-tunes of the people to whom they belong; not by using *these tunes* baldly, as themes, but by composing *in their vein*." Thus, he allowed the spirit of old plantation songs, and of Indian tunes, to take complete possession of his conceptive spirit, and out of their emotional fullness he brought forth his own themes.

The structural designs in this Symphony are absolutely orthodox, and are handled with super craftsmanship; masterly are also the stirring melodies—those which impress by their vigor and original fire; those which attract by their quaint beauty; and those whose simple, tender appeal deeply touches the heart.

Each one of the four Movements has an introductory sentence; in the first Movement this is fairly long, but thematically almost totally independent of the *Allegro*. The Themes of the first Movement are as follows:

The principal thematic melody runs through the entire Symphony, bursting forth unexpectedly here and there with tremendous effect.

The Introduction to the second (slow) Movement is a brief procession of chords in very broad tempo, of so unusual a nature that they might be uncanny, were they not so skilfully blended. The principal melody was engendered by reflections of Longfellow's *Hiawatha*, for which Dvořák entertained profound admiration. The form is First-Rondo, based upon these Themes:

The third Movement, a *Scherzo*, is obviously conceived in the spirit of some rude *Indian* dances and chants. It is a Song-form with *two* Trios, the melodies of which run thus:

The Finale is a splendidly vigorous, spirited Movement, tense with vitality, but held in fine restraint by auxiliary Themes of a milder, more touching quality. These thematic components are as follows:

Ex.138. IV Finale

The principal motive of the second Movement reappears in the course of the third and fourth; that of the third Movement glitters once or twice in the Finale; and thus the last Movement becomes a fascinating network of the foregoing motives of the Symphony, binding the whole work together in masterly continuity. The magnificent climax near the end is a companion-piece to the Coda of the first Movement of Brahms' Fourth Symphony; that of Dvořák is almost barbaric in its free, unbridled emission—that of Brahms is more scholarly, despite its white heat, more scrupulously controlled.*

* * *

*See the *Analytic Symphony Series*, No. 9.

Sibelius

The very first, and practically the only distinguished Finnish composer, assuredly the most eminent one, is *Jean* (or *Jan*) *Sibelius*. It is he who has placed Finland at last upon the musical map. Being nationally affiliated with the Russian race, the Finns share many characteristics with the Russian people; but their climatic conditions, farther north, force upon them greater ruggedness, and their temperament and life are more rigorous and harsh. This quality is stamped upon their music, and Sibelius is a true son of the soil. His music is robust, severe, often harsh and uncompromising, for his outstanding quality is sincerity; and he loves Nature—his whole being is absorbed by this primitive passion. He said: "The voices of nature are the voices of God, and if an artist can gain a mere echo of them in his creations, he is rewarded for all his efforts." Thus, his melodies exhibit familiar Russian traits, but in the more stark, rugged form that they derive from the bleak Finnish existence. Again he says: "I have never used actual folk-melodies, but always freshly conceived motives"—precisely the thought expressed by Dvořák about the melodies in his *New World* Symphony.

In the seriousness of his artistic attitude, his absolute command of all the technical essentials of his art, Sibelius measures up to the stature of the best musical masters of Russia, and is one of the most original, powerful, individual geniuses in present musical history.

Jan Sibelius was born in Finland, December 8, 1865; and is now living there. The following biographic sketch is from his own pen: "It is true, I am a dreamer and poet of Nature. I love the mysterious sounds of the fields and forests, water and mountains. My father was a surgeon of the rank of Major in the Finnish army. I was educated by my grandmother, who insisted on my studying particularly Greek and Latin. I was graduated from the University of Helsingfors, and studied law, but I did not care to be a lawyer or judge. I determined to become a musician, and began to take lessons on the violin. I had already studied music systematically from my fourteenth year, and even composed simple pieces of chamber music . . . . My first composition to be performed was *Variations for String-quartet*, played in Helsingfors in 1887 . . . . In 1889 I left Finland to study in Berlin. Prof. Albert Becker instructed me there in composition, and there I started my larger orchestral works. In 1891 I went to Vienna and continued my studies with Karl Goldmark. I also studied awhile with Albert Fuchs. These are in brief the principal facts of my musical career. It pleases me greatly to be called an artist of nature, for nature has been truly the book of books for me."*

Sibelius visited America in 1914, and while here received the degree of Doctor of Music from Yale University. He has also been in London on various occasions.

The First and Second Symphonies

Sibelius completed his First Symphony, E minor, Op. 39, in 1899. Though it was his first effort in this type of composition, it was immediately successful in gaining recognition and almost unchallenged admiration. Its Themes

*Quoted from *Musical America* of January 14, 1914.

are simple; national in spirit; inclined to the melancholy and even sombre moods; intrinsically patriotic in conception.

The first Movement opens with the intonation of a weird melody as clarinet solo; the *Allegro* (6/4 measure, in G major) which follows, displays tremendous vigor and determination, and—as details which contribute to the distinctive character of the music—the frequent, nearly prevailing, rhythms of eighth-notes, and the multifold repetitions of brief figures, so inherent in the natural musical habits of the Finns.

The usual slow Movement, an *Andante,* assumes its conventional location as second in order, and contains attractive picturesque touches. This is followed by the *Scherzo,* as third Movement. The true *Scherzo* quality is apparent in its rhythm only; its mood is dark, and harsh dissonances are plentiful. The Trio, however, is kindlier and more tender in tone.

The Finale, entitled *Quasi una Fantasia,* begins with the clarinet solo of the first Movement, pronounced with great force by the whole body of strings, in unison, and then unfolds a somewhat gloomy perspective, ending in a broad hymn of sadness.*

The Second Symphony of Sibelius, in D, Op. 43, is no less popular than the First—perhaps it is even more generally admired, because of its brighter countenance, and friendlier aspect; though it is less effective, less volcanic, imbued with less elemental power.

*See the *Analytic Symphony Series,* No. 29.

The Third, Fourth, and Fifth Symphonies

The Third Symphony, Op. 52, in C major, appeared in 1907. Its structural designs are free, though not wholly unconventional; the melodies frequently end with a semicadence, which imparts a querying inflection to them. The dominating quality is cheerfulness, but the texture is complex, and sharp dissonances—the indispensable and overabundant spice in modern musical repasts—abound.

It consists of three Movements only. The first Movement, a sonata-allegro design, utilizes these Themes:

The second Movement is lyric in quality and represents the softer contrasting mood which the "slow" Movement is designed to supply; it is tinged with melancholy, but is neither sentimental nor sorrowful. Its somewhat irregular structural plan approximates the Second-Rondo form, although there is actually only one real Theme, which alternates with two different brief motives. These thematic factors are as follows:

The third, and last, Movement is even more fantastic in design; there is no genuine subordinate Theme; the burden of the structure rests upon the initial Theme — or rather "Motive," for the thematic material is fragmentary. The most striking auxiliary motive occurs late in the course of the Movement; it is not a subordinate Theme, nor is it a Codetta; and yet it is vital, and *final*, since the last pages of the score are developed out of it. The motives are thus conceived:

Ex.141. III Finale Introductory Motive

Additional Motive (Final)

The Fourth Symphony, Op. 63, A minor, deals with the poetic aspects of nature. It is, from an artistic viewpoint, more interesting than the foregoing Symphonies. The Themes are finely characterized and skilfully handled, in the distinctive, rather severe manner of this great and decidedly individual genius of tone—a giant of the North, discoursing of a remote, heroic past. Many original, startling, almost grotesque details enliven its pages; for instance, a Ground Motive repeated no fewer than thirty-six times.

Sibelius composed his next Symphony, the Fifth, Op. 82, in Eb, shortly before the great war—in 1913; it was performed early in 1914, and is said to have been subsequently subjected to revision. It is intensely human, replete with passion, and its message is delivered with the force, directness, and utter indifference to embellishment or mitigation, that is so typical of the man.

It embraces four Movements, but the first two (*Molto moderato*, and *Allegro moderato*—the latter representing the *Scherzo*) are curiously interlocked by a sort of thematic Motto of four tones which runs through both, so that, while contrasting in mood, these two Movements are practically one, and are played thus.

The third (slow) Movement is an *Andante, quasi Allegretto*, beautifully designed and engaging, but of singularly meagre thematic contents.

The Finale is a frank expression of human emotion; its subordinate Theme is passionate, and leads, with the Coda, to a superb, overpowering, conclusion.

Worthy of addition to this list is one of Sibelius' symphonic Suites, *Karelia*, a Tone-poem of many resplendent qualities.

* * *

QUESTIONS FOR REVIEW

1. Which race has produced the majority of Classic masters?
2. Who were the earliest two non-Teutonic symphonists of the classic era?
3. Outline the biography of Liszt.
4. Define Liszt's attributes as a romantic composer.
5. What title did he originate for his new style of expression?

LISZT, TCHAIKOVSKY, DVOŘÁK, SIBELIUS

6. Which of his Tone-Poems is the most popular?
7. How many Symphonies did Wagner write; what is their general quality, and why?
8. What attributes pervade the music of Tchaikovsky?
9. Outline his biography.
10. For what phase of his art had Tchaikovsky a strong predilection?
11. How do his early Symphonies compare with the later ones?
12. Is his last Symphony as "pathetic" as its title implies?
13. In what respect is the order of the four Movements exceptional in this Sixth Symphony?
14. What national element does the music of Dvořák represent?
15. What qualities are conspicuous in his music?
16. Outline his biography.
17. Which is his best known Symphony?
18. What primitive musical utterances enter into the fabric of the *New World* Symphony?
19. Through whom has Finnish music become significant?
20. What are the predominating traits in the musical spirit of Sibelius?
21. Outline his biography.
22. What is the character of his music?
23. What peculiarity is seen in the nature of the Themes in his Third Symphony?
24. In what manner are the four Movements of his Fifth Symphony practically reduced to three?

References

Hervey	Franz Liszt and his Music.
Huneker	Franz Liszt.

Pourtales	Franz Liszt.
Wallace	Liszt, Wagner and the Princess.
Evans	Tchaikovsky.
Lee	Tchaikovsky.
Tchaikovsky, Modest	Life and Letters of P. I. Tchaikovsky.
Newmarch	Tchaikovsky's Life, and Analyses of his Works.
Hofmeister	Dvořák.
Newmarch	Sibelius

ILLUSTRATIVE RECORDS AND ROLLS

Records: B—Brunswick; C—Columbia; E—Edison; H—His Master's Voice; O—Odeon; Pa—Parlophone; Po—Polydor; V—Victor; Vo—Vocalion.

Rolls: A—Ampico; D—Duo-Art; M—Melodee; Pl—Pleyela; Q—QRS; U—Universal; W—Welte-Mignon.

Music Mentioned in Chapter VI:

Liszt—Les Préludes   Pa, V; A, W.

Tchaikovsky Symphonies
  No. 4, in F minor   C, V; M, U.
  No. 5, in E minor   C, V; M, Q, U.
  No. 6, in B minor (*Pathetic*)   C, V, O; M, Q, U, A, D.

Dvořák—Symphony No. 5, in E minor (*New World*)   C, V, E; M, Q, U, A, D.

Chapter VII

BERLIOZ, FRANCK, SAINT-SAËNS, d'INDY

THE student has seen how the symphonic type of composition was brought to life in the Latin countries of Italy and France;—how it soon passed over, suddenly and almost completely, to the Teutonic peoples of Austria and Germany, and there bore classic fruits that have never been excelled, nor as yet equalled;—and how, as the supremacy of this race in symphonic art began to wane, the Slavonic and other non-Teutonic races adopted it with ardor, and produced works of striking originality, power and enduring worth.

From this the student must not infer that the type passed out of existence among the Latins: it is true that France has not, as a rule, and still less has Italy, evinced active sympathy for the classic domain of symphonic art, but all the more assiduously have French composers pursued the romantic, poetic, subjective and realistic trend of musical thought and expression, and this style they have aided in developing to an eminent degree of vitality and genuine effectiveness.

The first son of French soil to conceive this attitude toward music was *Hector Berlioz*, probably the greatest and most influential musical genius that France has given to the world. He may confidently be acclaimed as the originator of the Romantic movement (for while credit is given to Carl M. von Weber for the earliest recognizable impulses in this direction, his achievements therein are utterly incomparable with those of Berlioz) and he demonstrated his convictions with unfaltering, unbending, often vehement energy, and ultimately with complete triumph.

The attitude of Berlioz toward the orchestra, and his incredible development, enlargement and refinement of its resources, would alone suffice to place him in the front rank of musical path-breakers. Nor was he, notwithstanding his absorbing romantic tendencies, disloyal to classic forms and methods; these he embraced unquestioningly, and he employed them with as much fidelity as his expansive, nervous, unalterably poetic disposition and purpose would permit.

Hector Berlioz was born December 11, 1803, near Grenoble in France. His father was a physician, and decreed that Hector should study medicine; but the youth defied the decree, and sacrificed parental assistance, in order to gratify his unquenchable passion for music. His first compositions were rejected with ridicule, as too original and unintelligible. But he had the courage of his convictions, which were enlisted fearlessly in the cause of romantic, realistic musical expression, or Program-music, and in 1830 he won the *Grand prix de Rome* with his Cantata *Sardanapal*. His first Symphony, the *Phantastique*, shortly followed; then his Second, *Harold en Italie* (1834), and the dramatic Symphony *Romeo and Juliet* (1839), which were highly praised by the critics, but not accepted by the public.

In 1839 he was appointed "Conservator" of the Paris Conservatory, and later its Librarian. In 1843 he visited Germany, and extended his travels during the next few years to Hungary, Bohemia and Russia, meeting everywhere with that recognition and applause which were strangely withheld from him in his own country. In 1852 he conducted, in London, the New Philharmonic Concerts, and the next year his *Benvenuto Cellini* was given at Covent Garden.

After his death, March 9, 1869, his countrymen heaped honors upon his memory, but it was chiefly through the unselfish efforts of Schumann, Liszt and others in Germany, that the very great power of Berlioz' genius was apprehended, and his fame established. He was compelled to turn to journalism at times for his livelihood, and he proved to be remarkably fitted for this activity; from time to time he produced literary writings of great acuteness and power.

The dominating force among Berlioz' musical tendencies was the dramatic, though this was paired with a scarcely less insistent lyric and poetic inclination. His strength lay in the wealth and originality of his ideas, and his persistency in their expression in his own manner. His weakness may be felt in a tendency to exaggerate, though it must be conceded that he was usually successful in obtaining precisely the effects for which he aimed. His influence upon succeeding generations, as the herald of a new sphere of musical thought, a new purpose for the language of tone, was incalculable. His extension and enrichment of the orchestra were conspicuous among the daring innovations which gave the first mighty impulse toward the momentous achievements of the Romantic composers who followed him.

The Fantastic Symphony

The First Symphony of Berlioz, which he called *Episodes in the Life of an Artist*, or *Fantastic Symphony*, in C major,

Op. 14, was written in 1831. The subject, which was of Berlioz' own invention, could scarcely be adjusted to the classic lines of the traditional symphonic form, since it presented a definite poetic program, and involved of necessity those modifications that gave being to the Symphonic-Poem.

The idea is defined by Berlioz in these words: "A young artist, in love, and tired of life, takes opium; the dose, too weak to kill, intoxicates him, and in his fevered dreams he reviews his own imaginary love-history, which culminates in a fantastic and dreadful ending." This poetic material is divided into five Episodes or Movements:

1. *Reveries, Passions.* For this first Episode Berlioz adopts the sonata-allegro design, and follows it as best he may, for it must be well understood that he himself had no intention of violating or rejecting the classic structural traditions, and was doubtless unaware of the vital consequences that were to attend his novel artistic purpose. There is a stately Introduction, followed by the regular *Allegro,* the principal melody of which is what Berlioz called the *idée fixe* of the youth's hallucinations, and which recurs as "Leading Motive" in every Movement of the Symphony. Thus Berlioz unconsciously conceived the germ of the *Leit-Motif,* that later assumed such immense artistic significance in the works of Liszt and Wagner. This *idée fixe* has the following thematic shape:

Ex.142.

2. *The Ball*, Waltz, A major.
3. *Scene in the Country*, Adagio, F major.
4. *March to the Scaffold*, Allegretto, G minor.
5. *Witches' Sabbath*, Allegro, C major. This Finale contains a remarkable Fugue which is a masterpiece of contrapuntal skill, but as music repulsive.

The melodies of Berlioz, not alone in this work, but everywhere, are original, radically different from those of any other composer. Compared with the bland melodic lines of the great classic leaders, the melodies of Berlioz seem, on a first hearing, singularly uninviting, stiff and angular; but they are true to his musical purpose, and impress the unprejudiced hearer more and more upon closer acquaintance, until their signal beauty is at last revealed. His harmonies and modulations are normal; his counterpoint baffling; his structure generally convincing—though in many respects his music betrays the lack of thorough early discipline. Above all, his instrumentation is phenomenal: he enriched the orchestra extensively, adding harp, English horn, ophicleide (or tuba) and other instruments, multiplying the bassoons and trumpets, thus increasing the resourcefulness of the orchestral body, and demonstrating himself with superb vision how its resources might be utilized.

Harold in Italy

This is the title of his Second Symphonic-Poem, Op. 16, in G, written in 1834, and based upon scenes from Byron's

Childe Harold. Similarly to the preceding symphonic epic, it has a Leading Theme which runs through all four Movements of the work, and it is here everywhere assigned to a solo-viola. The origin of this peculiar feature is explained by Berlioz as the result of a visit from Paganini, who begged Berlioz to write a viola Concerto for him. Paganini was dissatisfied with the product, since it did not gratify his ambition as virtuoso; and Berlioz decided to remodel it into a symphonic scheme, to which he gave the above name. The pervading viola-voice represents, in the poetic plan, the hero, Harold, and the Leading Theme which signalizes this idea runs thus, at the opening of the Symphony:

Ex.143.

The first Movement is called "Harold in the Mountains; Scenes of Melancholy, Happiness and Joy." It is molded in the sonata-allegro form, with a long and impressive Introduction, during which the "Harold-Motive" is announced—first by the full wood-wind, and in minor; then by the solo-viola, in major. The succeeding *Allegro* is a broad *Pastorale*, of thoroughly cheerful character.

The second Movement, "March of the Pilgrims, chanting their Evening Prayer," is realistic, frankly and charmingly descriptive, and extremely beautiful in conception and formulation.

The third Movement bears the title "Serenade of a Mountaineer in the Abruzzo," an amiable *Scherzo*, into the fabric of which the Harold-Motive is delightfully woven.

The Finale: "Harold's End—Orgy of Brigands," is a masterpiece of realistic structure. Its Introduction is a retrospect of the preceding scenes, similar to the plan of the Finale of Beethoven's Ninth Symphony, though totally different from this in its poetic relations. The *Allegro* which follows is an Orgy, but a genuinely *musical* one, set forth in perfectly clear form—a most salutary model for many a modern composer, whose prodigious travail brings forth a—mouse!

Romeo and Juliet

The next symphonic epic of Berlioz, known as the *Dramatic* Symphony, in B, Op. 17, was written in 1838. It is based upon Shakespeare's drama *Romeo and Juliet*, and carries the same title. It is his largest and most pretentious symphonic creation. In it he aims to widen still further his sphere of vivid musical expression by adding the human voice to his orchestral apparatus.

The Symphony embraces eight Numbers, or Movements, to which the following titles are given: 1. Introduction; 2. Prologue; 3. Ball scene; 4. Garden scene; 5. Queen Mab; 6. Juliet's Burial; 7. Romeo at the Grave; 8. Finale.

The first Number (orchestral) is not an Introduction in the accepted sense, but prefigures the opening Scene of the Tragedy—the feud between the houses of Montague and Capulet. The ensuing Prologue, partly orchestral and partly vocal, consists of three definite Sections, which narrate in brief form the coming events of the Drama.

Hereupon follow the four actual *symphonic Movements*: the first Movement (*Andante; Allegro*) deals with a mournful soliloquy of Romeo; the appearance of Juliet; and the grand festival and ball at the Capulets'. Despite its obviously festive character, this Movement is handled with fine moderation, is noble in conception and dignified in execution.

The second Movement (the slow Movement of the Symphony) is the Garden scene, ardently emotional, but discreet—an admirable example of poetic musical expression.

The third Movement (the *Scherzo*) is the famous music entitled *Queen Mab*, the *Fairy of Dreams*. It is the finest and most individual episode of the whole Symphony; very few, if any, specimens of absolute music can compare with it in originality, ingenuity and tonal beauty, among all the products of the Romantic school. The form is Song with Trio, and its principal Theme runs thus:

Ex. 144. BERLIOZ (1838)

Queen Mab

The next two of the total eight Numbers, "Juliet's Burial" and "Romeo at the Grave," are usually regarded as included in this third Movement, although they are detached. It is quite impossible to point out, here, all the remarkably ingenious, significant, and inescapably impressive details of these Numbers. The student will find his efforts abundantly rewarded on a careful examination of the music itself.

The Finale scarcely maintains the high standard of excellence that distinguishes all the preceding Movements. It is undisguisedly operatic, almost theatrical, in plan and execution (with its mixture of orchestra, vocal solo, and triple-chorus), and seems out of place in a work of symphonic dignity. Concerning its tremendous dramatic effect, however, there can be no question.

* * *

César Franck

Next after Berlioz, in France, came *César Franck*. They were equally original, each in his own direction, and both attained singular eminence as exponents of the tone-language; and yet nothing could be more striking than the contrast between these two masters: Berlioz, the robust, virile, aggressive realist, who went about the realization of his lofty, absorbing artistic ideals in the most straightforward, practical manner; and Franck, the gentle-minded, shy, devout dreamer, whose soul seemed to lose contact with the earth, in the mystic realm of spiritual visions. While Berlioz excelled in dramatic intuition and in his command of orchestral technic, Franck was far more scholarly, more thoroughly trained in the technic and structure of musical composition.

César Franck was born December 10, 1822, in Liége. Thus he was of Belgian descent; but as early as 1844 Paris became his permanent home, and he is so inseparably identified with the musical life of the French, that he is claimed by that nation as one of their own sons. He studied at the Conservatory in Liége until his fifteenth year, then at the Paris Conservatory, becoming in 1872 a Professor at that institution. In 1853 he was appointed Choirmaster at Ste. Clothilde, in 1857 organist there.

Equally famous as organist, instructor, and composer, he exerted a strong and enduring influence upon the younger school of French writers; among his distinguished pupils were Lekeu, Debussy, Vincent d'Indy, and many others. Franck was especially noted for his improvisations at the organ, which are said to have been, as the unhampered effusions of his richly gifted poetic and religious nature, of indescribable beauty and impressiveness. Having gained comparatively late in his modest career the recognition due him in his adopted country, Franck died, in Paris, November 8, 1890.

Franck was not a hasty or prolific composer, and the list of his (invariably fine) works, though not meagre, is not as long as might have been expected. He left only one Symphony, but a number of Symphonic-Poems, five Oratorios, three Operas, several Chamber-music works, many organ pieces and other compositions, and a few Songs.

Franck's methods of musical expression, particularly as concerns melody and harmony, were distinctive, not to be confounded with those of any other great master. His harmonies are incomparably sinuous, iridescent; his modulations incredibly flexible; his counterpoint fluent but firm; and the structure of his larger forms, while not everywhere in absolute conformity with traditional models, is always logical, finely balanced, clear, and effective.*

His one and only Symphony, in D minor, was written in 1889, a year before his death, and represents therefore a fully mature product of his long artistic life. It contains three Movements only, thus reverting to the original type of the symphony. Its first Movement is cast in the sonata-allegro mold, but the method of its presentation is unique: the principal Theme is stated *twice*, in succession, the first time in slow, stately tempo, with strong emotional emphasis, and after the manner of an Introduction, and then in rapid tempo, in more concise, passionate, dramatic tones. Immediately after this the entire twofold presentation is *restated, in sequence* (a third higher), but otherwise literally. A brief Transition leads over into the subordinate Theme, and from this point on, the form of the whole Movement is normal. Its Themes run thus:

*See further the article *César Franck* by Julien Tiersot in the *Musical Quarterly* of January, 1923.

It cannot escape the observant student that Franck makes frequent use of the Sequence (a "repetition" on other, higher or lower steps); its shifting motions seemed to be more congenial to his conceptive habits than the more stable effect of actual repetitions. The latter, it will be recalled, was a strikingly persistent and essential feature in the music of Beethoven, and that of all the classics.

The second (slow) Movement is a genuine, characteristic specimen of Franck's musical conception, especially as regards melodic delineation. Its principal Theme, a complete lyric Double-period, is of a haunting, indescribably touching quality, introspective, sorrowful but not despairing. The design is Second-Rondo, and both of the subordinate Themes are cheerful in mood. The structural manipulation of this Movement is masterly to the last degree: an ingenious and unique adjustment of novel methods to classic traditions.* The Themes are as follows:

Ex.146. II Principal Theme

First Subordinate Theme (in B♭)

Second Subordinate Theme (E♭)

The Finale is fundamentally sunny in spirit; vigorous at times, but nowhere boisterous, and contemplative rather than vivacious. The insertion of the sombre chief melodic period of the slow Movement (as second Codetta, and again in the Coda) effectually subdues the optimistic as-

---

*See the *Analytic Symphony Series*, No. 10, for full details of this Movement, and of the others.

pirations of the Movement; and the allusions to important thematic units of the opening Movement—in the third and fourth Sections of the Coda—have an excellent unifying effect. The Themes are as follows:

The form, sonata-allegro, is curiously abbreviated: the Recapitulation presents *only* the principal Theme—the subordinate one is omitted.

* * *

Saint-Saëns

The musical conception and methods of *Saint-Saëns* were thoroughly typical of the French people, to whom he belonged. That accounts for the character of his music: extremely ingenious, clever, always piquant and alluring, polished, preponderantly bright and vivacious; by no means wanting in pathetic and passionate impulses, but these of a more sentimental than profoundly tragic quality. He is adjudged by many critical observers as one of the most brilliant and eminent of French tone-masters, if not the foremost.

Charles Camille Saint-Saëns was born in Paris, October 9, 1835. He was astonishingly precocious; is said to have begun the study of the piano before he was three years old; and at the age of five he was able to play light operas from the score. He entered the Paris Conservatory when only seven, taking courses in piano, composition and organ. When sixteen, he gained the first prize in organ-playing; in 1853 became organist of Saint-Méry; in 1858 organist at the Madeleine. After 1870 he gave his entire time to composition and public performances. Although he had become famous chiefly as pianist, organist, and instrumental composer, his strong predilection for the drama impelled him to turn his attention very seriously to the stage, and he brought forth, in rapid succession, numerous (about fourteen) dramatic works, among them the justly celebrated sacred drama *Samson and Delila* (1877), and the equally distinguished operas *Étienne Marcel* (1879) and *Henry VIII* (1883)—also oratorios, cantatas and many other sacred choral works.

In 1881 Saint-Saëns took Reber's place in the *Académie;* in 1892 he received the honorary degree of Doctor of Music from Cambridge University; and a host of decorations, and honors of many kinds bore witness to the universal esteem in which he was held, throughout the musical world.

He was always an enthusiastic traveler, visiting many countries in the threefold capacity of pianist, organist, and conductor of his own works. He visited America twice, in 1906 and 1915.

Saint-Saëns was prolific, versatile (his literary writings were numerous and brilliant), acutely intellectual, quickly responsive to poetic suggestion, and meticulous in his artistic methods. Doubtless less profound than the great classic masters, he contributed all the more to the development and refinement of Romantic Music. His fame rests mainly upon his instrumental works, his Symphonies and his original and skilfully depicted Tone-Poems (*Le Rouet d'Omphale, Phaéton, Danse Macabre, La Jeunesse d'Hercule*). Retaining his vigor and enthusiasm in a remarkable degree to the end, he passed away December 16, 1921.

Early Symphonies

Saint-Saëns made his first symphonic experiment in his sixteenth year; but the one of which he acknowledged the parentage and proudly issued as "Number One"—in E♭, Op. 2—was composed in 1855, in his twentieth year. It is of greater historical than artistic consequence, and aroused but little interest or attention. It is orthodox and by no means devoid of innocent attractions.

With his Second Symphony, in A minor, Op. 55, written much later, the case was decidedly different; for in this work Saint-Saëns placed on record some of the finest and most engaging fruits of his genial powers of musical expression, and the work attracted respectful attention, and won cordial recognition, at home and abroad.

It embraces the usual four Movements: an *Allegro appassionato* (with Introduction), concise in form, sparkling in character, smooth, and finely impelled in its structural unfolding; an *Adagio* of superior merit; a *Scherzo;* and a vivacious Finale, *prestissimo,* in the major mode, in the conventional Rondo-form.

The Third Symphony (with Organ)

Saint-Saëns wrote his Third Symphony, C minor, Op. 78, in 1885-6, very shortly before the death of Franz Liszt, to whose memory the work is dedicated—signifying the warm friendship and sincere admiration that Saint-Saëns cherished for his older colleague.

It is the most extensive and imposing of his symphonic creations, broad in design, and at intervals strongly dramatic; on the whole, however, distinguished more for ingenuity of design and execution than for spontaneity of melodic conception, and for that clearness, directness and unimpeded evolution of structural purpose that proclaim the supreme master of the situation. At the same time, it does contain very many episodes of lovely tonal quality, of unaffected emotion, and of equally genuine heroic emphasis.

It is superbly scored, with a fuller instrumental body than Saint-Saëns was accustomed to employ. Following the stimulating lead of Berlioz, and profiting by the acquisitions of the intervening years, Saint-Saëns contributed in no small measure to the eloquence and vividness of the orchestra. To the ordinary full score he here adds the organ and the piano—the latter in one place for four hands.

The Symphony comprises the usual four Movements, in their conventional order; but the first two, and again the last two, are connected, so that the work as a whole is presented in two large Divisions.

The first Movement opens with a brief Introduction (*Adagio*). The principal Theme which thereupon follows is carried through the entire Symphony, in an almost incredible variety of rhythmic forms, some of which are here shown:

The design of the first Movement is sonata-allegro, regular, and clear. The subordinate Theme is easily recognizable.*

The second (slow) Movement, connected with the first, as above stated, is a lyric tone-picture of very great melodic and harmonic beauty, warmth and dignity. The form is First-Rondo, with the following principal Theme:

The subordinate Theme is short, in effect only an Interlude, developed out of the chief motive of the first Movement, as noted in Ex. 148.

The third Movement is a *Scherzo*, with Trio; spirited, ingenious, and extremely effective. Its Themes run thus:

*See the *Analytic Symphony Series*, No. 28, for detailed exposition of all the Movements.

An elaborate and lengthy Transition, of six Sections, leads from the *Scherzo* over into the *Finale;* and the latter continues the free, in a sense capricious, sectional formation, which functions as an Introduction, embracing three Sections (based mainly upon the principal motive of the first Movement) before the actual *Allegro* begins—with a *fugato* upon this same motive, as indicated in Ex. 148. Hence, the first and last Movements of the Symphony have the same principal Theme, only differing in mode (minor and major respectively), in rhythm, and in tempo.

The subordinate Theme, however, is new, most attractive, and affords an admirable contrast. It runs thus:

To this a Codetta is added, in G, upon exactly the same melodic motive. The design of the Finale is sonata-allegro; slightly irregular, inasmuch as the Recapitulation begins with the *Second* Part of the principal Theme—omitting the so vitally essential *First* Part (the actual identifying "beginning") of the Theme.*

* * *

*In conclusion, the student is urged to read the penetrating "critical estimate" of *Camille Saint-Saëns*, by D. C. Parker, in the *Musical Quarterly* of October, 1919. Also the article, *Camille Saint-Saëns*, by J.-G. Prod'homme, in the *Musical Quarterly* of October, 1922.

Vincent d'Indy

A collective and very general survey of the four musical master minds of the nineteenth century, whose headquarters were Paris, affords something like the following comparison—by no means critically accurate in every respect, but of value to the student in his broader estimate of historical values: Berlioz' musical impulses and habits were cosmic, universal in character and scope; those of Franck were spiritual; those of Saint-Saëns national, defined by the inherent qualities of his people; and those of d'Indy are intellectual.

If extraordinary acumen, keenness of mental power, rigorous artistic judgment, the utmost measure of theoretical knowledge and consummate technical skill constitute the real, or the only essential requirements of the master in music, then d'Indy assuredly heads the list in France, if not in the musical world. But the majority of music lovers will insist that the heart must speak as well as the head; and that music may be never so perfectly patterned and fashioned and welded, and still leave the listener cold. It would be absurdly incorrect to impute to d'Indy a lack of emotional warmth, of poetic grace, or of genuine human sympathy; for he possesses a large measure of all of these; and his works, large and small, contain passages of unforgettable charm and elegance; seriousness, dignity and profundity distinguish and vitalize all of his compositions. But the fact remains, that his music, taken as a whole, is more erudite than emotionally engaging.

Vincent d'Indy was born March 27, 1851, in Paris, as a descendant of an ancient noble family. His early studies in music were directed by Diémer, Marmontel and Lavignac, and supplemented by private study, of which the famous treatise on orchestration by Berlioz, and the music of Wagner, were most stimulating and fruitful objects. In 1870 he composed his first pieces for the piano, Op. 1 and 2, and sketched a Grand Opera *Les Burgraves*. In 1870-71 he served in the Franco-Prussian war, after which he resumed his musical occupations, and submitted to César Franck a quartet; the latter recognized the eminent talent of the youth, who from that day became a pupil, and ultimately the most distinguished representative disciple, of that master. From 1872 to 1876 d'Indy was organist in the town of St. Leu, and later the chorus-trainer for the Colonne Concerts. He was now definitely committed to a musical career, and thereafter devoted himself wholly to composition and conducting.

His Overture *Piccolomini* was performed under Pasdeloup at one of the popular concerts in January, 1874. This Overture, to which were later added the *Camp de Wallenstein* and *Wallenstein's Death*, led to the trilogy *Wallenstein* (Op. 12), the most remarkable of d'Indy's creations up to that time—first given, entire, in February, 1888. This was followed, in 1875, by his first Symphony, *Jean Hunyade;* in 1878 by a symphonic Ballade, *Le Forêt enchantée;* and another Symphony, now listed as his First, in G, Op. 25, with piano, entitled *Cévenole* (in 1886); then a set of symphonic Variations, *Istar*, Op. 42, and his Second Symphony, in B♭, Op. 57 (1903-1904). His Third Symphony, *De Bello Gallico*, was produced in 1918.

In 1894, d'Indy, with Bordes and Guilmant, founded the *Schola Cantorum*, designed at first to promote Gregorian and *a cappella* church-music, but soon expanding into a full Conservatory, of which he has been, since 1911, the sole Director. His whole life, as composer, conductor, lecturer, critic and editor, is devoted zealously to his art. He has published, with A. Sérieyx, a monumental Course in Composition, and recently issued *100 Harmonic Themes* (Op. 71). He has been an extensive traveller, acting as guest-conductor in various countries (in Spain and Russia, and, in 1905, 1921, and 1925 in America). Honors have been heaped upon him; he has been Secretary, and later President, of the National Musical Society; is a member of the Legion of Honor, and one of its officers since 1912; and is a member of numerous foreign Academies.

D'Indy's virile mentality impels him to employ complex means, apparently in preference to a more spontaneous and unsophisticated mode of expression. He has a strong predilection for novel harmonic effects, often of a biting, almost reckless quality, very different from the suave, velvety manner of his illustrious teacher César Franck. But he is absolutely sincere; his original and often startling utterances are those of an aggressive but serious mind of tremendous vigor, prefering the abstruse, and yet always justified by the conviction that every conceivable tone-effect may have its place and validity in the musical scheme.

The Second Symphony

Passing over d'Indy's remarkable early symphonic Epic *Wallenstein* (Op. 12, referred to in the biography), the unlisted Symphony *Jean Hunyade*, the authentic "First" Symphony *Cévenole*, and several other significant orchestral compositions, it will suffice to concentrate upon his Second Symphony, in B♭, Op. 57, wherein are recorded his most distinctive and excellent creative qualities.

This Second Symphony was written in 1903-4, and first publicly performed in February, 1904. It exemplifies the modern subjective trend of romantic music, but follows no program, adhering strictly to the methods of absolute musical presentation, though with those differences in result which the increasingly insistent demand for freedom of self-expression, free rein for personal emotions and passions, have inevitably brought about. Like the greater part of modern compositions, it tolerates no comparison with the sober objective art of the great classic masters; the latter, as is sufficiently apparent, aimed at the production of a unified structure to be viewed as a Whole, whereas the moderns achieve their effects more through the Details, contenting themselves with a procession of passing images, often supremely lovely, but bound rather loosely together. This trait is recognizable among the later "classics" as early as Schumann, with whom, as we have seen, beauty of detail supersedes firmness of structure. The distinction is obvious in d'Indy's music, though he, and others, have the happy custom of welding the panoramic details into an effective and perspicuous unit through the employment of Leading Motives. Thus, in this Symphony, the entire work rests upon a figure of four tones, announced portentously in the Introduction, and interwoven through the fabric of all the Movements, in multifold rhythmic shapes.*

The first Movement, in sonata-allegro form, utilizes these Themes:

*For an exhaustive elucidation of the entire Symphony, see the *Analytic Symphony Series*, No. 27.

D'INDY (1903)

Ex.152. I Introduction

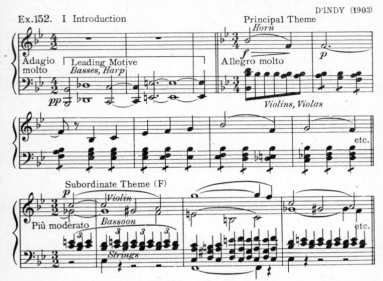

The second (slow) Movement is a First-Rondo form, augmented by *two* alternations of the principal Theme with the same subordinate one (somewhat modified). The chief Theme is a lyric sentence of unusual melodic character, typical of d'Indy's thought, weird, but not without a certain strain of loveliness; the other Theme is frankly unmelodious, in jerky dotted rhythm. These Themes are as follows:

Ex.153. II Principal Theme

A brief Introduction opens this slow Movement with an echo of the first figure of the Theme of the preceding one. Into the subordinate Theme the Leading Motive (in extended form) is here and there inserted.

The third Movement is essentially the *Scherzo,* but its chief, opening, Theme is a *Romanza* of simple, tender beauty. The other, alternating, Theme (the design approximates the First-Rondo) is evolved from the Leading Motive, in fantastic miniature rhythmic shape, wild, bacchantic, insistent—used ostensibly as accompaniment to other wild melodic phrases, one of which resembles the jerky subordinate Theme of the slow Movement. The lyric Theme is drawn for a time into the orgiastic, dizzy whirl, but regains its composure near the end. The Themes run thus:

The Finale is a marvel of thematic artifice and astoundingly ingenious combinations. It corresponds to none of the conventional designs, though the presence of two essential Themes is vaguely evident. The form can therefore claim no more accurate designation than a fanciful *Series of Episodes*, utilizing all the motives of the foregoing Movements, and one or two new ones, interlaced with dazzling skill, admirably controlled, and effectively presented.

An exhaustive analysis of it may be scrutinized in the *Analytic Symphony Series*, No. 27.

This Symphony is appraised by many critics as too cerebral. One commentator of wide orchestral experience declares his conviction that it just misses being a truly great work, because it lacks spontaneity. Unquestionably it displays a greater proportion of mental reflection than of genuine human sentiment, and of that quality, absolutely indispensable, in a work of art, especially of the Tone-art, namely, *Beauty*—a quality for which no degree of technical skill can compensate.

But be all that as it may, this Symphony is a creation to be reckoned with. It is, in many respects at least, a "great" Symphony—great in its scope, in its originality, in its supreme craftsmanship, in its sincerity; the product of an extraordinary musical genius.

* * *

QUESTIONS FOR REVIEW

1. Outline the course of symphonic progress from the beginning to the present.
2. Who was the first great French symphonist, and what were his innovations?
3. Outline the biography of Berlioz.
4. What novel structural factor originated with him; what is it called in his First Symphony, and what in his later works?

BERLIOZ, FRANCK, SAINT-SAËNS, d'INDY

5. Recount the origin of his Second Symphony.
6. What famous Number occurs in his Third Symphony?
7. Outline the contrast between the artistic dispositions of Berlioz and César Franck.
8. Outline Franck's biography.
9. What unusual structural feature distinguishes the first Movement of his Symphony?
10. What does Franck often substitute for "Repetition," and for what probable reason?
11. Of what was the musical conception of Saint-Saëns typical, and how was this element exhibited?
12. Outline the biography of Saint-Saëns.
13. Give some details of his Third Symphony.
14. How is the orchestral apparatus enlarged in this work?
15. In what manner does Saint-Saëns apply the *principle* of a Leading Motive?
16. How may the respective attitudes of the four symphonists of this chapter be roughly defined?
17. In which creative attributes does d'Indy excel, and what is the ruling element in his works?
18. Outline the biography of d'Indy.
19. What imposing orchestral works preceded his Second Symphony?
20. What structural feature is here again exhibited?
21. Describe the peculiar character of the *Scherzo* of this Symphony.
22. What is the "form" of the Finale?
23. What conflicting opinions are current, concerning the Symphony as a whole?

REFERENCES

BERLIOZ	Autobiography.
BERLIOZ	Life as Written by Himself.
BENNETT	Hector Berlioz.
BERNARD	Berlioz' Life and Letters.
D'INDY	César Franck.
SAINT-SAËNS	The Ideas of d'Indy (In *Outspoken Essays on Music*).
HERVEY	Saint-Saëns.
LYLE	Camille Saint-Saëns. His Life and Art.
MASON	Romantic Composers.
NEWMAN	Berlioz, Romantic and Classic (In *Musical Studies*).
MASON	d'Indy. (In *Contemporary Composers*.)
ROLLAND	Musicians of Today.
HILL	d'Indy. (In *Modern French Music*.)

ILLUSTRATIVE RECORDS AND ROLLS

Records: B—Brunswick; C—Columbia; E—Edison; H—His Master's Voice; O—Odeon; Pa—Parlophone; Po—Polydor; V—Victor; Vo—Vocalion.

Rolls: A—Ampico; D—Duo-Art; M—Melodee; Pl—Pleyela; Q—QRS; U—Universal; W—Welte-Mignon.

MUSIC MENTIONED IN CHAPTER VII:
 BERLIOZ—Fantastic Symphony H, C; Pl.
 BERLIOZ—Romeo and Juliet. French Phonograph Co.
 FRANCK—Symphony in D minor C, V; M, Pl, U, W.
 SAINT-SAËNS—Symphony No. 3, in C minor (with *Organ*) Pl.
 D'INDY—Symphony No. 2, in B♭ M.

Chapter VIII

BRUCKNER, ELGAR, MAHLER, STRAUSS, AND OTHER SYMPHONISTS OF THE NINETEENTH CENTURY, AND THE MODERN ERA.

BEFORE concluding our studies, with the present era of symphonic activity, it is necessary to turn backward a step, and complete the record of composers who produced more or less distinguished Symphonies, particularly during the second half of the nineteenth century. And this list, in keeping with all those that have gone before, is arranged chronologically. The following names therefore continue the roll of composers given as "Pioneers" at the end of the Fifth Chapter, and lead successively down to the present hour:

A venerable name, contemporaneous with that of Berlioz, is *Franz Lachner* (1803-1890), the eldest of three brothers of Bavarian birth, almost equally famous as musicians, whose steadfast support of the best classic ideals exerted a powerful influence for good. Franz wrote eight Symphonies, one of which (Op. 52, 1835) was awarded a prize by the Society of the Friends of Music; and another (No. VI, in D), which was highly praised by Schumann.

Ferdinand Hiller (1811-1885), a distinguished and prolific German composer, author of three Symphonies of the elegant type, that were admired for a certain ingenuity and excellent workmanship, though they are not weighty.

Next in chronological order came the highly accomplished English composer *George A. Macfarren* (1813-1887), the author of eight Symphonies (the First, in C, produced in his fifteenth year), which evince conscientious and skilful technic, but are wanting somewhat in original and vigorous conception. Further:

Robert Volkmann (1815-1883), a native of Saxony, whose two Symphonies compensate in grace and refinement for what they appear to lack of that larger and firmer grasp which goes with true genius.

William Sterndale Bennett (1816-1875), the eminent English pianist and composer, whose one Symphony (in G minor) was extremely popular in Great Britain, also admired abroad, and is still placed occasionally on concert programs. It is unpretentious; he himself said, "It is little more than a long Overture, on a Symphony plan."

Niels W. Gade (1817-1890), the leading exponent of Danish music, and an outstanding figure in symphonic history in his day. He was gentle-minded, romantic, sincere, conservative rather than outreaching; and his music is graceful, delicate, technically refined; in its modest fashion, truly delightful. Of his eight Symphonies, the

Fourth, in B♭, Op. 20 (1850) is most widely known and esteemed.*

Joachim Raff (1822-1882), the most famous composer that Switzerland has produced; a prolific and facile writer, whose musical ideas alternate oddly between frequent flights into the realm of genuine nobility, and lapses into an apparently hasty and superficial manner that borders on the commonplace. Hence, while his Third Symphony (*In the Forest*, Op. 153), and his Fifth (*Lenore*, Op. 177) have enjoyed great and deserved popularity, and still hold their own among the most excellent orchestral products of his day, those that followed (up to No. XI) have none of the sterling qualities that challenge attention and compel admiration. The first Movement of the (earlier) Second Symphony (C major, Op. 140) is decidedly significant and strongly attractive; and his entire Fourth Symphony (G minor, Op. 167), though neglected, is the best of them all. His last four (Nos. VIII, IX, X and XI) represent the four Seasons.

Friedrich Smetana (1824-1884) divides with Dvořák the musical honors of Bohemia. Smetana is best known through his beautiful opera *The Bartered Bride* (1866), but his creations in the orchestral domain are no less felicitous. These, however, are chiefly Symphonic-Poems, of which he wrote nine, including a remarkable series of six national Tone-pictures entitled *My Country*. Only one Symphony (*Triumph*—1853) came from his pen.

* * *

*See the interesting sketch *Niels W. Gade*, by his pupil and intimate friend Cornelius Rybner, in the *Musical Quarterly* of January, 1917.

Anton Bruckner

An imposing figure, for a time comparatively obscure, though early recognized as an organist of superlative ability, and almost suddenly, late in life, elevated to great prominence by enthusiastic admirers, was Anton Bruckner.

Bruckner was born September 4, 1824, in Upper Austria. Circumstances compelled him to study by himself, but so great was his talent, and his diligence, that he soon became an organist and contrapuntist of extraordinary ability. In 1855 he was appointed organist at Linz, prevailing over many rival applicants. In 1867 he became Court-organist in Vienna; in 1875, lecturer at the Vienna University, receiving from that institution the honorary degree of Doctor of Music in 1891. In 1869 he journeyed to France, and in 1871 to England, establishing his reputation as the greatest organist of his time. His First Symphony was composed in 1868; the Seventh, the first to engage the serious attention of the musical public, in 1884. His death occurred October 11, 1896, in Vienna.

There are certain points of contact between Bruckner and his close contemporary, César Franck. Both were of a shy, gentle disposition, devoutly religious, with less sense of the realities of life than of poetic or spiritual visions; both were eminent organists and consummate contrapuntists. Both were assiduous and influential teachers: among the numerous pupils of Bruckner were Felix Mottl, Arthur Nikisch, Gustav Mahler and Emil Paur.

The strongest artistic prepossession of Bruckner was his overwhelming reverence for the personality and the music of Wagner; and despite the uncommon vigor of his own genius, he was unable to withstand Wagner's influence, and to avoid rather frequent obvious imitation of his style. Bruckner's conception was fitful, unsteady, not always subjected to proper control; in consequence, his Movements are almost all too long, and devoid of balance and essential contrast. But he was profoundly sincere and earnest, and his style manifests much genuine power, dignity, nobility, at times even grandeur.

Bruckner produced nine Symphonies, each in the traditional four Movements, and almost without exception molded after classic designs. The First (1866) and Second (1872), both in C minor, are unimportant. The Third, in D minor (1873), dedicated to Wagner, is a noteworthy specimen of masterly orchestration. The Fourth, in E♭, called the *Romantic,* lives up to its title, and contains many truly beautiful episodes. His most important Symphony is the Seventh, in E major, finished in 1883. Opinions concerning it diverge widely; some regard it as "the loftiest and noblest expression of emotions that are too deep and subtle for any other than the musical medium of utterance;" others find "at least two of its four Movements dull, involved, bold in idea, tiresome in treatment." Still, all critics—and the public—agree that the slow Movement of this Seventh Symphony is one of the most imposing, lovely and impressive *Adagios* in symphonic literature. The first Movement of this (Seventh) Symphony begins with the following inviting principal Theme:

And the inspired *Adagio* opens thus:

Ex. 156. Principal Theme

Of his Ninth Symphony (1894) Bruckner completed only three Movements, the Finale remaining unfinished. Its second Movement (the *Scherzo*) was declared by one writer to be probably the most barbarous and oppressive *Scherzo* that symphonic scores can show. This dictum may have appeared quite reasonable and true forty years ago— but times, and tastes, have changed vastly since then.

* * *

Contemporaneous with Bruckner was *Karl Reinecke* (1824-1910) a widely known and cordially admired North German, of whose three Symphonies, the Third, in G minor, Op. 227, best reflects his refined, conservative, romantic disposition, and his lucid and skilful structural method. A fourth, *Kindersymphonie*, followed these as Op. 239.

Waldemar Bargiel (1828-1897), related by marriage to Schumann, and a sympathetic follower of the latter; noted for the refinement of his style, rather than for vigor or depth. He produced one Symphony.

The name of *Anton Rubinstein* (Russia, 1829-1894) no doubt sends a warm glow to the heart of many music lovers, especially those old enough to have heard him at the piano. As a composer, his strength lay in the spontaneity, Oriental warmth and emotional fervor of his melody and harmony. His readiness in conceiving Themes, often unique, always beautiful, was not unlike the manner of Schubert. His weakness may be detected in a lack of critical discipline, a sort of indifference that seemed to steal over him in the process of developing his themes, and a consequent looseness of structure that at the end often disappoints the hearer. Of his six Symphonies, the best known and most popular is his Second, the *Ocean* Symphony, in C major, Op. 42, dedicated to Liszt. It consisted originally of the usual four Movements, to which he later added two others as fourth and fifth, the original Finale remaining in its customary place. To the present writer he once said that he had no intention of following a descriptive program, but concurred passively in the titles suggested for the original Movements: Play of Wind and Wave; Soul as Ocean Depth; Neptune's Procession; and Man as Conqueror of the Ocean.

The Fourth Symphony, called the *Dramatic* (D minor, Op. 95), is conceded to be his most successful one. The

Fifth is known as the *Russian* Symphony, because of its extensive use of Slavonic melodies.

Karl Goldmark (1830-1915), of Hungarian descent, is most familiar to music lovers through his singularly engaging *Sakuntala* Overture, and his one Symphony, *The Rustic Wedding*, in E♭, an ingenious creation of great charm.

Salomon Jadassohn (Silesia, 1831-1902) produced four Symphonies, noted more for fine technical finish than for inspiration. His fame rests mainly upon his fruitful activity as a teacher and as an author of theoretical treatises.

Alexander Borodin, an eminent Russian composer (1834-1887) and almost equally noted scientist, wrote three Symphonies of unquestionable artistic distinction, the most popular one of which is the Second, in B minor, of strong Oriental and Russian flavor. Of the Third, in A minor, he finished only two Movements.

Another Russian, *César Cui* (1835-1918), was, similarly, distinguished both as composer and as military engineer. In his music he excelled in delicacy, neatness of structure, and lyric conception. His orchestral works were chiefly Suites; no Symphonies stand to his credit.

Felix Draeseke (Saxony, 1835-1913) was a musician of great power, at times eccentric, but usually serious and always technically refined, the recognition of whom was not commensurate with his merit. Of his four Symphonies, the Third, the *Tragica*, in C minor, Op. 40, is a creation of imposing qualities.

The extraordinarily gifted French composer *Georges Bizet* (1838-1875), famous author of the opera *Carmen*, wrote only a fragment (two Movements) of a Symphony, but contributed significantly to orchestral literature with his admirable Suites, *L'Arlésienne, Roma, Jeux d'Enfance*, and other works.

Max Bruch (Germany, 1838-1920), a sturdy supporter of classic ideals, best known through his numerous and eminent Choral compositions (*Frithjof, Schön Ellen, Odysseus*, etc.) and his sterling violin Concertos. He produced three Symphonies. No. I, in E♭, Op. 28, is a creation that stands worthily beside the classics, heroic in style but simple in conception, exhibiting the serious spirit and supreme mastership of its author. The Second, in F minor, Op. 36 (in three Movements), and the Third, in E major, Op. 51 (1887), have not succeeded in making their way into the knowledge and sympathy of the public.

Josef Rheinberger (Munich, 1839-1901), whose memory as a genial teacher of composition is cherished by many American students, is celebrated mainly for his organ works (twenty Sonatas, etc.), though he was astonishingly diligent and fruitful in other types of composition. He composed only two Symphonies: No. I, *Wallenstein*, D minor, in the usual four Movements, but tracing a definite program, as indicated by the given titles; and No. II, Op. 87, the *Florentine*. His writings, while not attaining inspired heights, possess genuine value and distinction, and confirm everywhere the master hand.

Another German master, *Friedrich Gernsheim* (1839-1916), was of like mind with his two contemporaries, Bruch and Rheinberger, in his thoroughly conservative attitude toward classic ideals and methods. His four Symphonies are decidedly serious in purpose, and classic in spirit; and while not strikingly original, they display fine taste and effective structure. No. III, in C minor, Op. 54, *Miriam*, is less genuinely symphonic than it is unique in its scheme.

Johan S. Svendsen (Norway, 1840-1911) was the first to add the Symphony to Norway's copious list of distinguished musical products. His conception was noble, his emotional range somewhat peculiar, dominated by a dreamy mood, his craftsmanship solid and refined. He wrote two Symphonies: No. I, in D, Op. 4, distinctly Scandinavian in character and contents; and No. II, in B♭, Op. 15, which is of greater emotional depth than the former.

Hermann Goetz (Prussia, 1840-1876), author of the justly celebrated Opera *The Taming of the Shrew*, and of one Symphony, in F major, Op. 9,—an extremely and deservedly popular work, delightfully fresh, exhilarating and winning in spirit and in presentation; its second Movement, an *Intermezzo*, is indisputably one of the most charming and ingenious sketches in modern symphonic literature.

Heinrich Hofmann (Berlin, 1842-1902), wrote one Symphony, *Frithjof*, of substantial merit; and several effective orchestral Suites and Serenades.

Arthur Sullivan (London, 1842-1900), the well-known and universally beloved creator of many light Operas or Operettas (among them *Pinafore*), that defy the tooth of time, and still gratify with dignity a popular musical craving that is fundamentally legitimate, composed one Symphony, in E minor, known as the *Irish* Symphony; it is a youthful work (1866), mentioned by Parry with genuine approval; not profound, but thoroughly musicianly.

Edvard Grieg (Norway, 1843-1907). The specific character of Scandinavian music has become universally familiar to music lovers chiefly through the masterly, exceedingly attractive and consequently popular, piano compositions of Grieg. But while he always asserted his Norwegian individuality, he possessed an indomitably personal musical propensity, a harmonic and modulatory idiom that was wholly unique and irresistibly charming; an idiom that was at first viewed with disfavor by the conservatives, but which speedily captured the rank and file of the musically discriminating community, and to this day, though its startling novelty naturally fades, maintains its strong hold upon those sensitive, poetic natures that love abundant color. His sinuous harmonies remind one vaguely of César Franck, but of a Franck transferred from mild and genial Parisian surroundings to the rugged, bleak North. Grieg wrote a few orchestral pieces (the *Peer Gynt* Suites, Overtures, etc.), but ventured only once upon symphonic ground, early in life (1864); his Symphony, Op. 14, owes its perpetuation solely to a four-hand piano arrangement.

Heinrich von Herzogenberg (Styria, 1843-1900), another staunch champion of the classic attitude, whose musical utterance was marked by nobility, freedom and ease of contrapuntal method, individuality of conception and skill in orchestration, but somewhat lacking in warmth and inspiration. He and his wife (a musical nature of very exceptional keenness) were most intimate and loyal friends of Brahms. Herzogenberg wrote two excellent Symphonies: in C minor, Op. 50; and in B♭, Op. 70.

Nikolai Rimsky-Korsakov (1844-1908), an outstanding and leading figure in the music of Russia, an eminent master of orchestral expression, a fervent devotee of the quality of Beauty in music, and preponderantly true to the spirit and the idiom of his nation. His whole active life was devoted to the promotion of the musical art of his native land. Though not the oldest nor the first Russian master, there is something patriarchal in Rimsky-Korsakov's position; he is cited as the father of the Russian school of orchestration; and, as teacher of many later celebrities, his strong and beneficent influence was far-reaching. His most widely known instrumental works are his superb orchestral Suite *Shéhérezade* (from the *Arabian Nights*), Op. 35; and the Oriental Suite *Antar* ("Poet and beloved Hero of the Desert"), Op. 9 (1881); both of these consist of four Movements, though the latter are not strictly analogous to those of the symphony. In their character they show that, despite his devotion to Russian folk-lore and folk-song, he had a decided taste for the Oriental in music, and caught its idiom most successfully.

Antar is generally listed as Rimsky-Korsakov's Second "Symphony," though the title *Suite* is more accurate.

The story runs thus: *Antar* rescues the Fairy *Gul-Nazar* (as a gazelle) from the pursuit of a giant bird. As a reward, she promises him three great Delights of Life: Revenge, Power, and Love. These episodes form the basis of the four Movements, of which the Finale is the best—the exceedingly skilful combination of the Fairy-theme and an Oriental Dance.

The Fairy-theme is a Leading-Motive, which appears near the beginning and runs through all the Movements. It appears thus in its original form:

Ex. 157. The Fairy-Theme (Gul-Nazar) RIMSKY-KORSAKOV (1881)

The Symphonies of this master (not to mention the Suites) are three in number: the First, in E major (1865); the Second, in C; and a Symphonietta in A minor—all admirable, but not on a plane with the Suites.

Charles-M. Widor (born in 1845), distinguished French organist, composer, and teacher; author of five Symphonies: in F minor (Op. 16); A major (Op. 54)—the utterance of a wholesome, cheerful spirit; F minor (with Organ); *Antique* Symphony (with closing Chorus); and *Sinfonia Sacra* (with Organ). Widor originated the idea of *Symphonies for the Organ*, and composed eight such, noted for originality and vigor; also two with specific titles:

Romane, and *Gothique*. This novel, and surely not inconsistent species of symphonic expression has found several imitators.

Alexander Mackensie (born in 1847) of Scotland, produced no Symphonies, but has written a number of Overtures (*Britannia*, 1894) and orchestral Rhapsodies, that possess enduring qualities.

August Klughardt (Saxony, 1847-1902), the author of four notable Symphonies, and a fine Symphonic-Poem, *Lenore*.

Philipp Scharwenka (1847-1917), an eminent Polish-Prussian composer and teacher; in 1891-2 in New York, with his equally famous brother Xaver Scharwenka. Philipp wrote two Symphonies and two excellent Symphonic-Poems, of which *Traum und Wirklichkeit* was most favorably received.

England, following the brilliant era of Henry Purcell (1658-1695), the greatest musical genius that Great Britain has given to the world, produced a goodly number of respectable, though not outstanding composers. Then, about a half-century later, that nation began a march of progress in matters musical that proved to be as significant as it was vigorous.

Probably the first master to confirm this momentous upward movement was *Charles Hubert H. Parry* (1848-1918), one of the finest and most eminent musicians of whom England can boast, equally distinguished as a prolific composer of instrumental and choral works of many types, and as an exceptionally keen, serious and erudite literary writer. His well-known book, *The Art of Music* (1893-6) is a genuine masterpiece of literary criticism and reflection. Parry produced five Symphonies (the first one in 1882), which reveal the musical master mind, fertile, virile, akin to Bach in polyphonic solidity and acuteness. The most popular one of the five in England is probably the Third, in C, known as the *English* Symphony (1889).*

Frederic H. Cowen (1852), born in Jamaica of English parents, and distinguished as a composer and conductor. Of his six Symphonies, the Third, in C minor (*Scandinavian*—1880), and the Fourth, in B♭ minor (*Welsh*—1884), are the best known. Arresting and individual melodic conception, fine poetic sensibility, and scholarly use of orchestral resources, invest his music with great charm.

Hans Huber (1852-1921), a Swiss composer of distinction; conservative, true to classic principles though poetically minded. His music does not often reveal the vital spark, but it is unaffected and wholesome, often vigorous, and structurally above criticism. Six Symphonies stand to his credit: No. I, D minor, Op. 63, *Tell*—"Oppression and Liberation of Switzerland;" No. II, E minor, Op. 115, *Böcklin* (named for a Swiss landscape painter) —the Finale of which is an admirable set of Variations inscribed "Metamorphoses, inspired by pictures of Böcklin;" No. III, C minor, Op. 118, *Heroic*, introducing "God save

---

*See the fine tribute to *Hubert Parry* by his close friend J. A. Fuller-Maitland, in the *Musical Quarterly* of July, 1919.

the King" in its first Movement; further, the *Academic*, the *Romantic* and the *Swiss*—each one bearing a characteristic title, but all true to the spirit of absolute music.

The progressive trend of music in Great Britain is further signalized by *Charles Villiers Stanford* (Dublin, born in 1852), a very eminent Irish composer and conductor, the author of seven distinguished Symphonies, which testify to his fertile and genial melodic conception and other meritorious musical qualities. No. I, in B♭, appeared in 1876; No. II, in D minor, *Elegiac*, in 1882; his Third, in F minor, *Irish* (1887), is probably the best known and most admired, at home and abroad; No. IV, in F (1889); No. V, in D, *L'Allegro ed il Pensieroso;* No. VI, in E♭ (1904); and No. VII, in D minor (1904)—all creations of superior worth.

Moritz Moszkowski (1854-1925), Polish-Silesian composer of the amiable, effectful type, elegant and brilliant, though somewhat superficial, produced one Symphonic-Poem, *Joan of Arc*, that was extremely well received in its day.

Ernest Chausson (1855-1899), an eminently endowed French composer, whose career was lamentally brief. He wrote one Symphony, a Symphonic-Poem *Viviane*, and other orchestral works of arresting quality and singular merit, distinguished by a degree of originality, a delicacy of fancy and technical proficiency that betoken true genius.

Christian Sinding (Norway, born in 1856), another notable exponent of Norwegian musical thought and expression, a worthy national counterpart of Grieg; though broader than the latter in his views and methods. Sinding wrote two Symphonies: No. I, in D minor, Op. 21, which reflects a vigorous dramatic spirit; and No. II, in D major, Op. 85 (1890), containing three Movements only, and of a bright, friendly character.

* * *

Edward Elgar

Edward William Elgar (born in 1857) is an imposing figure in the present-day musical history of Europe, a composer whose contributions further confirm the strong upward swing of the musical art in England. His conception is original, his manner somewhat severe, at first sight apparently abstruse and obscure; but he is eminently sincere, steadfast in his pursuit of that which is true and noble, and his absolute domination of every technical condition of musical structure assures his art solidity and enduring quality. Hence, his music makes a more and more profound and convincing impression at every renewed hearing. Of his two splendid Symphonies, No. I, in A♭, Op. 55 (1908), is no doubt the most popular; although the Second, in E♭, Op. 63 (1911—a *Memorial to King Edward*) is conceded to be more masterly, and, despite the charge of a lack of thematic interest, compels increasing recognition and admiration. Besides these, Elgar has composed two Concert-Overtures of symphonic proportions: *Froissart*, a picture of the days of Chivalry; and *In the South*, the fruit of a visit to Italy; further, the symphonic Study

Falstaff (1913), two Suites, and the unique and masterly orchestral Variations, *Enigma* (1899).*

Gustave Charpentier (born in 1860) an eminently gifted French composer, who also found time to engage in philanthropic activities. He has written no Symphony of the traditional type, but a Symphonic-Poem *Napoli* (1891), a symphonic drama *La Vie du Poëte* (1892), and an orchestral Suite *Impressions d' Italie*, that have been received with very great favor.

* * *

Gustav Mahler

This extraordinary musician, equally famous as composer and conductor, added another brilliant name to Bohemia's proud list of masters of music. Mahler attracted attention primarily through his complete and powerful equipment for the art of conducting; but he soon developed an absorbing ambition to become a composer as well, and about 1890 he began to astonish the musical world with elaborate orchestral works, some of them truly colossal in scope.

Gustav Mahler was born in a Bohemian village, July 7, 1860; he studied in Vienna, at the Conservatory (Anton Bruckner being one of his teachers) and also at the University. In 1880 he began a series of engagements as conductor—Hall (in Upper Austria), Kassel (1883), Prague (1885), Leipsic (1886), Pest (1888), Hamburg (1891), Vienna (1897)—where his efforts were crowned

*See *A Study of Elgar* by D. G. Mason in the *Musical Quarterly* of April, 1917.

with phenomenal success, and his reputation as a conductor of rare genius, energy, and judgment grew apace. In 1907 he came to New York, as chief conductor at the Metropolitan Opera, and in 1909 became the leader and reorganizer of the Philharmonic Symphony Orchestra. Early in 1911 his health began to fail, and later in that same year death overtook him, in Vienna.

Great men, whose conception and methods are of bewildering originality and force, almost invariably—especially in music—give occasion for more or less violent partisanship; but rarely have differences in judgment and opinion been more acute than in the case of Mahler the *composer*—about his unrivalled genius as a conductor there has never been any question. His advocates proclaim him and his creations as gigantic; the opposing group calls them merely bombastic.* The truth, as in all such controversies, probably lies midway between the two extremes. It is undeniable that Mahler was sincere in his artistic aspirations, and that it was the heroism and magnitude of his spirit that impelled him to select, naturally, the broadest canvas for his musical projects. A vein of pessimism, even misanthropy, seems to course through his musical utterance, which is at times downright ironical. But those who knew him declare that this was not inherent in his nature; that he was noble-hearted, a loyal friend, sensitive, and profoundly poetic. In his music he seeks to reflect human life, which we all know has its tragedies and its harsh discords.

Mahler composed nine Symphonies,—besides sketches for a tenth, which he wished to have destroyed. No. I, D major (1891), called *Titan*, is romantic, pastoral, in general character. No. II, C minor (1895) is serious and pathetic throughout its six Movements, and, side by side with episodes of unquestionable beauty, there are some (in the

*See the Review by Carl Engel in the *Musical Quarterly* of January, 1923, pages 150—153.

third Movement) that are grotesque; an Alto solo is interwoven in the fourth Movement, and vocal solos and Choruses in the Finale. No. III, D minor (1896) presents two large Divisions, the first of which consists of one Movement only, while the other embraces five—six Movements in all; the fifth one is a parody: a Chorus for boys' voices relates a meeting between Jesus and Peter in Heaven. No. IV, G major (1901) appears to lend confirmation to those who accuse Mahler of misanthropy: it is a travesty (replete with scorn and ridicule) on the Learned Pedant, pictured in four Scenes—(1) Contemplative, (2) Deliberate, (3) Reposeful, (4) Very slow (with a Soprano solo). No. V, (1903), known as the *Giant* Symphony, begins in C♯ minor and ends in D. It is a thoroughly serious work, in five Movements, which portray the emotions of a sorrowing Soul, finally emerging from pain and despair into the light of life. The first Movement is a kind of Funeral March, opening with this Theme:

No. VI, in A minor (1906) will scarcely admit of any other designation than the determined utterances of a misanthropic, almost cynical nature. No. VII (1908) begins in B minor and ends in C; it contains five Movements, is powerful, and comes to a joyous conclusion.

No. VIII, in E♭ (1910), is Mahler's most famous Symphony. It is called the *Symphony of the Thousand*, in view of the enormous apparatus it engages, and the stupendous scope of the work. In truth, it is not a "Symphony" at all, but a Cantata, and should be so named. To the fullest orchestral contingent are added seven Soloists, and three Choruses, one of Boys. Its chief Theme is a vocal intonation of the famous ninth-century hymn, *Veni, Creator Spiritus*.

The Ninth, and last, Symphony, in D, was written in 1911, the year of his death.

It is difficult, almost impossible, to appraise and characterize each one of Mahler's remarkable Symphonies with a degree of accuracy. While each one exhibits some distinctive traits, they are all fundamentally similar, and indefinable save in a general way, as pointed out.*

* * *

Claude Debussy (1862-1918) of French birth, marks the opening of a new and most significant epoch in the history of music. Not that Debussy was the sole originator of his novel language (or dialect?) of tone, for since the days of

---

*The student is warmly urged to read Allan Lincoln Langley's valuable article, *Justice for Gustav Mahler*, in the *Musical Quarterly* of April, 1926.

César Franck, and even earlier, there were vague foreshadowings of a different spirit in the tone-realm. But Debussy is a very conspicuous figure in the newer movement, and doubtless the most important and influential one.

The new (modern) epoch is simply one of greater *personal freedom* in the choice and presentation of musical ideas; the classic traditions, and historic formulas, are more or less radically abandoned, as barriers to the unhampered expression of intensely subjective, original, poetic, mystic, impressionistic or realistic conceptions. The modern manner is signalized by the unrestrained use of tone-resources; it repudiates time-honored structural regulations, often dislocates and jumbles the consistent rhythmic patterns, multiplies dissonances to an apparently exaggerated extent, and ignores the dictates of natural, sustained melody. In its extremest phases it characterizes the *Ultramodern* trend (not alone in France, but in Germany, Russia and other European countries as well).

Debussy has left no genuine Symphony, but a number of fascinating Symphonic-Poems, Suites, and other orchestral pieces (like *L' Après-midi d'un faune*), among which the "Symphonic Sketches," *La Mer* (1903-5), most nearly resemble the symphonic type, and are exceedingly popular. The latter consist of three Movements, every one of which presents many passages of exquisite beauty.*

---

*See the articles, the first by G. Jean-Aubry, and the second by J.-G. Prod'homme: *Claude Debussy*, and *Claude Achille Debussy*, both in the *Musical Quarterly* of October, 1918.

Felix Weingartner (born in 1863), Dalmatian conductor and composer of distinction and authority, familiar to concert-goers in America as a brilliant orchestral leader, has written three Symphonies: in G, Op. 23; in E♭, Op. 29; and in E, Op. 49—besides an unlisted Fourth; all of which display an eminent grade of musicianship.

Frederick Delius, born (1863) in England of German parents, has written no Symphony, but his compositions include Symphonic-Poems and many other works for orchestra, that manifest unique and remarkable original traits, and rare command of the orchestra. His strange and fascinating genius stands alone. Of his Tone-Poems, *The Song of a Great City* (Paris) is especially admirable.

* * *

Richard Strauss

This eminent musical master mind, whose extraordinary genius seemed for a time destined to make him the successor of Richard Wagner, was born in Munich, Germany, in 1864. During his earlier creative period he adhered loyally to classic traditions and methods; later, the individual quality and tremendous energy of his musical spirit impelled him beyond these limits, and he soon proved himself to be one of the most original and forceful exponents of the modern school of composition.

Strauss has not attained to the universal importance of Wagner, nor has he reached the level of the great classic masters; a certain whimsicality, reckless originality, structural inconsistency, have stood in his way. Still, he has gained, justly, world-renown. His style is refreshing, and calculated to impress at once; every line he draws is strikingly vivid; his rhythms are singularly alert and vital; his melodies unique, yet by no means abnormal—his song *Traum durch die Dämmerung* is one of the most exquisite lyrics ever penned;—and his control of every factor of musical material, and of the orchestra, is unsurpassable.

The attention of the musical world was first arrested by his Symphonic-Poems: *Aus Italien* (1886)—more properly a Suite, but with the usual four Movements, in traditional designs; *Macbeth* (1886); *Don Juan* (1888); *Tod und Verklärung* (1889), which made a most powerful impression, partly skeptical and adverse, but generally favorable and even enthusiastic; *Till Eulenspiegel* (1894); *Also sprach Zarathustra* (1894); *Don Quixote* (1897); and *Ein Heldenleben* (1898).*

His first Symphony, in D minor, was composed earlier than all of these (1881), and afforded many proofs of the unusual genius of the youth, though still obviously undeveloped. The Second Symphony, in F minor, came in 1884; the Third—*Sinfonia Domestica*, a picturesque, capricious, but at times extremely beautiful, and in all of its parts a clever musical portrayal of domestic life—did not appear until twenty years later (1903), all of the Symphonic-Poems have intervened. His Fourth, and latest, the *Alpine* Symphony, was written in 1915. This has been

*See *A Study of Strauss* by Daniel G. Mason, in the *Musical Quarterly* of April, 1916.

variously adjudged; it is noisy, and presents but little of lasting value; the instrumentation, naturally, is superb, dazzling (serving as a mantle of charity), but many of the ideas seem lacking in novelty and force. It is less of a Symphony than a Suite, consisting, as it does, of a numerous series of descriptive Episodes ("Night, Sunrise, The Ascent, ... On the Summit, Vision, Elegy, Calm before the Storm, ... Descent, Sunset, Night"—to mention the chief pictures). The "Ascent" is initiated with this splendid, spirited Theme:

Ex. 159. "The Ascent" — R. STRAUSS (1915)

* * *

Alexander Glazounov (born in 1865), a prominent personality in Russian music history, was a pupil of Rimsky-Korsakov. He was distinguished as a prolific composer of music of many types, with the larger forms liberally represented; also he was a successful teacher. His music is extremely scholarly, founded upon classic conceptions and methods, fascinating in its thematic manipulation, clear and effective in its structure; and yet it conveys the impression of emanating somewhat more largely from the mind than from the emotions.

Glazounov has produced eight excellent Symphonies, the first one, in E, as early as 1882 (at the age of seventeen), the others following at fairly regular intervals. They are all virile, thoroughly interesting, harmonious and ingratiating, preponderantly cheerful in mood, and present very frequent episodes of unique charm and enduring beauty. No. II, F♯ minor, Op. 16 (1886), is dedicated to Liszt; the Third, D major, Op. 33 (1890), to Tchaikovsky. No. V, in B♭, Op. 55 (1896), one of his best and most widely esteemed Symphonies, is genial, sunny and vigorous, exerting a powerful appeal to the interest and sympathy of the hearer. The first Movement is skilfully built upon this Theme:

The second Movement is a delightful *Scherzo*, akin to the Fairy-visions of Mendelssohn; the third Movement is a beautiful lyric, intimate in mood, and glowing in tone; the Finale has a military character. Glazounov's later Symphonies all attest his superb technical proficiency, and his advancing maturity. Besides these Symphonies, Glazounov has composed a number of Symphonic-Poems, Suites and Overtures.

Paul Dukas (Paris, born in 1865) is another noteworthy exponent of the progressive modern trend in France. He has written an excellent Symphonic-Poem, *L'Apprenti-Sorcier* (1897), a Symphony (1896), and several Overtures.

Granville Bantock (London, born in 1868), an uncommonly gifted composer, who has exerted a marked influence upon English music, not alone by his own writings, but also through his unselfish and powerful advocacy of the works of younger English composers. He has created two Choral Symphonies; also the Festival Symphony *Christus,* a *Hebrides* Symphony, a *Pagan* Symphony, a number of Tone-Poems, Suites and Overtures—all highly effective, picturesque, and aglow with orchestral color, of which he is a consummate master.*

Alexander Scriabin (Moscow, 1872-1915) was one of the most revolutionary, daringly original exponents of ultra-modern musical tendencies that Russia has brought forth. His methods exhibit steadily increasing antagonism to the principles and traditions of organized, conventional tone-association. More and more he employed music as a medium for the exposition of his mystical speculations, a subtle subject, with which ordinary musical ways and means are not concerned. Hence, he saw himself con-

---

*See the article *Granville Bantock* by Herbert Antcliffe in the *Musical Quarterly* of July, 1918.

strained to invent new forms, and he even emphasized the relation of colors and perfumes to musical effects.*

Scriabin wrote three Symphonies: No. I, in E, with Chorus; No. II, in C minor, Op. 29, a work which may claim unique significance (in its way), and that won recognition beyond Russian borders. It consists of five Movements, the first one a brief Fantasy; the second sombre, disquieting, though including passages of winning quality; the third an Idyl; the fourth a picture of inner and outer storms; the Finale heroic in tone. No. III, in C major, Op. 43, traces a program of which the title is *The Divine Poem;* it embraces three Movements: "Conflict; Voluptuousness; Divinity," connected without pauses. One commentator finds this work "as far as mere beauty of sound is concerned, superior to almost anything else he has written." This was followed, as a kind of sequel, by the *Poem of Ecstasy* (1908), which is said "to express the joy of untrammeled activity."

Another stage in the ascending course of musical aspiration and solid achievement in Great Britian, is represented by *Ralph Vaughan Williams* (born in 1872). His methods are bold and original. Of his Symphonies, the one entitled *London* (1917) has been much lauded in England and elsewhere. It is not Music in the abstract sense of the classic masterworks, and one searches in vain for real Beauty. It is more like an intricate, incredibly clever geometrical drawing, of which the lines are pointed in

*See *The Significance of Scriabin*, by Herbert Antcliffe, in the *Musical Quarterly* of July, 1924.

tones. It pictures a great city, with its dull, sombre, throbbing base, occasional flashes of light, and all its din and turmoil by night and by day; and the extensive infusion of cockney strains locates it geographically as London. A sort of Leading Theme, with which it opens, and which recurs as the impressive ending, has the following pregnant form:

Besides this, Williams has composed a *Pastoral* Symphony, a *Sea* Symphony (choral), Suites, Impressions, and other orchestral works.

Max Reger (Bavaria, 1873-1916), a much discussed personality, who made a deep impression by his stupendous contrapuntal mastership (tempting comparison with Bach), and whose most successful field was that of organ music. He wrote a remarkable *Sinfonietta*, A major, Op. 90, that strikes one observer as a "deluge of notes, without music."*

Sergei Rachmaninov (Russia, born in 1873), one of the most richly endowed and serious minded of the younger Russian school, whose three Symphonies (1895, 1906, 1915 —*The Bells*, with Chorus) bear testimony to the origin-

*See *The Two Reger-legends*, by Ernest Brennecke, in the *Musical Quarterly* of July, 1922.

ality, superb craftsmanship and nobility of his creative style.*

Gustav Holst (born in 1874), an Anglo-Swedish composer of distinction; the author of a Symphony *Cotswolds* (1900), a Symphonic-Poem *Indra* (1903), and several orchestral Suites, the most popular one of which is *The Planets* (1915), a work of superior merit.

Josef Suk (Bohemia, born in 1874), an uncommonly gifted composer and violinist, in some of whose creations a strong spiritual relationship to Schubert's spontaneous and fertile melodic conception is recognizable. He has produced two Symphonies, one in E, and another, *Asrael*, in E minor, Op. 27, besides Symphonic-Poems and Overtures. *Asrael* comprises five Movements; its character is preponderantly sombre, at times tragic.

* * *

Our final group of notable present-day composers embraces names that are almost exclusively identified with Modern and Ultramodern tendencies. In common with a few earlier writers, cited above, they can hardly claim recognition as Masters of the Symphony, and yet their historic importance cannot be denied or overlooked.

Very prominent among these Ultramoderns is *Arnold Schönberg* (Vienna, born in 1874), an eccentric but interesting, perhaps momentous composer. His harmony textbook is regarded with mistrust, as crude and boastfully

---

*See *Sergei Rachmaninov*, by Victor Balaiev, in the *Musical Quarterly* of July, 1927.

iconoclastic. He has written a *Kammersymphonie* in E; a Symphonic-Poem, and other orchestral pieces.*

Then follow, chronologically, as usual:

Maurice Ravel (born in 1875), an uncommonly gifted, original and adroit French composer, who has written no Symphonies, but in other forms has produced numerous orchestral works of unique merit.

Ernest Bloch (Geneva, born in 1880), since 1916 a citizen of the United States, an eminently gifted composer, of ardent poetic and imaginative temperament, profound musical erudition and great skill. To his two earlier Symphonic-Poems, *Orientale* (1896), and *Vivre—Aimer* (1900), he has added a Symphony in C♯ minor (1902), and one in F (1918—*Israël*, with Hebrew themes). Two other Symphonic-Poems followed in 1905, *Hiver—Printemps;* and quite recently an ambitious *American* Symphony (1928), which he calls an Epic Rhapsody "written in love for this country," concluding with an original Anthem which "as its apotheosis, symbolizes the Destiny, the Mission of America." The Symphony is constructed entirely upon this Anthem, which the composer "hopes will become known and beloved." Critical estimates of the work differ (as usual) but that it has moments of great beauty and genuine impressiveness is generally conceded.†

Igor Stravinsky (Russia, born in 1882), a composer of very marked originality, extreme in his views regarding the

*See the article *Schönberg and Beyond*, by Egon Wellesz, in the *Musical Quarterly* of January, 1916.
†See *Ernest Bloch*, by Guido Gatti, in the *Musical Quarterly* of January, 1921. 1921.

future of music, and displaying remarkable force and skill in putting them into practice. He has produced a Symphony in E♭, orchestral Suites (*Le Rossignol*, 1914), six Ballets (*Pétrouchka*, 1911; *Le Sacre du Printemps*, 1913), and various other orchestral numbers, all of which have compelled keen interest and (with some hearers) genuine enthusiasm.*

Sergei Prokofiev (born in 1891), a Russian composer of ultramodern aims, whose recent orchestral Ballet *Le Pas d' Acier* (1920)—representing (1) "The Stories and Legends of the Countryside," and (2) "The Mechanism of the Factories"—has been called a Bolshevik Ballet, and is so noisy that "its frightful din was a continuous reminder of General Sherman's definition of War" (to cite the words of a sufficiently trustworthy observer). This impression, which is concomitant with a hearing of his works, is somewhat softened by an earlier composition, *Classical* Symphony Op. 25 (1917), the result of "an idea of catching the spirit of Mozart, and putting down that which, if he were now living, Mozart might have put into his scores" (Felix Borowski).

Arthur Honegger (born in 1892), a French composer of Swiss parentage, author of a "Mimic Symphony" *Horace Victorieux;* a Symphonic-Poem *Pastorale d' Été;* and, recently, an orchestral sketch, *Pacific 231*—the musical description of the course of a locomotive, very cleverly executed, but devoid of beauty.

---

*See *Impressions of I. Stravinsky*, by C. Stanley Wise, in the *Musical Quarterly* of April, 1916.

Paul Hindemith (born in 1895), gifted Hessian violinist and promising composer, who appears to strike a happy medium between reaction and progress, writing at times in the controlled vein of the older, more sober conception, and again adopting the extravagant methods of the ultra-moderns. He has written an orchestral Suite (Dances from one of his Operas), but as yet no genuine Symphony.

Erich W. Korngold (born in 1897), a singularly precocious Moravian composer; he is the youngest, and therefore the last upon our list. He has written a *Sinfonietta*, which, in common with his other works, has aroused decided interest and met with no little approval. The appraisal of his extremely promising talent, and of his possible artistic significance, must rest with the future. The same is true of the other younger men in the last pages of our list; a list, which, be it here admitted, *does not claim to be an exhaustive one.*

* * *

Modern and Ultramodern music seem to mark but little if any real advance, but rather an increasing weakness, and retrograde movement. The classic ideals have not been furthered. No actual progress has been made beyond Beethoven; Brahms is apparently the only master of the post-Beethoven period who earnestly and single-mindedly fostered the classic reality of absolute music.*

The multiplication of dissonant, harsh, ugly, cacophonous sounds, and the open defiance of a central tonality

---

*See *The Symphony since Beethoven*, by Felix Weingartner.

(which would seem to be as essential as the indispensable protecting law of a planetary system)—these traits in modern music are disquieting and unpromising enough. But the most fatal element is its formlessness. The sane domination of order and organization is supplanted by the impulses of fretful, unguarded imagination. Consequently, modern music is diffuse instead of compact, eccentric instead of concentric, elusive instead of comprehensible and inviting. These attributes militate against the hoped-for "return to Mozart," and lead the art farther and farther away from its pure, orderly mission; their influence makes for disintegration; the subjective completely overpowers the needful objective.*

However, as we said near the end of the Fifth Chapter: Some good will come from all this; these experiments, though often painful to witness, mean Progress in certain directions. "God is Love," but, also "God is Law;" and some day a divinely-minded (i.e., Law-abiding) Genius of a new era will appear, who will guide all these new impulses into the proper channels, and produce Symphonies as great as those of Beethoven—perhaps even, by just so much as he does so, greater than Beethoven's.†

* * *

*Ernest Newman, in a recent article in the *New York Times* says: "The 'new music' is plainly not making much progress with Everyman." And: "Everyman's objections resolve themselves finally into these two: he feels that much of this 'new music' is a purely cerebral exercise on the part of the composer . . . . and he feels that even when the language is perfectly lucid, the mental state it reveals is not one that attracts him . . . . "

†See *Modernists, Classics and Immortality in Music*, by O. G. Sonneck, in the *Musical Quarterly* of October, 1925.

THE MODERN ERA

QUESTIONS FOR REVIEW

1. Group the names given in this Chapter according to nationality. Which composers were of Austrian descent?
2. Which represent Germany?
3. Which were of French descent?
4. Which represent Great Britain?
5. Which were Russian?
6. Which were Scandinavian?
7. Which were Swiss?
8. Which were Bohemian?
9. Which other nationalities are represented?
10. Who wrote a *Forest* Symphony?
11. Outline the biography of Anton Bruckner.
12. What qualities distinguish Bruckner's music?
13. Who wrote an *Ocean* Symphony?
14. Who wrote the *Rustic Wedding* Symphony?
15. Who wrote *L'Arlésienne* Suite?
16. Who wrote the *Peer Gynt* Suite?
17. Who wrote the *Antar* Symphony?
18. Who wrote Symphonies for the Organ?
19. Mention some of Elgar's creations.
20. Outline the biography of Gustav Mahler.
21. What qualities distinguish his music?
22. Who wrote *L'Après-midi d'un faune?*
23. What qualities characterize the music of Richard Strauss?
24. Mention some of the Tone-Poems of Strauss.
25. What are the characteristics of Scriabin's music?
26. Who wrote a famous *London* Symphony?

27. Who wrote *Le Sacre du Printemps*?
28. What differentiates the Modern and Ultramodern schools from the Classic?

References

Rosenfield	The Musical Chronicle (Bruckner).
Weingartner	The Symphony since Beethoven.
Weissmann	Problems of Modern Music.
Buckley	Sir Edward Elgar.
Newman	Elgar.
Finck	Richard Strauss: the Man and his Works.
Newman	Richard Strauss.
Rolland	Richard Strauss; Debussy. (In *Musicians of Today*.)
Porte	Sir Edward Elgar.
Mason	Elgar. (In *Contemporary Composers*.)
Montagu-Nathan	Rimsky-Korsakov. History of Russian Music.
Stefan, Gustav	Mahler; A Study of his Personality and Work.
Rosenfield	Musical Portraits (Mahler).
Rimsky-Korsakov	My Life.
Liebich	Debussy.
Hill	Debussy; Ravel. (In *Modern French Music*.
Aubrey	French Music of Today.
Hull	Dictionary of Modern Music and Musicians.

See also:
  Index to *The Musical Quarterly*.
  Index to *La Revue Musicale*.

THE MODERN ERA

Oxford History of Music (new edition, *Bibliography* by Calvocoressi).

Subject Index to Periodicals. Library Association, London.

Current Magazine Contents.

Readers' Guide.

Blom. General Index to Modern Musical Literature in the English Language.

ILLUSTRATIVE RECORDS

Records: B—Brunswick; C—Columbia; E—Edison; H—His Master's Voice; O—Odeon; Pa—Parlophone; Po—Polydor; V—Victor; Vo—Vocalion.

Music Mentioned in Chapter VIII:

Bruckner—Symphony No. 7, in E major   Po.
Rimsky-Korsakov—Antar   C.

EPILOGUE

American Symphonists

A TREATISE on "Masters of the Symphony" would be unfairly incomplete without respectful mention of the achievements of American composers in the significant field of orchestral production.

Admitting that no rival of Beethoven has yet arisen in America, it is indisputable that the best products of this country in the larger musical forms are fully as valuable and encouraging as very many of those of even celebrated contemporary European composers.

But before stating the important case of our musical countrymen, the student is urged to give earnest attention to an article upon *The American Composer: The Victim of his Friends*, by John Tasker Howard, in the *Musical Quarterly* of July, 1922; and the trenchant and impartial essay by O. G. Sonneck, *The American Composer, and the American Music Publisher*, in the *Musical Quarterly* of January, 1923 (pages 122 to 125, 132).

Our list, chronological as usual, begins with a musical personage of considerable importance in his day, and one of the first American-born composers to employ the larger forms: *William H. Fry* (Philadelphia, 1813-1864), author of two Operas, four Symphonies (performed in New York in 1853), Overtures, etc.

Equally noted was *George F. Bristow* (Brooklyn, 1825-1898) violinist, organist and composer. He produced five Symphonies, of which the *Arcadian* (1874) was deservedly popular.

Ellsworth C. Phelps (Connecticut, 1827-1913), author of two Symphonies, *Hiawatha* (New York, 1880), and *Emancipation*, four Symphonic-Poems and numerous other works.

The Dean of American symphonists was *John K. Paine* (Portland, Maine, 1839-1906), an eminent organist, teacher and composer, thoroughly serious, and firm in his adherence to classic aims. Besides two Symphonies (in C minor, 1876; and in A, *Spring*, 1880), he created two Symphonic-Poems, and other orchestral works.

W. W. Gilchrist (Jersey City, 1846—Easton, Pa., 1916), conductor, organist and composer. His First Symphony, in C, was played by the Philadelphia Symphony Orchestra in 1910. He also wrote a second Symphony, in D, besides Chamber-music, Choral works and many songs and anthems.

F. Grant Gleason (Connecticut, 1848-1903), author of a Symphonic-Poem, *Edris*, Op. 21 (1896), two symphonic Cantatas, Op. 17 and Op. 20, and a number of other noteworthy compositions, instrumental and vocal.

Arthur Foote (Salem, Massachusetts, born in 1853), one of J. K. Paine's many pupils who achieved distinction. He has written no Symphony, but several Suites, an Overture and other orchestral pieces, which reveal marked individuality and a fine sense of structural proportions.

Adolph M. Foerster (Pittsburg, 1854—), has composed a fine Symphonic-Poem, *Sigrid*, and additional orchestral works.

George W. Chadwick (Lowell, Massachusetts, 1854—), one of the first American composers to study abroad, has written three Symphonies of outstanding excellence, in C major (1882), B♭ (1886), and F (1894), besides a *Sinfonietta* in D (1904), and a *Suite Symphonique* (1910), a large number of Symphonic-Poems, and other orchestral works, greatly esteemed, both at home and abroad, for their sterling qualities, their distinction, solidity, and genuine beauty.*

Arthur Bird (Massachusetts, 1856—), gifted American composer, has produced an excellent Symphony, in A (New York, 1886), three orchestral Suites, and other notable works.

George Templeton Strong (New York, 1856—), has spent much of his life in Europe. He composed three Symphonies, one of which, in F, *In den Bergen*, was performed in New York in 1887; also a Symphonic-Poem, and other orchestral works of distinction.

Henry Schoenefeld (Milwaukee, 1857—), the able author of two Symphonies, *Pastoral* and *Springtime*.

Edgar Stillman Kelley (Wisconsin, 1857—), who was also among the first to turn Eastward and seek to deepen his

---

*See the article *George W. Chadwick*, by Carl Engel, in the *Musical Quarterly* of July, 1924.

musical consciousness by contact with European teachers. He has produced three Symphonies, *Gulliver* (1896), *New England* (1913), and *California;* two orchestral Suites; and many other instrumental works. His music attests superior natural endowment, individuality, solidity, and eminent command of all technical resources.

Harry Rowe Shelley (Connecticut, 1858—), noted organist and composer, the author of two Symphonies (one, in E♭, performed in New York in 1897), and other orchestral works.

Edward A. MacDowell (New York, 1861-1908), an opulently gifted composer and excellent pianist, whose sensitive poetic musical nature and subtle subjective manner of expression, always exquisite and refined in his smaller sketches and equally adequate in larger forms, has endeared him to the hearts of his people. Some critics regard him as the leading exponent of American music; certain it is, that he is the most widely known and universally esteemed tone-poet of this nation. MacDowell's orchestral creations consist of three admirable Symphonic-Poems; two Suites, of which the *Indian* (1897) enjoys great popularity; and fragments of a Symphony based on the *Chanson de Roland* (1891), which was not completed.

Arthur B. Whiting (Cambridge, Massachusetts, 1861—), author of an Overture (1885), and a few other orchestral compositions.

Henry Holden Huss (Newark, New Jersey, 1862—), has produced no Symphony, but his compositions include Concertos and Chamber music.

Ernest R. Kroeger (St. Louis, 1862—), author of a Symphony in B♭, six excellent Overtures, and a Suite, *Lalla Rookh*.

Horatio W. Parker (Massachusetts, 1863-1919), an outstanding personality in the history of American music, distinguished for the seriousness of his aims and his fidelity to the principles of classic art; and for the solidity of his artistic workmanship, especially in choral composition; also for his success as teacher. His two exceptionally fine Oratorios, and other works, brought him international fame. One Symphony, in C minor (1885), stands to his credit; to which are added a Symphonic-Poem (Op. 50), and three Overtures.

Turning for the first time to the consideration of woman's achievement in the sphere of musical creation, we encounter the distinguished name of *Mrs. H. H. A. Beach* (Henniker, New Hampshire, 1867—), who has manifested her very unusual power of origination, individuality, and a superb mastery of all the details of tone-language, technical and structural, in a great variety of larger and smaller forms. Her one Symphony, *Gaelic* (1896), has been cordially received and lauded on both sides of the Atlantic.

Exactly contemporaneous with Mrs. Beach is another woman-composer, *Margaret Ruthven Lang* (Boston, 1867—), who has not ventured upon symphonic ground, but who has produced several very creditable Overtures and other orchestral pieces.

Henry F. Gilbert (Massachusetts, 1868-1928), an eminently gifted and skilful composer, who labored successfully to arouse deeper interest in the Indian and Negro music of this country; he wrote a symphonic Prologue, *Riders to the Sea* (1915), a symphonic Ballet, *The Dance in Place Congo* (1918), and other interesting and effective orchestral creations.*

Louis A. Coerne (New Jersey, 1870-1922), a musician of estimable qualities, the composer of a Symphonic-Poem, *Hiawatha* (1893), two orchestral Tone-Poems, and other instrumental works.

Howard A. Brockway (Brooklyn, 1870—), a composer of substantial merit; the author of a Symphony (1895), an orchestral Suite (1903), and other pieces that excel in conception and execution. His special study has been the folk-songs of Kentucky. His Symphony in D was first given in Boston in 1907.

Henry K. Hadley (Massachusetts, 1871—), an eminent writer and conductor, whose orchestral compositions include four Symphonies, the last one of which, in D minor (1911), *North, East, South, West*, presents many admirable features; further, several Overtures, two Tone-Poems, an Oriental Suite, and various other works.

Bertram Shapleigh (Boston, 1871—), a versatile artist, of keen mentality and lively imagination. He has produced two Symphonies; also Tone-Poems, Suites, and smaller orchestral compositions.

*See the article, *An American Composer*, by Olin Downes, in the *Musical Quarterly* of January, 1918.

Frederick S. Converse (Massachusetts, 1871—), a musician of pronounced individuality, whose arresting creations exhibit both vigor and refinement. Among these there is a Symphony in D minor (1898), one in C minor (1920), and one in E; also five Symphonic-Poems, two Overtures, etc. His opera, *The Pipe of Desire* (1906), was the first American work to be presented at the Metropolitan Opera in New York.

Rubin Goldmark (New York, 1872—), a worthy successor to his distinguished uncle Karl Goldmark. No Symphony has come from his pen; but an Overture *Hiawatha* (1900), and two Tone-Poems, *Samson* (1914), and *Requiem* (1919), attest his superior musicianship, rare endowment, serious and poetically disposed temperament.

Edward Burlingame Hill (Massachusetts, 1872—), a composer and teacher of outstanding artistic qualities; he has recently written a Symphony, in B♭, Op. 34 (1927), that has been received with great favor. His earlier orchestral works include a Symphonic-Poem, Symphonic Pantomimes, and pieces, of substantial merit.

Daniel Gregory Mason (Massachusetts, 1873—), a versatile, exceedingly conscientious and earnest artist, exceptionally endowed musically and in other intellectual respects as well. He has produced one Symphony, in C minor, Op. 11 (1916), and a few Chamber-music works of sterling quality, besides a number of valuable, scholarly books and critical essays on musical subjects.

Arne Oldberg (Ohio, 1874—), an eminently gifted composer and pianist, the author of three excellent Symphonies, in F minor, C minor and (again) F minor, respectively; two Overtures, and other works, orchestral and concerted, of marked merit.

Mortimer Wilson (Iowa, 1876—), noted teacher and composer, the author of five valuable Symphonies, a Suite *A Country Wedding*, an Overture *New Orleans* (1920), besides a number of compositions of Chamber-music type.

Ernest H. Schelling (New Jersey, 1876—), spent the first thirty years of his life almost entirely in Europe, where he pursued his musical studies and developed his extremely ample and pronounced artistic gifts. Since 1905 he has made America his home. He has written one Symphony, and a limited number of other thoughtful compositions that manifest distinction and skill.

John Alden Carpenter (Illinois, 1876—), has attracted serious attention with his Songs, the conspicuous merits of which are likewise evident in his few orchestral compositions, which include one Symphony (1917).

David Stanley Smith (Ohio, 1877—), distinguished organist, composer and educator, the author of three notable Symphonies, in F minor (1912), in D (1918), and in C minor (1928); also a Symphonic-Poem *Darkness and Dawn*, several Overtures, and a number of other orchestral compositions.

Eric DeLamarter (Lansing, Michigan, 1880—), organist, composer and conductor, has two Symphonies to his credit, one in D (1914), the other in G (1920), besides Chamber-music, organ compositions, songs, etc.

Arthur Shepherd (Idaho, 1880—), a composer of very marked originality, vigor and scholarship, emphatically progressive in his attitude, but thoroughly serious in conception and expression. He has created no Symphony of the regular type, but has written an orchestral Suite, and interesting Overtures.

John Powell (Richmond, Va., 1882—), an eminently gifted composer and pianist, whose *Negro Rhapsody* (1918) has challenged the unqualified admiration of music lovers. He has not produced an authentic Symphony, but has written masterly Concertos and Chamber-works.

Charles T. Griffes (Elmira, New York, 1884-1920), a most promising composer, whose career was all too brief, but who created a profound impression by the originality and distinction of his musical utterances. He wrote no genuine Symphony; but a remarkable Symphonic-Poem, *The Pleasure-Dome of Kubla Khan,* and a few Chamber-music works confirm his uncommon power.

Emerson Whithorne (Ohio, 1884—), has produced two notable Symphonic-Poems, and various compositions of the Chamber-music type.

Deems Taylor (New York, 1885—), one of the most serious-minded and proficient of our younger composers, the author of an excellent Symphonic-Poem *The Siren Song* (1913), a Suite, Choral works, and recently an Opera *The King's Henchman,* that has swiftly gained deserved popularity.

Philip Greeley Clapp (Boston, 1888—), the composer of three Symphonies, No. I, in E minor (1911), No. II, in E♭ (1916), and No. III, in A (1919), besides Tone-Poems, an orchestral Prelude, a String-quartet, etc.

Leo Sowerby (Michigan, 1895—), an extremely gifted young writer, who has already achieved marked success. He has written two Symphonies (1922, 1929), and a number of other orchestral works; also Chamber-music.

Howard H. Hanson (Nebraska, 1896—), the youngest, and possibly the most promising representative of American symphonic art. He is exceptionally gifted, original, possesses a spirit of very pronounced, almost vehement vitality, and is fully equipped with the necessary scholastic requirements. His First Symphony, Op. 21, in E minor, *Nordic* (1922) has been performed in many American and European cities with great success. His Second Symphony, Op. 30, *Romantic*, is nearing completion. Besides these, Hanson has composed three Symphonic-Poems, and several other works in the larger forms, both instrumental and vocal.

*   *   *

To this list must be appended the names of those foreign-born composers who have made America their home, and have thus more or less directly contributed to the musical wealth and standing of our country.

Heredity, and their native environment, have undeniably equipped these composers with a background of musical advantages, which are essentially European in kind. Still, since they have brought their talent here and have given them to us, they have become ours.

The list, chronological, as usual, begins with the pre-eminent name of *Leopold Damrosch* (Posen, 1832—New York, 1885). This excellent master of the Tone-art, who, in his own work, and through that of his eminent sons Frank and Walter, has exerted so mighty and widespread an influence upon the musical destiny of America, came to New York in 1871. He wrote one Symphony, in A, a Festival Overture, and various other works, orchestral and choral. His eldest son: *Frank Damrosch* (Breslau, 1859—), has established an imperishable reputation, not as composer, but as organizer and educator. The other son: *Walter Damrosch* (Breslau, 1862—), one of the most prominent orchestral conductors, has written no Symphony, but has produced three Operas of superior merit, besides a number of other compositions.

Ludwig Bonvin (born, 1850, in Switzerland, came to America in 1887), the author of one accredited Symphony, in G minor, and a few other orchestral works.

Victor Herbert (born, 1859, in Dublin, came to America in 1886, died in New York, 1924). His orchestral works embrace a Symphonic-Poem *Hero and Leander*; three Suites, an *Irish Rhapsody*, a Serenade, and other pieces, but no Symphony. Herbert's renown, as a fertile, spontaneous composer, was gained through his numerous, universally popular, light Operas.

Pietro Floridia (Sicily, 1860—), in America since 1904, a finely equipped musician, author of five Operas, one Symphony (D minor, given in Cincinnati in 1907, and in New York), and other effective compositions.

Charles Martin Loeffler (born in Alsace in 1861, came to America in 1881), a musical master mind, that has spread its lustre far beyond the boundaries of his adopted land; noted equally for his strong progressive inclination, his ardent and exquisitely refined poetic spirit, and his absolute command of technical and orchestral requirements. He has created four Symphonic-Poems, of which the first one, *La Mort de Tantagiles* (1897), is perhaps the best known; also a Symphony in one Movement *Hora Mystica* (1916), with male chorus; a Suite (with Violin), and other compositions, orchestral, concerted and vocal of fascinating originality and enduring worth.*

Worthy of mention are, further:

Hugo Kaun (Berlin, 1863—), a precocious, prolific, original and able composer, who vitalized the musical atmosphere of Milwaukee from 1887 to 1902, and then returned to his native country. He has created three Symphonies, in D, C minor, and E minor (1915), several Symphonic-Poems, Suites, and other works, orchestral and choral.

Gustav Strube (Saxony, 1867; in America since 1891), author of three Symphonies, the second of which, in B minor (1909), contains many excellent and engaging traits.

Frederick A. Stock (Rhenish Prussia, 1872; in America since 1895) has written two Symphonies, No. I, in C minor

*See the article, *Charles Martin Loeffler*, by Carl Engel, in the *Musical Quarterly* of July, 1925.

(1909), and No. II, in E♭ (1915); a Symphonic-Poem *Life* (1905); Overtures, symphonic Sketches, Variations, and other works of outstanding quality.

Ernest Bloch (1880) has been assigned to our foregoing principal list, as his sojourn in America—since 1916—has been comparatively brief, and none of his recent works (not even the "American" Symphony) exhibit any specific American attributes.

Percy Grainger (Australia, 1882; since 1915 in the United States), eminent pianist, and composer of exceptional vitality and distinction. He has written a number of orchestral works, but no Symphony.

Leo Ornstein (Russia, 1895; since 1907 in America), a meteoric apparition, whose musical productions seemed at first problematic and baffling, and still defy reasonable classification, or reliable artistic appraisement.*

References

Separate Biographies

GOETSCHIUS	Mrs. H. H. A. Beach.
SAERCHINGER	Ernest Bloch. (In *Modern Music and Musicians*.)
GATTI	Ernest Bloch (*Music Quarterly*, January, 1921).
CHADWICK	Horatio Parker.
ENGEL	George W. Chadwick (*Musical Quarterly*, July, 1924).
DOWNES	An American Composer (Henry F. Gilbert). *Musical Quarterly*, January, 1918.
PARKER	Percy Aldridge Grainger: A Study.

*See *Ornstein and Modern Music*, by Charles L. Buchanan, in the *Musical Quarterly* of April, 1918.

AMERICAN SYMPHONISTS

SCOTT	Percy Grainger, The Music and the Man (*Musical Quarterly*, July, 1916).
HOWARD	Charles Tomlinson Griffes.
HOWARD	Deems Taylor.
ENGEL	Charles Martin Loeffler (*Chesterian*, March, 1920).
ENGEL	Charles Martin Loeffler (*Musical Quarterly*, July, 1925).
GILMAN	Phases of Modern Music (Loeffler).
GILMAN	Nature in Music (Loeffler).
GILMAN	Edward Mac Dowell: A Study.
BROWN	Boyhood of Edward Mac Dowell.
PAGE	Edward Mac Dowell: his Works and Ideals.
PORTE	Edward Mac Dowell: a great American Tone-Poet.
SONNECK	Catalogue of First Editions of Edward Mac Dowell.
CURRIER	Edward Mac Dowell as I knew him (*Musical Quarterly*, January, 1915).
MARTENS	Leo Ornstein: the Man—his Ideals—his Work.
BUCHANAN	Ornstein and Modern Music (*Musical Quarterly*, April, 1918).

* * *

Collective Biographies

GILMAN	Stories of Symphonic Music (Chadwick, Converse, Hadley, Loeffler, Mac Dowell).
HUGHES AND ELSON	American Composers.
KEY	International Music Year Book.
—	Musical America's Guide.

SAERCHINGER	International Who's Who in Music (New York, 1918).
MARTENS	Composers of America (Chadwick, Kelley, Parker, Oldberg, Goldmark, Brockway, Hadley, Converse, Gilbert, Powell, Wilson, Hill, Smith, Coerne, and others. (In *Modern Music and Musicians*.)

* * *

American Orchestras

HOWE	The Boston Symphony Orchestra.
HUNEKER	The Philharmonic Society of New York, and its seventy-fifth anniversary (1917).
KREHBIEL	The Philharmonic Society of New York.
OTIS	The Chicago Symphony Orchestra, 1891-1924.
WISTER	Twenty-five years of the Philadelphia Orchestra.
RUSSELL	The American Orchestra and Theodore Thomas.
THOMAS	A Musical Autobiography.
DAMROSCH, W.	My Musical Life.

* * *

General History

RITTER	Music in America.
DWIGHT	History of Music in Boston. (In Windsor's *Memorial History of Boston*.) Chapter VII.
ELSON	History of American Music.
MADEIRA	Music in Philadelphia; and the Musical Fund Society
SIMPSON	America's Position in Music.
SONNECK	Suum Cuique. (A survey of Music in America.)

MASON	Music in America. (In *Contemporary Composers*.)
MARTENS	Music in America. (In Landormy's *A History of Music*.)
UPTON	Musical Memories.
GROVE	Dictionary of Music and Musicians. (*American Supplement*.)
HUBBARD	American History and Encyclopedia of Music.
—	The Art of Music, volume IV: *Music in America*.

ILLUSTRATIVE RECORDS

GRAINGER	Scotch Strathspey and Reel. C
SCHELLING	Victory Ball. V

AMERICAN SYMPHONIES

WITH DATES OF FIRST PERFORMANCE

BEACH, MRS. H. H. A.
   Gaelic Symphony, in E minor.   Boston, October 31, 1896.

BIRD, ARTHUR
   Symphony No. 1, in A.   New York, November 5, 1886.

BLOCH, ERNEST
   Symphony No. 1, in C♯ minor.   New York, March 8, 1918.
   Symphony No. 2, in F.
   Symphony No. 3 (*America*).   New York, December 20, 1928.

BONVIN, LUDWIG
   Symphony, in G minor.   Op. 67.

BRISTOW, GEORGE F.
   Symphony (*Arcadian*).   New York, February 14, 1874.

BROCKWAY, HOWARD A.
   Symphony No. 1, in D.   Boston, April 6, 1907.

CARPENTER, JOHN ALDEN
　　Symphony No. 1, in C.　Norfolk, Conn., June 5, 1917.

CHADWICK, GEORGE W.
　　Symphony No. 1, in C.　Boston, February 23, 1882.
　　Symphony No. 2, in B♭.　Boston, December 11, 1886.
　　Symphony No. 3, in F.　Boston, October 20, 1894.
　　Sinfonietta, in D.　Boston, 1904.
　　Suite Symphonique.　Philadelphia, March 29, 1911.

CLAPP, PHILIP GREELY
　　Symphony No. 1, in E minor.　Boston, April 11, 1914.
　　Symphony No. 2, in E♭.　Boston, April 6, 1917.
　　Symphony No. 3, in A.

CONVERSE, FREDERICK S.
　　Symphony No. 1, in D minor.　Munich, June, 1898.
　　Symphony No. 2, in C minor.　Boston, January 30, 1920.
　　Symphony No. 3, in E.　Boston, April 21, 1922.

DAMROSCH, LEOPOLD
　　Symphony, in A.

DELAMARTER, ERIC
　　Symphony No. 1, in D.　Chicago, January 23, 1914.
　　Symphony No. 2, in G (*After Walt Whitman*).　Philadelphia, June 5, 1920.

FLORIDIA, PIETRO
　　Symphony No. 1, in D minor.　Cincinnati, March 22, 1907.

FRY, WM. H.
　　Four Symphonies: *Christmas, or Santa Claus; The Breaking Heart; Childe Harold; A Day in the Country.*

GILCHRIST, W. W.
　　Symphony No. 1, in C.　Philadelphia, February 8, 1910.
　　Symphony No. 2, in D.

HADLEY, HENRY
    Symphony No. 1 (*Youth and Life*). New York, December 2, 1897.
HADLEY, HENRY (*Continued*)
    Symphony No. 2 (*The Four Seasons*). New York, December 20, 1901.
    Symphony No. 3, in B minor. Boston, April 11, 1908.
    Symphony No. 4 (*North, East, South and West*). Norfolk, Conn., June 6, 1911.
HANSON, HOWARD
    Symphony No. 1, in E minor (*Nordic*). Rome, 1922.
    Symphony No. 2 (*Romantic*).
HILL, EDWARD BURLINGAME
    Symphony No. 1, in B♭, Op. 34. Boston, March 30, 1928.
KAUN, HUGO
    Symphony No. 1, in D. Op. 22.
    Symphony No. 2, in C minor. Op. 85.
    Symphony No. 3, in E minor. Op. 96.
KELLEY, EDGAR STILLMAN
    Symphony No. 1 (*Gulliver*). New York, April, 1896.
    Symphony No. 2 (*New England*). Norfolk, Conn., June 3, 1913.
    Symphony No. 3 (*California*).
KOLAR, VICTOR
    Symphony No. 1, in D. New York, January 28, 1916.
KROEGER, ERNEST R.
    Symphony No. 1, in B♭. St. Louis, 1896.
LOEFFLER, CHARLES MARTIN
    Symphony (*Hora Mystica*). Norfolk, Conn., June, 1916.
MASON, DANIEL GREGORY
    Symphony No. 1, in C minor. Op. 11. Philadelphia, February 18, 1916.

OLDBERG, ARNE
    Symphony No. 1, in F minor.   Op. 23.
    Symphony No. 2, in C minor.   Los Angeles, June, 1915.
    Symphony No. 3, in F minor.   Chicago, March 18, 1927.

PAINE, JOHN K.
    Symphony No. 1, in C minor.   Op. 23.   Boston, January 26, 1876.
    Symphony No. 2, in A (*Spring*).   Op. 34.   Cambridge, March 10, 1880.

PARKER, HORATIO W.
    Symphony No. 1, in C minor.   Munich, 1885.

PHELPS, ELLSWORTH C.
    Symphony No. 1 (*Hiawatha*).   New York, May 10, 1880.
    Symphony No. 2 (*Emancipation*).

SCHELLING, ERNEST H.
    Symphony No. 1, in C minor.

SCHOENEFELD, HENRY
    Symphony (*Pastoral*).   1892.
    Symphony (*Springtime*).

SESSIONS, ROGER HUNTINGTON
    Symphony No. 1, in E minor.   Boston, April 22, 1927.

SHAPLEIGH, BERTRAM
    Symphony No. 1, in B minor.   Op. 62.
    Symphony No. 2, in A.   Op. 68.

SHELLEY, HARRY ROWE
    Symphony No. 1, in E♭.   New York, June 25, 1897.

SMITH, DAVID STANLEY
    Symphony No. 1, in F minor.   Op. 28.   Chicago, December 14, 1912.
    Symphony No. 2, in D.   Op. 42.   Norfolk, Conn., June, 1918.
    Symphony No. 3, in C minor.   Op. 60.   (Composed in 1928).

AMERICAN SYMPHONISTS

SOWERBY, LEO
    Symphony No. 1, in E.   Chicago, April 7, 1922.
    Symphony No. 2, in B minor.   Chicago, March 29, 1929.

STOCK, FREDERICK A.
    Symphony No. 1, in C minor.   Chicago, December 31, 1909.
    Symphony No. 2, in E♭.   Chicago, 1915.

STRONG, TEMPLETON
    Symphony No. 1, in F (*In den Bergen*).   New York, November 24, 1887.
    Symphony No. 2 (*Sintram*).   New York, April 12, 1892.
    Symphony No. 3 (*An der See*).

STRUBE, GUSTAV
    Symphony No. 1, in C minor.   Boston, April 4, 1896.
    Symphony No. 2, in B minor.   Boston, April 3, 1909.
    Symphony No. 3 (*Homage to Lanier*).   Washington, March 17, 1925.

WAGENAAR, BERNARD
    Symphony No. 1.   New York, October 7, 1928.

WILSON, MORTIMER
    Five Symphonies.

INDEX

ABEL, KARL F., 38
Absolute music, 8
Academic Symphony (Huber), 338
ALBRECHTSBERGER, JOHANN G., 92
L'Allegro ed il Pensieroso (Stanford), 338
Alpine Symphony (Strauss), 346
Also sprach Zarathustra (Strauss), 346
AMATI, NICCOLO, 14
American Symphony (Bloch), 353, 372
American symphonies with dates of first performance, 375-379
An der See (Strong), 379
Antar (Rimsky-Korsakov), 334, 335
Antique Symphony (Widor), 335
L'Apprenti-Sorcier (Dukas), 349
L'Après-midi d'un faune, 344
Arcadian Symphony (Bristow), 361
Asrael Symphony (Suk), 352
Aus Italien (Strauss), 346
Ave verum corpus (Mozart), 1

BACH, JOHANN CHRISTIAN, 38
BACH, JOHANN SEBASTIAN, 7, 16, 27, 30, 36, 82, 93, 249
Brandenburg Concertos, 36
Mass in B minor, 7
Well-Tempered Clavichord, 48, 91
BACH, PHILIPP EMANUEL, 30, 38, 41, 44, 48, 72

BANTOCK, GRANVILLE, 349
Christus Symphony, 349
Hebrides Symphony, 349
Pagan Symphony, 349
BARGIEL, WALDEMAR, 329
Bartered Bride, The, (Smetana), 325
BEETHOVEN, LUDWIG VAN, 3, 7, 30, 62, 72, 89-157, 158, 160, 165, 167, 171, 176, 179, 180, 185, 189, 197, 205, 209, 248, 253, 259, 299, 356, 360
Eroica Symphony, 105-112, 120
Fidelio, 7, 93
Funeral March, 109
Mass in C, 93
Mass in D, 8
melodies of, 98
Missa solemnis, in D, 93, 146
Pastoral Symphony, 124-132
Prometheus, 106
Symphony No. 1, in C, 94-100
Symphony No. 2, in D, 100-105
Symphony No. 3 (Eroica), 105-112, 120
Symphony No. 4, in B♭, 113-117
Symphony No. 5, in C min., 118-124
Symphony No. 6 (Pastoral), 124-132, 133
Symphony No. 7, in A, 133-140
Symphony No. 8, in F, 140-146

381

INDEX

Symphony No. 9 (Choral), 146-154

his use of kettledrums, 115, 128, 149

BEACH, MRS. H. H. A., 364, 375
Gaelic Symphony, 364, 375

BENNETT, WM. STERNDALE, 324

BERLIOZ, HECTOR,
biographical sketch of, 294, 295
Benvenuto Cellini, 295
Dramatic Symphony (Romeo and Juliet), 299-301
Harold in Italy, 297-299
Symphony No. 1 (Fantastic), 295-297

BIRD, ARTHUR, 362, 375
Symphony No. 1, 362, 375

BIZET, GEORGES, 331

BLOCH, ERNEST, 353, 372
American Symphony, 353
Hiver—Printemps, 353
Israël Symphony, 353
Orientale, 353
Vivre—Aimer, 353

Böcklin Symphony (Huber), 337

BONVIN, LUDWIG, 370
Symphony, in G minor, 370, 375

BORODIN, ALEXANDER, 330

BRAHMS, JOHANNES, 8, 49, 63, 72, 104, 112, 221, 223, 258
biographical sketch of, 226-227
German Requiem, 8, 227
Symphony No. 1, in C minor, 227-234
Symphony No. 2, in D, 234-239
Symphony No. 3, in F, 239-245
Symphony No. 4, in E minor, 49, 245-250

Brandenburg Concertos (J. S. Bach), 36

BRISTOW, GEORGE F., 361
Arcadian Symphony, 361

BROCKWAY, HOWARD A., 365
Symphony No. 1, in D, 365, 375

BRUCH, MAX, 331

BRUCKNER, ANTON,
biographical sketch, 326
Symphony No. 7, in E, 327, 328

CALIFORNIA SYMPHONY (Kelley), 366, 377

Candle Symphony (Haydn), 53-56

CANNABICH, CHRISTIAN, 34

CARPENTER, JOHN ALDEN, 367, 375
Symphony No. 1, in C, 375

CHADWICK, GEORGE W., 362
Sinfonietta, in D, 362
Symphony No. 1, in C, 362, 376
Symphony No. 2, in B♭, 362, 376
Symphony No. 3, in F, 362, 376
Suite Symphonique, 362

Chamber music, 3, 4

Chanson de Roland (MacDowell), 363

CHARPENTIER, GUSTAV, 340

CHAUSSON, ERNEST, 338

CHERUBINI, LUIGI, 252, 259

CHOPIN, FRÉDÉRIC, 183

Christus Symphony (Bantock), 349

Chronological list of Early Symphonists, 38

CLAPP, PHILIP GREELEY, 369, 376
Symphony No. 1, in E minor, 369, 376

Symphony No. 2, in E♭, 369, 376
Symphony No. 3, in A, 369, 376

Classic School, 181, 182

INDEX

Classical Symphony (Prokofiev), 354
COERNE, LOUIS ADOLPHE, 365
   Hiawatha, 365
Concerto grosso (Handel), 36
CONVERSE, FREDERICK S., 366
   Pipe of Desire, 366
   Symphony No. 1, in D minor, 366, 376
   Symphony No. 2, in C minor, 366, 376
   Symphony No. 3, in E, 366, 376
CORELLI, ARCHANGELO, 30
Cotswolds Symphony (Holst), 352
Country Wedding, A (Wilson), 367
COUPERIN, FRANÇOIS, 24, 25, 26, 27, 30, 47
   Réveille-matin, Le, 24-26
COWEN, FREDERIC H., 337
   Scandinavian Symphony, 337
   Welsh Symphony, 337
Creation, The, (Haydn), 46
CUI, CÉSAR, 330
CZERNY, CARL, 259

DAMROSCH, FRANK, 370
DAMROSCH, LEOPOLD, 370
   Symphony in A, 370, 376
DAMROSCH, WALTER, 370
Dance in Place Congo (Gilbert), 367
Dante Symphony (Liszt), 261, 262
Darkness and Dawn (Smith), 367
DEBUSSY, CLAUDE, 343-344
   L'Après-midi d'un faune, 344
   La Mer, 344
DELAMARTER, ERIC, 367, 376
   Symphony No. 1, in D, 367, 376
   Symphony No. 2, in G (After Walt Whitman), 367, 376

DELIUS, FREDERICK, 345
   Song of a Great City, 345
DES PRÉS, JOSQUIN, 91
Development, 27, 32, 34, 35
   of orchestral instruments, 10-39
DITTERSDORF, KARL D. VON, 38
Divine Poem, Symphony (Scriabin), 350
Don Giovanni (Mozart), 66
Don Juan (Strauss), 346
Don Quixote (Strauss), 346
DRAESEKE, FELIX, 330
   Tragica Symphony, 330
Dramatic Symphony (Romeo and Juliet) (Berlioz), 299-301
Dramatic Symphony (Rubinstein), 329
DUFAY, GUILLAUME, 91
DUKAS, PAUL, 349
   L'Apprenti-Sorcier, 349
DVOŘÁK, ANTON, 278-283, 284, 325
   biographical sketch of, 279
   Symphony, No. 1, in D, 279
   Symphony No. 2, in D minor, 279
   Symphony No. 3, in F, 280
   Symphony No. 4, in G minor, 280
   Symphony No. 5 (New World), 280-283

EDRIS (Gleason), 361
Ein Heldenleben (Strauss), 346
Elegiac Symphony (Stanford), 338
ELGAR, EDWARD, 339
   Memorial Symphony, 339
Elijah (Mendelssohn), 184
English Symphony (Parry), 337
Eroica Symphony (Beethoven), 105-112, 120

INDEX

ESTERHAZY, PRINCE, 46, 54, 56
Evolution of the symphony, 10-39
Exposition, 32, 34, 35

FANTASTIC SYMPHONY (Berlioz), 295-297
Farewell Symphony (Haydn), 53-56
Faust Symphony (Liszt), 261, 262
Fidelio (Beethoven), 7, 93
Figaro (Mozart), 66
Florentine Symphony (Rheinberger), 331
FLORIDIA, PIETRO,
    Symphony No. 1, in D minor, 370, 376
FOERSTER, ADOLPH M., 362
    Sigrid, 362
FOOTE, ARTHUR, 361
Form of symphony, 31
Forms, rondo-, 63
Four Seasons, The, Symphony (Hadley), 377
FRANCK, CÉSAR, 301-306, 333, 344
    biographical sketch, 302
    Symphony, in D minor, 303-306
French Overture, 21
Frithjof Symphony (Hofmann), 332
FRY, WILLIAM H., 360
Funeral March (Beethoven), 109

GABRIELI, ANDREA, 30
GABRIELI, GIOVANNI, 13
GADE, NIELS W., 324
Gaelic Symphony (Beach), 364, 375
German Requiem (Brahms), 8, 227
GERNSHEIM, FRIEDRICH, 332
    Miriam Symphony, 332
Giant Symphony, The, (Mahler), 342

GILBERT, HENRY F., 365
    Dance in Place Congo, 365
    Riders to the Sea, 365
GILCHRIST, W. W., 361
    Symphony No. 1, in C, 361, 376
    Symphony No. 2, in D, 361, 376
GLAZOUNOV, ALEXANDER, 63, 347-349
    Symphony No. 5, in B♭, 348
GLEASON, F. GRANT, 361
    Edris, 361
GOETZ, HERMANN, 332
    Taming of the Shrew, The, 332
GOLDMARK, KARL, 330
    Rustic Wedding, Symphony, 330
    Sakuntala, 330
GOLDMARK, RUBIN, 366
    Hiawatha, 366
    Requiem, 366
    Samson, 366
GOSSEC, FRANÇOIS F., 34, 38
GRAINGER, PERCY, 372
GRÉTRY, ANDRÉ E. M., 36
    Richard Cœur de Lion, 36
GRIFFES, CHARLES T., 368
    The Pleasure-Dome of Kubla Khan, 368
GYROWETZ, ADALBERT, 38

HADLEY, HENRY, 365
    Symphony No. 1 (Youth and Life), 376
    Symphony No. 2 (The Four Seasons), 377
    Symphony No. 3, in B minor, 377
    Symphony No. 4 (North, East, South and West), 377
Haffner Symphony (Mozart), 70-72

INDEX

HANDEL, GEORG F., 36
   Concerto grosso, 36
HANSON, HOWARD, 369, 377
   Symphony No. 1, in E minor (Nordic), 369, 377
   Symphony No. 2 (Romantic), 369, 377
Harold in Italy (Berlioz), 297-299
HAYDN, FRANZ JOSEPH,
   Candle Symphony, 53-56
   Creation, The, 46
   Farewell Symphony, 53-56
   Military Symphony, 58
   Surprise Symphony, 56, 57
Hebrides Symphony (Bantock), 349
HERBERT, VICTOR, 370
   Hero and Leander, 370
   Irish Rhapsody, 370
Hero and Leander (Herbert), 370
Heroic Symphony (Huber), 337
HERZOGENBERG, HEINRICH VON, 334
Hiawatha (Coerne), 365
Hiawatha (Rubin Goldmark), 356
Hiawatha Symphony (Phelps), 361
HILL, EDWARD BURLINGAME, 366
   Symphony No. 1, in B♭, 366, 377
HILLER, FERDINAND, 324
HINDEMITH, PAUL, 355
Hiver—Printemps (Bloch), 353
HOFMANN, HEINRICH, 332
   Frithjof Symphony, 332
HOLST, GUSTAV, 352
   Cotswolds Symphony, 352
   The Planets, Symphony, 352
Homage to Lanier, Symphony (Strube), 379
HONEGGER, ARTHUR, 354
   Mimic Symphony, 354
   Pacific 231, 354
   Pastorale d'Été, 354
Hora Mystica, Symphony (Loeffler), 371, 377
HOWARD, JOHN TASKER, 360
HUBER, HANS, 337
   Academic Symphony, 338
   Böcklin Symphony, 337
   Heroic Symphony, 337
   Romantic Symphony, 338
   Swiss Symphony, 338
   Tell Symphony, 337
Hungarian Music, 260
HUSS, HENRY HOLDEN, 363

ILLUSTRATIVE RECORDS AND ROLLS, 39, 88, 156, 203, 256, 292, 322, 359, 375
In den Bergen, Symphony (Strong), 362, 379
Indian Suite (Mac Dowell), 363
D'INDY, VINCENT, 63, 313-320
   biographical sketch of, 314-315
   Symphony No. 2, 315-320
Instruments of the orchestra, 5, 6
In the Forest, Symphony (Raff), 325
Irish Rhapsody (Herbert), 370
Irish Symphony (Stanford), 338
Irish Symphony (Sullivan), 333
Israël Symphony (Bloch), 353
Italian Overture, The, 19
Italian Symphony (Mendelssohn), 188-193

JADASSOHN, SALOMON, 330
JOACHIM, JOSEF, 226
Jupiter Symphony, No. 49, in C (Mozart), 80-85

INDEX

KALLIWODA, JOHANN W., 254
  Kammersymphonie (Schönberg), 353
Karelia (Sibelius), 290
KAUN, HUGO, 371
  Symphony No. 1, in D, 377
  Symphony No. 2, in C min., 377
  Symphony No. 3, in E min., 377
KELLEY, EDGAR STILLMAN, 362, 363
  Symphony No. 1 (Gulliver), 363, 377
  Symphony No. 2 (New England), 363, 377
  Symphony No. 3 (California), 377
Kettledrums, Beethoven's use of, 115, 120, 149
King's Henchman, The, (Taylor), 368
KOLAR, VICTOR, 377
  Symphony No. 1, in D, 377
KLUGHARDT, AUGUST, 336
KORNGOLD, ERIC W., 355
  Sinfonietta, 355
KROEGER, ERNEST R., 364, 377
  Lalla Rookh, 364
  Symphony No. 1, in B♭, 364, 377
KUHNAU, JOHANN, 30, 47

LACHNER, FRANZ, 323
  Lalla Rookh (Kroeger), 364
LANG, MARGARET RUTHVEN, 364
Lenore Symphony (Raff), 325
Life (Stock), 371
Little Russia Symphony (Tchaikovsky), 268
LISZT, FRANZ, 134, 183, 258-264, 348
  biographical sketch of, 259-260
  Dante Symphony, 261, 262

  Faust Symphony, 261, 262
  Les Préludes, 262-264.
LOEFFLER, CHARLES MARTIN, 371
  La Mort de Tintagiles, 371
  Symphony, Hora Mystica, 371, 377
London Philharmonic Society, 154, 252
London Symphony (Williams), 351
LULLY, JEAN BAPTISTE, 21, 22
  Phaëton, 21, 22

MACBETH (Strauss), 346
MAC DOWELL, EDWARD A., 363
  Chanson de Roland, 363
  Indian Suite, 363
MACFARREN, GEORGE A., 324
MACKENZIE, ALEXANDER, 336
Madrigals, 12
Magic Flute, The, (Mozart), 66
MAHLER, GUSTAV, 340-343
  biographical sketch, 340-341
  Symphony No. 1, (Titan), 341
  Symphony No. 2, in C min., 341
  Symphony No. 3, in D min., 342
  Symphony No. 4, in G, 342
  Symphony No. 5 (The Giant), 342
  Symphony No. 6, in A min., 343
  Symphony No. 7, in B min., 343
  Symphony No. 8 (Symphony of the Thousand), 343
  Symphony No. 9, in D, 343
MASON, DANIEL GREGORY, 366, 377
  Symphony No. 1, in C minor, 366, 377
Mass in B minor (Bach), 7
Mass in C (Beethoven), 93
Mass in D (Beethoven), 8

INDEX

MÉHUL, ETIENNE, 252
Memorial Symphony (Elgar), 339
MENDELSSOHN, FELIX, 29, 48, 63, 72, 108, 181-200, 184, 348
    biographical sketch, 184, 185
    Elijah, 184
    Hymn of Praise, 193
    Italian Symphony, 188-193
    Reformation Symphony, 187
    St. Paul, 184
    Scotch Symphony, 192, 194-200, 211
Mer, La (Debussy), 344
MEYERBEER, GIACOMO, 252
Military Symphony (Haydn), 58
Mimic Symphony (Honegger), 354
Miriam Symphony (Gernsheim), 332
Missa solemnis, in D (Beethoven), 93, 146
Mitridate (Mozart), 66
MONTEVERDE, CLAUDIO, 13, 17, 19
Mort de Tintagiles, La (Loeffler), 371
MOSZKOWSKI, MORITZ, 338
MOZART, WOLFGANG A., 1, 8, 16, 17, 30, 44, 45, 59, 63, 64-86, 89, 90, 91, 92, 93, 94-95, 96, 97, 98, 101, 116, 159, 162, 166, 185, 186
    Ave verum corpus, 1
    Don Giovanni, 66
    Figaro, 66
    fundamental qualities of, 85
    Haffner Symphony, 70-72
    Jupiter Symphony, No. 49, 80-85
    last symphonies of, 70-85
    Magic Flute, The, 66
    Mitridate, 66
    Symphony No. 1, in E♭, 66, 67
    Symphony No. 12, in G, 68-70
    Symphony No. 35, in D (Haffner), 70, 71
    Symphony No. 38, in D, 72
    Symphony No. 47, in E♭, 74, 75
    Symphony No. 48, in G minor, 76-80
    Symphony No. 49, in C (Jupiter), 80-85
My Country (Smetana), 325

NEGRO *RHAPSODY* (Powell), 368
NEUKOMM, SIGISMUND, 253
New England Symphony (Kelley), 366, 367
New Orleans (Wilson), 367
New World Symphony (Dvořák), 280-283
Nordic Symphony (Hanson), 369, 377
North, East, South and West, Symphony (Hadley), 377

OCEAN *SYMPHONY* (Rubinstein), 329
Ode to Joy by Schiller, 151
OKEGHEM, JEAN DE, 91
OLDBERG, ARNE, 367
    Symphony No. 1, in F min., 367, 377
    Symphony No. 2, in C min., 367, 377
    Symphony No. 3, in F min., 367, 377
ONSLOW, GEORGE, 253
Opera, 1, 2
Oratorio, 1, 2
Organ, 3, 335
Orchestral color, 5, 6

INDEX

Orchestral instruments, development of, 10-39
Orientale (Bloch), 353
ORNSTEIN, LEO, 372
Overture, 19
    French, 21
    Italian, 19
Overture, Scherzo and Finale (Schumann), 206

PACIFIC 231 (Honegger), 354
    Pagan Symphony (Bantock), 349
PAGANINI, NICCOLO, 260, 298
PAINE, JOHN K., 361
    Symphony, No. 1, in C min., 361, 378
    Symphony No. 2 (Spring), 361, 378
PAISIELLO, GIOVANNI, 38
PARKER, HORATIO W., 364
    Symphony No. 1, in C min., 364, 378
PARRY, CHARLES HUBERT H., 336, 337
    English Symphony, 337
Le Pas d'Acier (Prokofiev), 354
Pastorale d'Été, (Honegger), 354
Pastoral Symphony (Beethoven), 124-132, 133
Pastoral Symphony (Schoenefeld), 362, 378
Pastoral Symphony (Williams), 351
Pétrouchka (Stravinsky), 354
275-278
Pétrouchka (Stravinsky), 354
Phaëton (Lully), 21, 22
PHELPS, ELLSWORTH C., 361
    Hiawatha Symphony, 361
    Emancipation Symphony, 361
Pianoforte music, limitations of, 3

PICHEL, W., 38
Pipe of Desire (Converse), 366
Planets, The, Symphony (Holst), 352
Pleasure-Dome of Kubla Khan, The, (Griffes), 368
PLEYEL, IGNAZ J., 38, 252
Poem of Ecstasy (Scriabin), 350
Polish Symphony (Tchaikovsky), 268
POWELL, JOHN, 368
    Negro Rhapsody, 368
Préludes, Les (Liszt), 262-264
PROKOFIEV, SERGEI, 354
    Classical Symphony, 354
    Le Pas d'Acier, 354
Prometheus (Beethoven), 106
PURCELL, HENRY, 336

QUESTIONS FOR REVIEW, 8, 37, 86, 154, 200, 254, 290, 320, 327

RACHMANINOV, SERGEI, 351
RAFF, JOACHIM, 325
    In the Forest, Symphony, 325
    Lenore Symphony, 325
RAMEAU, JEAN-PHILIPPE, 27, 47
RAVEL, MAURICE, 353
Recapitulation, 27, 32, 33, 35
Records and Rolls, Illustrative, 39, 88, 156, 203, 256, 292, 322, 359, 375
Reference books, 9, 38, 87, 156, 202, 256, 291, 322, 258, 372-375
Reformation Symphony (Mendelssohn), 187
REGER, MAX, 351
REINECKE, KARL, 328
REMENYI, EDUARD, 226
Repetition, 99, 128, 142, 165

INDEX

Requiem (Rubin Goldmark), 356
Réveille-matin, Le (Couperin), 24-26
RHEINBERGER, JOSEF, 331
    Florentine Symphony, 331
    Wallenstein Symphony, 331
Rheingold, Das (Wagner), 20
Rhenish Symphony (Schumann), 219-223
Richard Cœur de Lion (Grétry), 36
Riders to the Sea (Gilbert), 367
RIES, FRANZ, 91
RIMSKY-KORSAKOV, NIKOLAI, 334, 347
    Antar, 334, 335
    Scheherezade, 334
Romantic School, 182
Romantic Symphony (Hanson), 369, 377
Romantic Symphony (Huber), 338
ROMBERG, ANDREAS, 253
ROMBERG, BERNARD, 253
Romeo and Juliet, Symphony (Berlioz), 299-301
Rondo-forms, 63, 64, 132, 136
Rossignol, Le (Stravinsky), 354
RUBINSTEIN, ANTON, 329
    Dramatic Symphony, 329
    Ocean Symphony, 329
    Russian Symphony, 329
Russian Symphony (Rubinstein), 330
Rustic Wedding, Symphony (Karl Goldmark), 330

S*ACRE DU PRINTEMPS, LE* (Stravinsky), 354
St. Paul (Mendelssohn), 184
St. Matthew Passion (Bach), 7, 48, 184

SAINT-SAËNS, CAMILLE, 306-312
    biographical sketch, 307
    early symphonies of, 308
    Phaëton, 308
    Symphony No. 1, in E♭, 308
    Symphony No. 2, in A min., 308, 309
    Symphony No. 3, in C min., (with Organ), 309
Sakuntala (Karl Goldmark), 330
SALIERI, ANTONIO, 259
SAMMATINI, GIOVANNI B., 32
Samson (Rubin Goldmark), 366
Scandinavian Symphony (Cowen), 337
SCARLATTI, ALESSANDRO, 19
SCARLATTI, DOMENICO, 24, 27, 30
SCHARWENKA, PHILIPP, 336
Scheherezade (Rimsky-Korsakov), 334
SCHELLING, ERNEST H., 367, 378
    Symphony No. 1, in C min., 367, 378
SCHÖNBERG, ARNOLD, 352, 353
    Kammersymphonie, 353
SCHOENEFELD, HENRY, 362, 378
    Symphony No. 1 (Pastoral), 362, 378
    Symphony No. 2 (Springtime), 362, 378
SCHUBERT and MENDELSSOHN, 158-203
SCHUBERT, FRANZ, 2, 72, 158-181, 185, 205, 278, 283
    biographical sketch of, 159-161
    early symphonies of, 162-164
    Symphony No. 1, in D, 162
    Symphony No. 2, in B♭, 163
    Symphony No. 3, in D, 163

INDEX

Symphony No. 4, (Tragic), 163-166
Symphony No. 5, in B♭, 166-170
Symphony No. 8 (Unfinished), 170-175
Symphony No. 10, in C, 175-181
Tragic Symphony, 163-166
Unfinished Symphony, 163-166
SCHUMANN and BRAHMS, 204-223
SCHUMANN, ROBERT, 12, 175, 183, 226, 251, 258, 260
    biographical sketch of, 205-206
    Overture, Scherzo and Finale, 236
    Rhenish Symphony, 219-223
    Symphony No. 1 (Spring), 207-211
    Symphony No. 2, in C, 211, 214-219
    Symphony No. 3 (Rhenish), 219-223
    Symphony No. 4, in D min., 196, 211-214
Scotch Symphony (Mendelssohn), 192, 194-200, 211
SCRIABIN, ALEXANDER, 349, 350
    Symphony No. 1, in E, 350
    Symphony No. 2, in C min., 350
    Symphony No. 3 (Divine Poem), 350
    Poem of Ecstasy, 350
Seasons, The (Haydn), 46
Sea Symphony (Williams), 351
SESSIONS, ROGER HUNTINGTON, 378
    Symphony No. 1, in E minor, 378
SHAPLEIGH, BERTRAM, 365
    Symphony No. 1, in B min., 365, 378
    Symphony No. 2, in A, 365, 378

SHELLEY, HARRY ROWE, 363, 378
    Symphony No. 1, in E♭, 363, 378
SHEPHERD, ARTHUR, 368
SIBELIUS, JAN, 284-290
    biographical sketch, 285
    Symphony No. 1, in E min., 285-286
    Symphony No. 2, in D, 286
    Symphony No. 3, in C, 287-289
    Symphony No. 4, in A min., 289
    Symphony No. 5, in E♭, 290
    Karelia, 290
Sigrid (Foerster), 362
SINDING, CHRISTIAN, 338
Sinfonia Domestica (Strauss), 346
Sinfonia Sacra (Widor), 335
Sinfonietta (Chadwick), 362
Sinfonietta (Korngold), 355
Sintram, Symphony (Strong), 379
Siren Song, The (Taylor), 368
SMETANA, FRIEDRICH, 325
    Bartered Bride, The, 325
    My Country, 325
SMITH, DAVID STANLEY, 367
    Darkness and Dawn, 367
    Symphony No. 1, in F minor, 367, 378
    Symphony No. 2, in D, 367, 378
    Symphony No. 3, in C minor, 367, 378
Sonata, The, 27, 30
    -Allegro, 32, 51
    -Movement, 24
Song of a Great City (Delius), 345
Songs Without Words (Mendelssohn), 29
SONNECK, O. G., 360

INDEX

SOWERBY, LEO, 369
   Symphony No. 1, in E, 378
   Symphony No. 2, in B min., 378
SPOHR, LUDWIG, 253
Spring Symphony (Paine), 361
Spring Symphony (Schumann), 207-211
Springtime Symphony (Schoenefeld), 362, 378
STAMITZ, JOHANN KARL, 33, 38
STAMITZ, KARL, 33, 38
STANFORD, CHARLES VILLIERS, 338
   Elegiac Symphony, 338
   Irish Symphony, 338
   L'Allegro ed il Pensieroso, 338
Statement, 28
STOCK, FREDERICK A., 371
   Symphony No. 1, in C min., 371
   Symphony No. 2, in E♭, 371, 378
   Life, 371
STRADIVARIUS, ANTONIO, 14
STRAUSS, RICHARD, 345-347
   Also sprach Zarathustra, 346
   Aus Italien, 346
   Don Juan, 346
   Don Quixote, 346
   Ein Heldenleben, 346
   Macbeth, 346
   Symphony No. 1, in D min., 346
   Symphony No. 2, in F min., 346
   Symphony No. 3 (Sinfonia Domestica), 346
   Symphony No. 4 (Alpine), 346, 347
   Till Eulenspiegel, 346
   Tod und Verklärung, 346
STRAVINSKY, IGOR, 353, 354
   Pétrouchka, 354
   Rossignol, Le, 354

   Sacre du Printemps, Le, 354
   Symphony in E♭, 353
STRONG, GEORGE TEMPLETON, 362
   Symphony (In den Bergen), 362, 379
   Symphony No. 2 (Sintram), 379
   Symphony No. 3 (An der See), 379
STRUBE, GUSTAV, 371
   Symphony No. 1, in C min., 370
   Symphony No. 2, in B min., 379
   Symphony No. 3 (Homage to Lanier), 379
Suite, The, 23, 24
Suite Symphonique (Chadwick), 362
SUK, JOSEF, 352
   Asrael, Symphony, 352
SULLIVAN, ARTHUR, 333
   Irish Symphony, 333
Surprise Symphony (Haydn), 56, 57
SVENDSEN, JOHAN S., 332
Swiss Symphony (Huber), 338
Symphonic-Poem, 259, 261
Symphonies for the Organ (Widor), 335
Symphony
   -allegro form, 32
   evolution of, 10-39
   form of, 31, 53
   meaning of term, 18, 19
   structure of, 31, 32, 53
Symphony of the Thousand (Mahler), 345

TAMING OF THE SHREW, THE (Goetz), 332
TAYLOR, DEEMS, 368

INDEX

King's Henchman, The, 368
Siren Song, The, 368
TCHAIKOVSKY, PETER ILYITCH, 266-278
  biographical sketch, 266-267
  Manfred, 278
  Symphony No. 1 (Winter-Storms), 268
  Symphony No. 2 (Little Russia), 268
  Symphony No. 3 (Polish), 268
  Symphony No. 4, in F min., 268-272
  Symphony No. 5, in E min., 273-275
  Symphony No. 6 (Pathetic), 275-278
Tell Symphony (Huber), 337
Three-part song form, 27, 28, 29, 32, 35, 51, 55, 69, 111, 177
Till Eulenspiegel (Strauss), 346
Titan Symphony (Mahler)
Tod und Verklärung (Strauss), 346
Tone-poem, 261
Tragica Symphony (Draeseke), 330
Tragic Symphony (Schubert), 163-166
Transcriptions of Symphonies, 7
Twelfth Symphony (Mozart), 68-70
Two-part form, 24, 27, 28, 29, 30, 33, 34, 42

UNFINISHED SYMPHONY (Schubert), 170-175

VIVRE—AIMER (Bloch), 353
VOGLER, G. J., 252
VOLKMANN, ROBERT, 324
VON WEBER, CARL MARIA,
  Symphony No. 2, in C, 251

WAGENAAR, BERNARD, 379
  Symphony No. 1, 379
WAGENSEIL, G. C., 38
WAGNER, RICHARD, 8, 20, 134, 183, 264-266
  Rheingold, Das, 20
  Symphony, in C, 264, 265
Wallenstein Symphony (Rheinberger), 331
Walt Whitman Symphony (DeLamarter), 367, 376
WANHAL, J. B., 38
WEBER, CARL MARIA VON, 183, 251, 252, 294
WEINGARTNER, FELIX, 345
  Symphony No. 1, in G, 345
  Symphony No. 2, in E♭, 345
  Symphony No. 3, in E, 345
  Symphony No. 4, 345
Well-Tempered Clavichord (J. S. Bach), 48-91
Welsh Symphony (Cowen), 337
WHITHORNE, EMERSON, 368
WHITING, ARTHUR B., 363
WIDOR, CHARLES-MARIE, 335
  Antique Symphony, 335
  Sinfonia Sacra, 335
  Symphonies for the Organ, 335

INDEX

WILLIAMS, (RALPH) VAUGHAN, 350
    London Symphony, 350, 351
    Pastoral Symphony, 351
    Sea, The, 351
WILSON, MORTIMER, 367, 379
    A Country Wedding, 367
    five symphonies, 367, 379
    New Orleans, 367

WINTER, PETER VON, 252
Winter-Storms, Symphony (Tchaikovsky), 268
WRANITZKY, PAUL, 38

YOUTH AND LIFE, SYMPHONY (Hadley), 376

974-2
57T

DATE DUE

MAY 1 7 1971			
OCT 2 0 1972			
DEC 1 4 1974			
MAY 1 4 1977			
MAY 1 4 1977			
MAY 1 4 1977 / MAY 1 7 1983			
MAY 1 5 1984			
DEC 1 7 1985			
2-11-86 mending			
DEC 1 5 1987			
JUL 3 1 '95			
AUG 1 3 1998			
GAYLORD			PRINTED IN U.S.A.